# *The* RUSSIANS PLAY CHESS

*Fifty-six Master Games*

*Selected and Annotated*

*by*

IRVING CHERNEV 1900-

NEW YORK

DOVER PUBLICATIONS, INC.

This Dover edition, first published in 1964, is an enlarged version of the work first published by David McKay Company in 1947.

Library of Congress Catalog Card Number: 63–21903

Manufactured in the United States of America

Dover Publications, Inc.
180 Varick Street
New York 14, N. Y.

# Preface to the Dover Edition

Six games have been added to the collection of fifty in the original edition. They are games that have been won by four extremely gifted players: Bronstein, Smyslov, Tal and Petrosian. Of the four, the first-named tied for the title of World's Champion in a match with Botvinnik; the other three have held the proud title, "Chess Champion of the World." It says much for the progress of chess that nearly all of these great masters, each a genius in his own way, were almost completely unknown at the time *The Russians Play Chess* was first printed. We can be grateful for the individual style of their play. Their games provide a wealth of ideas in the strategy of winning, and a study of them will surely add pleasure to our lives.

New York                                                    IRVING CHERNEV
July 30, 1963

# Introduction

In 1945 and again in 1946, American chess fans were stunned by our team's losses to the Russians by decisive scores. These defeats were all the more unexpected in view of the formidable American line-up: Reshevsky, Fine, Denker, Horowitz, Kashdan, to name only the outstanding players.

The matches proved beyond a doubt that the Russians were the greatest chessplayers in the world. The natural consequence is that Americans are very curious to know more about these masters. What makes them so good? What is their method of play? Have they discovered a secret system? Where can we see some of their games?

This collection of fifty games is an effort to provide an answer to the questions. The writer has carefully examined thousands of games by hundreds of Russia's players, and selected these as the cream of the crop. The considerations which affected their choice were the following:

*Variety*: they must be representative. The games in this volume illustrate the winning styles of 36 masters.

*Utility*: they must be modern. The period covered is 1925–1946.

*Brevity*: they must be reasonably short. The average for the collection is 30 moves per game.

*Artistry*: they must be enjoyable. The accent throughout is on brilliancy.

All the games meet this exacting test; playing them over should assure richly satisfying entertainment.

October 25, 1946                                    IRVING CHERNEV

# Contents

## GAMES

*Contents*

## 1. LENINGRAD 1925

### French Defense

*"The whole game sparkles with life and beauty."*

> *Tartakover*

| WHITE | BLACK |
|-------|-------|
| P. Romanovsky | E. Rabinovich |

| | |
|---|---|
| 1 P—K4 | P—K3 |
| 2 P—Q4 | P—Q4 |
| 3 Kt—QB3 | B—Kt5 |
| 4 P—K5 | P—KB3 |

and the position is shown on the diagram below:

**1.** Black varies from the usual procedure of immediately attacking the base of White's Pawn chain by 4 . . . P—QB4.

| | |
|---|---|
| 5 Kt—B3 | P—QB4 |
| 6 B—Kt5*ch* | K—B1 |

Unnecessarily foregoing the cas-tling privilege. Black should simply have interposed his Bishop.

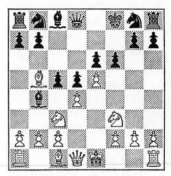

**2.** 7 QP×P     Q—R4

Bringing pressure on the pinned Knight, and threatening also 8 . . . Q×B.

     8 B—K2     P×P

The Pawn center looks good to Black. White cannot play 9 Kt× P, as 9 . . . B×Kt*ch;* 10 P×B, Q×P*ch* loses the Knight.

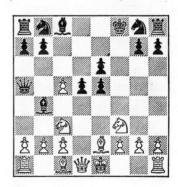

**3.** 9 O—O     Kt—QB3

And now all the center Pawns are well-protected—or are they?

    *10* Kt×QP !    . . . .

Not a sacrifice—just a loan.

**4.**
| 10 . . . . | P×Kt |
| *11* P—B3 | B×P(4) |
| *12* P—QKt4 | . . . . |

Regains the piece favorably.

    *12* . . . .    Kt×P

Or 12 . . . B×P; 13 P×B, Kt ×P (13 . . . Q×KtP; 14 Q× P); 14 Kt×P.

**5.**    *13* P×Kt    B×P

Black still seems to have a good game, as he is ahead in material and his center Pawn cannot be touched (if 14 Kt×P, B—B6 wins the exchange).

| *14* R—Kt1 | B—KB4 |
| *15* R×B !! | . . . . |

A sharp sacrifice, the purpose of which is to break up Black's center.

**6.**
| *15* . . . . | Q×R |
| *16* Q×P | . . . . |

Black cannot offer the exchange of Queens, as after 16 . . . Q— K5; 17 Q—Q6*ch*, Kt—K2 (on 17 . . . K—B2; 18 Kt—Kt5*ch* wins the Queen, or if 17 . . . K—K1; 18 B—Kt5*ch* wins); 18 B—KKt5, Q×B (if 18 . . . R— K1; 19 B—Kt5 wins); 19 B× Kt*ch*, K—K1; 20 B—Kt5, K— B2; 21 Kt×P*ch* forces mate or wins the Queen.

    The King Pawn cannot be saved. Black's best chances lie in getting his inactive pieces quickly into the fray.

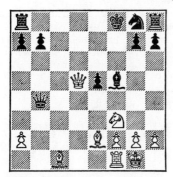

## 7.

| | | |
|---|---|---|
| 16 .... | | Kt—K2 |
| 17 Q×KP | | Q—K5 |
| 18 Q—Kt2 ! | | .... |

A very fine move, in spite of its awkward appearance. White threatens 19 Kt—Kt5, or 19 R—K1—and one thing more, as we shall see.

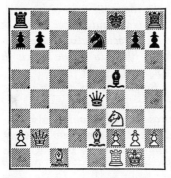

## 8.

| | | |
|---|---|---|
| 18 .... | | R—B1 |
| 19 B—KR6 ! | | |

This was White's third threat—the attack on the Knight Pawn.

| 19 .... | | R—KKt1 |

Not 19 . . . Q—KKt5 on account of 20 Kt—Kt5. After the text move, Black's game begins to look better. He even menaces 20 . . . R—B7.

With one Bishop attacked, and the other Bishop's life in danger, retreat would seem to be imperative. But White has a startling riposte.

## 9.

| 20 Q—B6ch ! |

This pretty stroke is the real reason behind White's previous move.

| 20 .... | | K—K1 |
| 21 B—Kt5ch | | .... |

Poses a problem for Black. If 21 . . . K—Q1; 22 Q—Q6ch forces mate, or if 21 . . . Kt—B3; 22 B×P threatening 23 R—K1 wins. On 21 . . . B—Q2; 22 B×Bch, K×B; 23 Kt—K5ch, K—B2; 24 Q×Ktch and 25 Kt—Q7ch wins the Queen.

Black must interpose his Rook. White will regain the material he sacrificed, but at the cost of parting with one of his powerful Bishops.

To strike at the Knight once more by 26 B—Kt5.

          25 . . . .          **K—Q1**

To reply to 26 B—Kt5 by 26 . . . R—K1.

        26 **B—B8**      **Resigns**

If 26 . . . R×B; 27 Q×R*ch*, B —K1; 28 Kt—Q4 !, K—Q2; 29 Kt—B5 is convincing.

**10.**   21 . . . .       **R—B3**
        22 **B×P**         **B—Q2**

White's Queen is attacked.

      23 **B×R**           **Q×B**
      24 **R—K1**         . . . .

White does not avoid the exchange of Queens, as after 24 . . . Q×Q; 25 B×Q he wins the pinned Knight, and the game.

## 2. LENINGRAD 1927

### Nimzovich Opening

*Romanovsky demonstrates the terrific potential power of a centralized position. Eventually he reaps the fruit of his position play and forces a break with a scintillating combination, liberally sprinkled with pins and Knight forks.*

*Ragozin, then a very young player, lost this game; but his present high reputation is evidence that one such defeat taught him more than would a hundred victories.*

    WHITE           BLACK

**V. Ragozin   P. Romanovsky**

    *1* Kt—KB3        Kt—KB3
    *2* P—QKt3        P—KKt3
    *3* B—Kt2         B—Kt2
    *4* P—Kt3         . . . .

**11.**   24 . . . .       **Q—B4**
        25 **B—R6**         . . . .

and the position is shown on the diagram below:

**1.** Evidently White intends to be even more original than Nimzovich, whose idea in this opening was, to control K5 by this sort of grouping: 4 P—K3, 5 Kt—K5 and 6 P—KB4.

| 4 .... | P—Q4 |
| 5 B—Kt2 | P—B4 |
| 6 O—O | O—O |

**2.**
| 7 P—Q3 | Kt—B3 |
| 8 P—B4 | .... |

This, which would have been an excellent move earlier, is now out of place.

|   | 8 .... | P—Q5 |

Naturally! The advanced Pawn cuts down the mobility of White's pieces and prevents the normal development of the Queen's Knight to B3.

White's impotent Queen Bishop is now, in the words of Nimzovich, "biting on granite."

**3.**
| 9 QKt—Q2 | Q—B2 |
| 10 P—KR3 | .... |

Probably planning to continue with P—KKt4, R—K1, Kt—B1 and Kt—Kt3.

|   | 10 .... | Kt—KR4 ! |

Now on 11 P—KKt4, Kt—B5 followed by 12 . . . P—KR4 would tear apart White's King-side position.

11 P—K3 fails after 11 . . . P×P; 12 B×B, P×Pch; 13 R×P, K×B, as Black wins a Pawn.

**4.**  *11 Kt—K4   P—Kt3*

Protecting the Bishop Pawn, and preparing to fianchetto the Queen Bishop.

*12 P—R3   B—Kt2*
*13 Q—B2   P—B4*
*14 Kt(K4)—Q2   P—K4*

Black builds up a powerfully centralized position.

**5.**  *15 P—QKt4   ....*

White's only chance of counter-action.

*15 ....   QR—K1*
*16 KR—Kt1   P—K5*

A vigorous break-through, which is much superior to winning a Pawn by 16 . . . P×P; 17 P×P, Kt×QKtP; 18 Q—Kt3, Kt—QB3; 19 P—B5*ch.*

It is noteworthy that this vigorous thrust is made only when all of Black's pieces are fully mobilized.

**6.**  *17 P×KP   ....*

Not at once 17 Kt—Kt5, as 17 . . . P—KR3 wins the Knight.

*17 ....   P×KP !*

Now White must not take the King Pawn, as after 18 Kt×KP, Kt×QKtP !; 19 P×Kt, B×Kt, and Black wins the exchange.

The previous exchange of Pawns has benefited Black enormously. His Bishop file was opened, and his King Rook now bears directly down on the opposing King.

**7.**    18 Kt—Kt5      R×P !

An unexpected sacrifice, which is as elegant as it is forcible. The prosaic 18 . . . P—K6 would also have won—another proof of the strength of Black's centralization.

**8.**    19 Kt(Q2)×P     . . . .

If 19 K×R, Q×Pch; 20 K—B1 (20 K—Kt1, Kt—B5 mates quickly), R—B1ch; 21 Kt(Kt5)—B3, Kt—B5; 22 B—R1, Kt×RP; 23 Kt×P, Q—Kt8 mate, or if

White interposes at move 21 by Kt(Q2)—B3, then 21 . . . Q×Kt, and the other Knight falls, as 22 Q×P would lose material by 22 . . . Kt—Kt6ch.

**9.**    19 . . . .      Kt×QKtP !

A fine point in the combination. It is important to open up the way for Black's Queen Bishop to take part in the attack.

    20 P×Kt      R×Bch

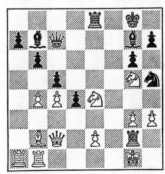

**10.**   White is given "choice." If 21 K—R1, Q×P; 22

Kt×Q, Kt×Kt mate, or if 21
K—B1, R×Kt; 22 Kt×R (22
K×R, R×P*ch*), B×Kt wins, as if
23 Q×B, Kt×P*ch* wins the Queen.

> 21 K×R        Q×P*ch*
> 22 K—B1       . . . .

Or 22 K—R1, R×Kt; 23 Kt×R,
B—K4; 24 P—K3, B×Kt*ch*, and
mate next move.

**11.**  22 . . . .      B×Kt
23 Q×B      . . . .

If 23 Kt×B, R—B1*ch* forces
mate.

> 23 . . . .      R×Q
> 24 Kt×R        Q×P*ch*

The last trump trick. White must
lose his Knight. If 25 K—Kt1,
Q—Kt5*ch*, or if 25 K—K1,
Q—R8*ch*, and if 25 K—B2,
Q—K6*ch*.

**25 Resigns**

An entertaining illustration of
the ease with which a King side
attack can be conducted, once
the center is fully controlled.

## 3.  LENINGRAD 1929

### Caro-Kann Defense

*After the first seven moves,
Black's game seems normally
developed and free of any visi-
ble weaknesses. But then with
amazing alertness Ilyin-Genevsky sees a glimmer of opportunity; soon his opponent is on
the ropes, fighting for his life.*

WHITE                BLACK

**A.Ilyin-Genevsky P.Romanovsky**

> 1 P—K4       P—QB3
> 2 P—Q4       P—Q4
> 3 Kt—QB3     P×P
> 4 Kt×P       Kt—Q2
> 5 Kt—KB3     KKt—B3

and the position is shown on the
diagram below:

**1.**  Modern  players  almost
invariably  avoid 1 . . .

P—K4 as a reply to 1 P—K4. One reason is that White cannot then play such openings as the Ruy Lopez, the Giuoco Piano, the Vienna Game or even the King's Gambit. Of the irregular defenses, the Caro-Kann shares in popularity with the Sicilian and the French.

**6 Kt×Kt*ch*        Kt×Kt**

6 . . . KP×Kt would have left Black with three Pawns to four on the Queen-side.

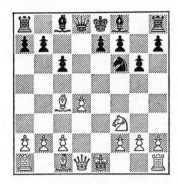

**3.**        **8 Kt—Kt5 !        . . . .**

Stronger than 8 Kt—K5.

**8 . . . .        Kt—Q4**
**9 Q—B3 !        . . . .**

Now we see the reason for White's previous move—9 . . . B—K3 defending the Bishop Pawn would be answered by 10 Kt×B and after 10 . . . P×Kt, Black would be left with a miserable position.

**2.** The recapture with the Knight looks more natural than 6 . . . KP×Kt; yet the subsequent course of the game tends to show it to be inferior, as White works up a quick attack.

**7 B—QB4        P—KKt3**

The pin by 7 . . . B—Kt5 would be premature because of 8 B×P*ch*, K×B; 9 Kt—K5*ch* winning a Pawn.

A beginner would make White's next move instinctively —a master, after much thought!

**4.**        **9 . . . .        P—B3**

An ugly move, but 9 . . .
P—KB4 does not look any more
attractive.

    10 Kt—K4        Kt—Kt3
    11 B—Kt3        . . . .

White offers a Pawn for the sake
of rapid mobilization.

    11 . . . .       Q×P
    12 B—K3         . . . .

And now another Pawn, with the
same object.

**6.**    13 O—O—O    . . . .

More accurate than 13 O—O,
as the Rook commands an open
file without loss of time.

    13 . . . .                Kt—Q4

Plugs up the file, and threatens to
remove one of the powerful
Bishops—but White finds a way.

    14 B×Kt        P×B
    15 R×P !       . . . .

**5.**    12 . . . .        Q—K4

He does not dare play 12 . . .
Q×P on account of 13 R—Q1.
White's threat would then be 14
B—Q4, Q—R6; 15 B×P, P×B;
16 Kt×P*ch*, K—K2; 17 Kt—
Kt8*ch*, R×Kt; 18 Q—B7 mate.
Or if 12 . . . Q—Q1; 13 R—Q1,
Kt—Q2; 14 Kt—Kt5, Q—R4*ch*;
15 B—Q2, Q—Kt4; 16 B—B7*ch*,
K—Q1; 17 Kt—K6 mate.
White's next is similar to
Morphy's idea in his game against
the Duke of Brunswick.

**7.**    The Queen file is re-opened
with gain of time. Black

must not take the Rook as 16 Kt×P*ch* would cost his Queen.

> 15 . . . .          **B—Kt5**

Moving the Queen to K3 is answered by 16 R—K1, threatening 17 Kt—Q6*ch*. Or if 15 . . . Q—B2; 16 R—QB5, Q—Kt1; 17 B—B4, P—K4; 18 Kt×P*ch* wins.

**8.**          16 Kt×P*ch* !          **Q×Kt**

Of course not 16 . . . P×Kt; 17 R×Q*ch*.

> 17 Q×B          . . . .

The threats are: 18 Q—Q7*ch*, and 18 B—Q4.

> 17 . . . .          **Q—B3**
> 18 KR—Q1          **B—Kt2**
> 19 R—QB5          . . . .

Black must be kept on the run. Should he be given time to castle, he would have an excellent game, barring the weakness of his isolated King Pawn. The idea is then to check quickly and root the King out.

**9.** White's object is to penetrate with his Queen at Q7.

> 19 . . . .          **Q—R3**
> 20 Q—Q7*ch*          **K—B2**
> 21 Q—Q5*ch*          **Q—K3**

21 . . . K—B1; 22 R—B7 leaves Black's pieces hopelessly scattered, while 21 . . . K—B3 permits mate on the move.

> 22 R—B7          . . . .

**10.** White welcomes an exchange of Queens, as

his control of the seventh rank is sufficient to win.

22 ....        B—K4
23 R×P*ch* !    ....

White's concentration on the endgame does not preclude his conjuring up a decisive mid-game combination!

23 ....        K×R
24 B—Kt5*ch*   K—B2

Or 24 ... B—B3; 25 Q×P*ch* and White captures the Rook with check.

**11.**   25 Q×P*ch*   B—B2

A King move permits 26 Q×R*ch*.

26 Q×B*ch*   **Resigns**

If 26 ... K—Kt1; 27 B—R6, Q—B3; 28 R—Q7 wins. Or if 26 ... K—K1; 27 Q—B3 (threatening 28 Q×R*ch*, or 28 R—K1), K—B2; 28 R—K1, Q—Q3; 29 Q—B3*ch*, K—Kt2; 30 Q—Kt7*ch* !! wins in masterly style.

## 4. MOSCOW 1931

### Scotch Game

*Riumin turns in a captivating, heart-warming classic—where the final maneuver ending in mate seems to have been part of one long combination planned by Riumin with his very first move!*

| WHITE | BLACK |
|-------|-------|
| **M.** Slonim | **N.** Riumin |
| 1 P—K4 | P—K4 |
| 2 Kt—KB3 | Kt—QB3 |
| 3 P—Q4 | P×P |
| 4 Kt×P | Kt—B3 |
| 5 Kt×Kt | KtP×Kt |

and the position is shown on the diagram below:

**1.**   6 Kt—B3   ....

White deviates from the route thousands have followed—6 B—Q3, P—Q4; 7 P×P, P×P; 8 B—Kt5*ch*, B—Q2; 9 B×B*ch*, Q×B; 10 O—O.

| | |
|---|---|
| 6 . . . . | **B—Kt5** |
| 7 **B—KKt5** | . . . . |

Looks aggressive, but is not as strong as it looks. Better is 7 B—Q3, defending the King Pawn, and enabling early castling.

## 3.

| | |
|---|---|
| 9 **B—Q2** | . . . . |

The Bishop retreats; a tacit acknowledgment that his seventh move was premature. 9 Q—Q2 instead would have lost a Pawn by 9 . . . B×Kt; 10 P×B, Kt×P.

| | |
|---|---|
| 9 . . . . | **P—Q4** |

Piles up more pressure on the pinned Pawn.

Black attacks—and at the same time develops!

## 2.

| | |
|---|---|
| 7 . . . . | **Q—K2** |

Again attacking the King Pawn.

| | |
|---|---|
| 8 **B—Q3** | . . . . |

White promptly defends.

| | |
|---|---|
| 8 . . . . | **Q—K4** |

With two new threats: 9 . . . B ×Kt*ch*, and 9 . . . Q×B.

Black's last move is stronger than 8 . . . P—Q4; 9 O—O, B× Kt; 10 P×B, P×P; 11 B×P!

## 4.

| | |
|---|---|
| 10 **Q—K2** | . . . . |

White could have safely castled here as after 10 . . . P×P; 11 Kt×P, or if 10 . . . P—Q5; 11 Kt—K2, B×B; 12 Q×B, Kt×P, 13 B×Kt, Q×B, 14 Kt×P, and the position favors White.

10 . . . .     O—O
11 O—O—O     . . . .

Dangerous policy with the Queen Knight file encouragingly open to Black.

**5.** Much safer is castling King side, but White is intent on avoiding routine situations.

11 . . . .     R—Kt1

Seizes the open file.

12 P—B4     . . . .

Misses his last chance to simplify by 12 P×P, which would lead to an exchange of Queens.

    Slonim is evidently under the impression that his position is safe, and that he can become aggressive.

**6.** 12 . . . .     Q—K2

Gives White two new worries: 13 . . . B—Kt5, and 13 . . . B—QR6.

13 P×P     B—QR6 !

The first move of a delightful winning combination.

**7.** 14 Kt—R4     . . . .

On 14 Q×Q, Black would have sacrificed his Queen, and won by 14 . . . B×P*ch;* 15 K—Kt1, B×

Ktch; 16 K—B1, B—Kt7ch; 17 K—Kt1, B—R6ch; 18 B—Kt4, B×B; 19 Q—K2 (the Queen must go to a white square), B—Kt5; 20 Q—B1, B×R; 21 Q×B, B—R6ch; 22 K—R1, B—Kt7ch; 23 K—Kt1, Kt×P, and the threat of 24 . . . Kt—B6 mate wins.

**8.** *14 . . . .*      **B×Pch !**

Black insists on giving up his Bishop.

    *15* **Kt×B**         **Q—R6**
    *16* **Q—K5**         **. . . .**

The only move to defend the Knight.

    *16 . . . .*        **R—K1**

Now seizing the open King file, and gaining time through the attack on the Queen.

The presence of the Rook on the open file will be an important factor in the final mating combination, as will be seen in the next few moves.

**9.** White's Queen must remain on the diagonal leading to his Knight.

    *17* **Q—Q4**        **P—B4 !**

Forcing the Queen to go to B3.

    *18* **Q—B3**        **Q×P**

**10.** Black threatens 19 . . . Q—R8 mate.

    *19* **B—K1**        **. . . .**

To make a flight square for the King.

    *19 . . . .*        **R—K7 !**

A problem-like move to keep the King from coming out.

**11.** White must capture the Rook, as a Knight move permits 20 . . . R—Kt8 mate.

*20 B×R　　　Kt—K5 !*

Now that the Bishop has been lured away, Black's Knight steps in, not to attack the Queen but to guard against the King's exit.

*21 Resigns,* as mate cannot be stopped.

## 5. MOSCOW 1931

### Sicilian Defense

*Sozin cleverly sacrifices his Queen to obtain a position where four of his pieces are aimed at his opponent's King. Curiously enough, Black's pieces are completely helpless to aid their King who is rooted to the spot, and threatened with a deadly discovered check.*

| WHITE | BLACK |
|---|---|
| **V.** Sozin | Nekrasov |
| 1　P—K4 | P—QB4 |
| 2　Kt—KB3 | Kt—KB3 |
| 3　P—K5 | Kt—Q4 |
| 4　P—QKt3 | . . . . |

and the position is shown on the diagram below:

**1.** White has varied from the more usual 4 Kt—B3. The idea of fianchettoing the Bishop has considerable merit, as, should the powerful King Pawn disappear, then the Bishop's scope on the diagonal is increased.

Alapin in a famous game against Rubinstein established a winning advantage with 4 Kt—B3, Kt×Kt; 5 QP×Kt, Kt—B3; 6 B—QB4, P—Q3; 7 B—B4, P×P; 8 Kt×P, Q×Q*ch;* 9 R×Q, Kt×Kt; 10 B×Kt, P—QR3; 11 B—B7.

| 4　. . . . | P—KKt3 |
|---|---|
| 5　B—Kt2 | B—Kt2 |

undeniable; he has a grip on the center, his pieces have more mobility than Black's and his Rooks will soon be able to seize the important center files.

White can either go in for a direct attack on the King, or concentrate on the weakness of Black's Queen Pawn.

**2.** Black naturally opposes his opponent's control of the long diagonal.

| 6 | P—B4 | Kt—B2 |
| 7 | Kt—B3 | P—Q3 |

A better plan was 7 . . . Kt—B3; and if 8 Kt—K4 then 8 . . . Kt—K3 preparing for 9 . . . P—Q4.

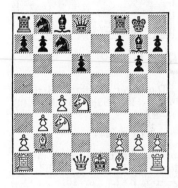

**4.** | 11 | B—K2 | P—Q4 |

A risky opening-up of the game, as his opponent is better developed.

| 12 | P×P | Kt×P |
| 13 | Kt×Kt ! | Q×Kt |

The exchange is in White's favor, as it enables him to post his Bishop powerfully at QB4, with a gain of time.

White will of course castle to get his King into safety, and then direct his fire against Black's Bishop Pawn—his weak point. Sozin carries out this plan with remarkable originality and verve.

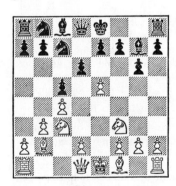

**3.** | 8 | P×P | P×P |
| 9 | P—Q4 | P×P |
| 10 | Kt×P | O—O |

Positionally White's superiority is

**5.** *14* O—O   R—Q1

Too eager to attack. Better is 14 . . . Kt—B3; 15 B—KB3, Q—KKt4.

*15* B—B4 !  . . . .

Initiating a delightful combination. If 15 . . . Q—QB4; 16 Q—B3, B×Kt (or 16 . . . Q—B1; 17 QR—Q1 followed by 18 B—R3); 17 Q×Pch, K—R1; 18 Q—B6ch!, B×Q; 19 B×B mate.

**6.** *15* . . . .  Q—K5

Black avoids the pretty loss by 15 . . . Q—Q2; 16 Q—B3, B×Kt; 17 B×B, Q×B; 18 QR—Q1, Q—Kt3; 19 Q×Pch, K—R1; 20 R×Rch, Q×R; 21 R—K1, B—Q2; 22 R—K8ch! Q×R (or 22 . . . B×R; 23 Q—B8 mate) 23 Q—B6 mate.

*16* R—K1   Q—B5

16 . . . R×Kt loses by 17 B×R, Q×B; 18 R—K8ch, B—B1; 19 Q×Q.

**7.** *17* R—K7 !!  B×Kt

Black has won a piece, and threatens to win the Queen.

*18* R×BP !  B×Pch
*19* K—R1   R×Qch
*20* R×R   . . . .

Suddenly Black is helpless. If 20 . . . Q×R; 21 R—Q8 is mate. Or 20 . . . Q×B; 21 R—Kt7ch, K—R1; 22 R—Q8ch, and mate next move.

*20* . . . .  **Resigns**

## 6. LENINGRAD 1932

### Gruenfeld Defense

*Ragozin composes an artistic end-game—not a product of his imagination, but against an opponent, in actual over-the-board play!*

| WHITE | BLACK |
|-------|-------|
| V. Ragozin | P. Romanovsky |

| | | |
|---|---|---|
| 1 | P—Q4 | Kt—KB3 |
| 2 | P—QB4 | P—KKt3 |
| 3 | Kt—QB3 | P—Q4 |
| 4 | Kt—B3 | B—Kt2 |
| 5 | Q—Kt3 | P—B3 |

and the position is shown on the diagram below:

**1.** Black's last move is probably his best, even though it prevents his Queen Knight from occupying its most effective square. If instead 5 . . . P—K3, then 6 B—Kt5 is strong.

**6 P—K3** . . . .

White has an interesting alternative in 6 B—B4, P×P; 7 Q× BP, B—K3; 8 Q—Q3, Kt—Q4; 9 B—Q2, Kt—Kt5; 10 Q—Kt1.

**2.** | 6 . . . . | O—O |
| 7 B—Q2 | P—QR3 |

Better prospects were offered by 7 . . . P—Kt3; 8 B—K2, B—Kt2; 9 O—O, QKt—Q2.

**3.** 8 P—QR4 . . . .

Prevents the freeing maneuver 8 ... P×P; 9 B×P, P—QKt4; as then 10 P×P, BP×P; 11 B×P, Q—Kt3; 12 B—B4 costs Black a Pawn.

8 ....        **P—QR4**

Otherwise 9 P—R5 ties up Black's Queen side.

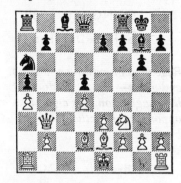

**5.** *12 R—QB1 !*    ....

Not only commanding an important open file, but also preventing a re-grouping by 12 ... Kt—B2 and 13 ... Kt—K1, as after 12 ... Kt—B2; 13 R—B5 wins either the Queen Pawn or the Rook Pawn.

12 ....        **P—K3**
13 O—O        ....

**4.** *9 B—K2*    ....

Not 9 B—Q3, Kt—R3; 10 P×P, Kt—QKt5; and Black gains a tempo by the attack on the unprotected Bishop.

9 ....        **Kt—R3**
10 P×P        **Kt×P**
11 Kt×Kt      **P×Kt**

On 11 ... Q×Kt; 12 Q×Q, P×Q; 13 B×P, Kt—B4; 14 B—Kt4 wins a Pawn.

In bygone days the way to win was by a direct King side assault. As defensive play became hardboiled, opportunities for such tactics dwindled. Today players fight for control of a file!

**6.** Black still cannot play 13 ... Kt—B2 as the reply

14 Q—Kt6 would cost him a Pawn.

$$13 \ldots \quad \text{R—K1}$$
$$14 \ \text{B—Kt5} \quad \ldots$$

Interposing by 14 . . . B—Q2 now loses a Pawn after 15 B×B, Q×B; 16 B×P.

Black must move his Rook, which interferes with his planned . . . B—B1 followed by . . . B —Kt5.

**8.** $\quad 16 \ldots \quad \text{B—Q2}$
$\quad 17 \ \text{Kt—K5 !} \quad \ldots$

On 17 . . . B—K1, White wins in exquisite style by 18 R—B8, R×R; 19 R×R, Kt—B2 (19 . . . K—B1; 20 B×B !, Q×Q; 21 B— Q7*ch* wins); 20 Q—R3, B—B1 (20 . . . K—B1; 21 Kt—Q7*ch* catches the Queen); 21 B×B, R×B (21 . . . Kt×B also loses); 22 R×R, Kt×R; 23 Q×B*ch!*, K×Q; 24 Kt—Q7*ch* regaining the Queen with a piece ahead.

**7.** $\quad 14 \ldots \quad \text{R—K2}$
$\quad 15 \ \text{R—B2} \quad \text{Q—Kt3}$
$\quad 16 \ \text{KR—B1} \quad \ldots$

Should Black try to get his Knight into play by 16 . . . Kt —B2, White gives up his Queen for three pieces as follows: 17 Q—R3, B—B1 (17 . . . K—B1; 18 R×Kt); 18 Q×R, B×Q; 19 R×Kt with an easy win, as one of the Bishops must fall.

Ragozin has played well positionally—as evidenced by the way he has tied up Black's pieces into knots. Now he demonstrates his combinative ability.

**9.** $\quad 17 \ldots \quad \text{B×Kt}$
$\quad 18 \ \text{P×B} \quad \text{B×B}$

| 19 | Q×B | Q×Q |
| 20 | P×Q | Kt—Kt5 |

The exchanges have left White with an important end-game advantage—complete control of the only open file.

The open file is usually a means to an end—a jumping off place to dominate the seventh rank, or to get behind the opposing Pawns.

**10.**    *21 R—B8ch*    . . . .

White's task will be easier with a pair of Rooks off the board.

| 21 | . . . . | R×R |
| 22 | R×Rch | K—Kt2 |
| 23 | B—B3 | P—Q5 |

Giving up a Pawn in order to centralize his Knight. Against other moves, White wins a Pawn by 24 R—QR8, P—Kt3; 25 R—Kt8.

In addition to his pieces having little mobility, Black suffers from the weakness of his black squares KB3, Q3 and Q5.

**11.**    *24 B×P*    Kt—Q4
        *25 P—Kt6*    . . . .

Threatens 26 B—B5, R—Q2; 27 B—B8*ch*, K—Kt1; 28 B—R6*ch* followed by mate.

     *25* . . . .    R—Q2

Prepared to answer 26 R—QR8 with 26 . . . Kt×KtP, as the Bishop would not dare capture the Knight.

**12.**    *26 K—B1*    P—Kt4
        *27 P—KKt4*    P—R3
        *28 K—K2*    K—Kt3
        *29 K—B3*    P—B3

Hope springs eternal! He threatens 30 . . . P×P; 31 B×P, Kt×KtP. There is also this possibility: 30 K—K4, P—B4ch; 31 P×Pch, P×Pch; 32 K—Q3, Kt×KtP; 33 P—K6, R×Bch! winning.

**34 R—B7** . . . .

Clearing the way for the passed Pawn's march. Black must not touch the Pawn, as 34 . . . Kt×P would be answered by 35 R—Kt7 mate.

**13.**
| | | |
|---|---|---|
| 30 | P×P | Kt×BP |
| 31 | R—B7 | R—Q4 |
| 32 | R—K7 ! | . . . . |

Intending to capture the King Pawn, and then win the pinned Knight.

**15.**
| | | |
|---|---|---|
| 34 | . . . . | P—K4 |
| 35 | P—Kt7 ! | . . . . |

Threatening 36 R×Kt, R×R; 37 P—Kt8(Q).

| | | |
|---|---|---|
| 35 | . . . . | P×B |
| 36 | R×Kt | R—Kt3 |
| 37 | R—Q6ch !! | Resigns |

An elegant conclusion. The Rook is lured away, and the Pawn Queens.

## 7. LENINGRAD 1933

### Queen's Indian Defense

*Chekover's play to win a piece is skillful, but interest in the game does not die there. Kan refuses to be subdued easily, and it requires all of Chek-*

**14.**
| | | |
|---|---|---|
| 32 | . . . . | R—Q3 |
| 33 | R×KtP | Kt—Q2 |

*over's ingenuity to weave an
air-tight mating net around
Black's King.*

| WHITE | BLACK |
|-------|-------|
| **V. Chekover** | **I. Kan** |

| | | |
|---|---|---|
| 1 | P—Q4 | Kt—KB3 |
| 2 | P—QB4 | P—K3 |
| 3 | Kt—KB3 | P—QKt3 |
| 4 | P—KKt3 | B—Kt2 |
| 5 | B—Kt2 | B—Kt5*ch* |

and the position is shown on the
diagram below:

**1.** The Indian defenses have tremendously livened up
the Queen's Pawn Openings.
They have converted games that
depended on careful maneuvering for position, into games featuring vigorous fighting chess.

| | | |
|---|---|---|
| 6 | B—Q2 | B×B*ch* |
| 7 | Q×B | . . . . |

The best way to recapture. The
Queen Knight belongs at B3 to
bring pressure on Q5.

**2.** | | | |
|---|---|---|
| 7 | . . . | O—O |
| 8 | O—O | . . . . |

A good alternative is 8 Kt—B3,
and if 8 . . . Kt—K5; 9 Q—B2.
Now if 9 . . . Kt×Kt; 10 Kt—
Kt5 (threatening mate) wins the
exchange.

| | | |
|---|---|---|
| 8 | . . . . | P—Q3 |

8 . . . P—Q4 blocks the action
of Black's Bishop.

**3.** | | | |
|---|---|---|
| 9 | Kt—B3 | QKt—Q2 |
| 10 | Q—B2 | . . . . |

To prevent 10 . . . Kt—K5.

| 10 . . . . | Q—K2 |
|------------|------|
| 11 P—K4    | P—K4 |
| 12 KR—K1   | . . . . |

White naturally does not play 12 P—Q5, as he wants that square for his pieces.

**4.**    12 . . . .    **P—B4**

To induce 13 P—Q5 or 13 P× KP, either of which would benefit Black.

*13 Kt—Q5 !*    Kt×Kt

White's Knight cannot be left there dominating the game.

| 14 KP×Kt | Q—B3 |
|----------|------|
| 15 P×KP  | P×P  |

If 15 . . . Kt×P; 16 Kt×Kt, P× Kt; 17 Q—K4, KR—K1; 18 P— B4 !

The recapture with the Pawn benefits White. To begin with he now has a passed Pawn. Black on the other hand cannot get his Knight into play, and is tied down as well to defending his KP.

**5.**    16 Q—K4    P—QKt4

If 16 . . . Q—Q3; 17 B—R3 (threatening 18 B×Kt, Q×B; 19 Q×P), P—B3; 18 B—B5, P— Kt3; 19 B×P, P×B; 20 Q×P*ch*, K—R1; 21 R—K4 wins.

*17 P—Kt3*    . . . .

On 17 P×P, Kt—Kt3 gives Black counter-play.

**6.**    

| 17 . . . . | P×P   |
|------------|-------|
| 18 P×P     | Q—QR3 |
| 19 Kt×P    | Kt×Kt |
| 20 Q×Kt    | Q×BP  |
| 21 Q—B7 !  | . . . . |

Now we see the reason for White's 19th move. If 21 . . . B×P; 22 KR—B1, Q—Q5 (or Q6); 23 R—Q1 wins a piece. Or if 21 . . . QR—Kt1; 22 QR—Kt1, Q—R3; 23 P—Q6 wins.

With White's Queen in a dominating position, and his Queen Pawn preparing to march on, new troubles loom up for Black.

**7.**

| | | |
|---|---|---|
| 21 | . . . . | B—R3 |
| 22 | P—Q6 | QR—Q1 |
| 23 | QR—Q1 | Q—QR5 |

23 . . . Q×P would have been too risky as White would play 24 B—B6 threatening 25 P—Q7 followed by 26 Q×R.

  24 Q×RP  . . . .

24 B—B6 would have been answered by 24 . . . B—Kt4.

Chekover's idea is to make Black give up a piece for his Queen Pawn. In the meantime he must keep an eye on Black's passed Pawn—a potential danger!

**8.**

| | | |
|---|---|---|
| 24 | . . . . | P—B5 |
| 25 | Q—Q4 | B—Kt4 |
| 26 | R—K3 | Q×P |

Certainly a plausible enough capture, as danger seems remote. White now wins a piece by a little combination.

  27 R—R1  R×P

Forced, as 27 . . . Q—B7 would lose by 28 B—K4.

**9.** 28 Q—K5  . . . .

If Black plays 28 . . . P—B3; White wins by the surprising 29

Q—Q5*ch!*, R×Q; 30 B×R*ch*, K—R1; 31 R×Q.

| 28 .... | Q—Q7 |
|---|---|
| 29 Q×B | .... |

White has won a piece, but Black can still put up a fight.

End-game composer Chekover is now in his element. He maneuvers the heavy pieces accurately and economically.

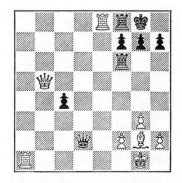

## 10. 29 ....       R—KB3

How does White defend against the threat of 30 ... Q× P*ch?* If 30 R—KB1, R×P; 31 R×R, Q×R; or if 30 R—KB3, R×R; 31 B×R, Q—B6 and Black wins a piece.

### 30 R—K8!      ....

The answer is that he doesn't defend!

He plays for mate instead by 31 R×R*ch*, K×R; 32 R—R8*ch*, K—K2; 33 R—K8*ch*, K—Q3, and mate by 34 Q—B6. Now comes a finale, entrancing in its cold precision.

## 11.
| 30 .... | Q×P*ch* |
|---|---|
| 31 K—R1 | P—Kt3 |

Forced.

| 32 R(R1)—R8! | K—Kt2!? |
|---|---|
| 33 Q—Kt4! | .... |

33 R×R? would be a terrible blunder as 33 ... Q—K8*ch* would force mate. Now White threatens 34 Q×R mate.

## 12.
| 33 .... | R×R |
|---|---|
| 34 R×R | .... |

Still threatening mate in one.

| 34 .... | P—Kt4 |
|---|---|

35 P—Kt4 !    . . . .

Now the idea is 36 Q—B8*ch*, K—Kt3; 37 B—K4*ch*.

35 . . . .          R—B5
36 Q—B8*ch*         K—Kt3

Now if White plays 37 B—K4*ch*?, then 37 . . . R×B; 38 R×R, Q—B8 mate.

A drowning man (on the chess board too) may snatch at a straw (in this case a two by four trap).

## 13.    37 Q—Q6*ch* !    K—Kt2

If 37 . . . R—B3; 38 B—K4*ch*, K—R3; 39 Q—B8 mate. Or 37 . . . P—B3; 38 R—Kt8*ch*, K—B2; 39 B—Q5 mate.

38 Q—K5*ch*          R—B3

If 38 . . . P—B3; 39 Q—K7*ch*, K—R3; 40 R—KKt8, R×P; 41 Q—Kt7*ch*, K—R4; 42 Q×RP mate.

Now White has the desired position. Chekover is not interested in the Knight Pawn. He's after big game.

## 14.    39 Q—K7 !    . . . .

Intending 40 Q—B8*ch*, K—Kt3; 41 B—K4*ch*.

39 . . . .          R—KKt3
40 Q—B8*ch*         K—B3
41 R—K7 !           R—Kt2
42 Q—Q8             . . . .

Threatening to win the Queen, or mate by 43 Q—Q6*ch*.

## 15.    42 . . . .          K—Kt3
43 Q—Q6*ch*         P—B3

On 43 . . . Q—B3; 44 B—K4*ch* wins.

| | |
|---|---|
| *44* R×R*ch* | K×R |
| *45* Q—K7*ch* | Resigns |

If 45 . . . K—Kt1; 46 B—Q5*ch*, and wins; or 45 . . . K—R3; 46 Q—B8*ch*, K—Kt3; 47 B—K4*ch* ending all resistance.

## 8. LENINGRAD 1934

### Nimzoindian Defense

*Belavienetz ties up his opponent's pieces, and then, according to theory, "the combinations should come of themselves." Nevertheless, Belavienetz adds some touches which are original and witty.*

*Belavienetz had great talent for chess. How far he might have gone we will never know, for unfortunately he as well as many other men of marked ability, gave their lives in the World War.*

| WHITE | BLACK |
|---|---|
| S. Belavienetz | V. Ragozin |

| | | |
|---|---|---|
| *1* | P—Q4 | Kt—KB3 |
| *2* | P—QB4 | P—K3 |
| *3* | Kt—QB3 | B—Kt5 |
| *4* | Q—B2 | Kt—B3 |
| *5* | Kt—B3 | . . . . |

and the position is shown on the next diagram:

**1.**    5 . . . .      O—O

Surprisingly timid, as it cedes the center without any struggle. More in the spirit of the variation would be 5 . . . P—Q3; 6 P—QR3, B×Kt*ch*; 7 Q×B, O—O.

| | |
|---|---|
| *6* P—K4 ! | B×Kt*ch* |
| *7* P×B | . . . . |

**2.** The exchange of pieces favors White. The far greater mobility of his pieces outweighs the theoretical drawback of his doubled Pawns.

| 7 .... | P—Q3 |
|---|---|
| 8 P—K5 | P×P |
| 9 P×P | Kt—Q2 |

**3.** See the previous note. The outlook for Black's development is bleak.

| 10 B—R3 | .... |
|---|---|

An attractive alternative was 10 Kt—Kt5, P—KKt3; 11 P—B4 followed by 12 Kt—K4.

| 10 .... | Kt—K2 |
|---|---|

**4.** 11 R—Q1   P—KR3

To stop White from playing 12 Kt—Kt5, P—KKt3; 13 Kt—K4, Q—K1 (otherwise 14 Kt—B6*ch*, K—Kt2; 15 Q—Q3 wins the pinned Queen Knight); 14 R× Kt!, B(or Q)×R; 15 Kt—B6*ch*, winning the Queen.

| 12 Q—K4 | .... |
|---|---|

White is now powerfully centralized.

**5.** Black cannot free his game by 12 ... P—KB4, as after 13 P×P e.p., Kt×P (13 ... R×P; 14 Kt—K5 followed by 15 Q—Q3 wins); 14 R×Q, Kt×Q; 15 B×Kt wins a piece.

| 12 .... | R—K1 |
|---|---|
| 13 B—Q3 | Kt—B1 |
| 14 O—O | R—Kt1 |

It is surprising that Ragozin who is skilled in the conduct of the black side of the Nimzovich Defense is here so curiously helpless. The text move defends the Knight Pawn so that the Bishop may be developed.

**6.** Black's pieces have been forced into awkward defensive positions.

*15* Q—Kt4     . . . .

Threatens to win the Queen by 16 B—R7*ch*.

*15* . . . .     B—Q2
*16* B—B1     . . . .

Increasing the pressure against Black's crowded King side.

**7.** White threatens 17 B×P.

*16* . . . .     Kt—B4
*17* Q—R3     . . . .

Making room for 18 P—Kt4 to drive away the Knight.

*17* . . . .     Kt—Kt3
*18* B—K4 **!**     . . . .

**8.** If Black plays 18 . . . Q—B1 (to free himself from the pin) White wins by 19 P—Kt4, Kt(B4)—K2; 20 B×RP, P×B; 21 Q×P followed by 22 Kt—Kt5 forcing mate.

*18* . . . .     Q—K2
*19* P—Kt4     . . . .

White dictates the tempo.

# 9. 19 ....      B—R5

On 19 . . . Kt(B4)—R5; 20 Kt×Kt, Kt×Kt; 21 R×B, Q×R; 22 Q×Kt and White, with two Bishops for a Rook, and the attack as well, has an easy win.

| 20 P×Kt | P×P |
| 21 Q×BP | B×R |
| 22 R×B | . . . . |

# 10. Black needs mobility for his Rooks. He can stop the threatened 23 R—Q7 by 22 . . . QR—Q1 but he wants to keep both his Rooks, as an exchange simplifies White's task.

22 ....      Q—K3

Of course not 22 . . . Kt×P?; 23 Q—R7*ch* and mate next move. But White welcomes the exchange of Queens, as he gets his Rook on the seventh rank.

Once there, the Rook will not only be in position to gobble up all of Black's Pawns, but will confine the enemy King to the last rank and thus prevent him from taking part in the ending.

# 11. 23 Q×Q      ....

More effective than the "brilliant" 23 Q×Kt, P×Q; 24 B—Q5, K—B2, and White's Rook does not get to the seventh.

| 23 .... | R×Q |
| 24 R—Q7 | Kt×P |
| 25 Kt×Kt | R×Kt |

Black hopes to break through with his Rooks by way of the King file.

# 12. 26 P—B3      R(Kt1)—K1
27 R×QBP      P—B4

28 B—Q5*ch*!  . . . .

**13.** 28 . . . .          K—R1

If 28 . . . R×B; 29 P×R, R—
K8*ch*; 30 K—B2, R×B; 31 P—
Q6, R—Q8 (31 . . . K—B1; 32
R—B8*ch*, K—B2; 33 P—Q7);
32 P—Q7 and White wins.

29 B—B4          R—K8*ch*
30 K—Kt2         R(K1)—K7*ch*
31 K—R3          P—KKt4

**14.** Black has faint hopes of
spreading a mating net,

somewhat as follows: 32 B—Kt3,
R—Q8; 33 R×P, R—Q6 (threat-
ening 34 . . . P—B5); 34 P—
B4, P—Kt5*ch*; 35 K—R4, R×
P*ch*; 36 B×R, R—R6 mate.

32 B—Q6          R—KKt8
33 R—K7 !        . . . .

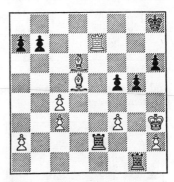

**15.** The threat of 34 B—
K5*ch* forces Black to exchange Rooks.

33 . . . .        R×R
34 B×R           P—Kt3
35 P—B5 !        P×P
36 B×BP          R—Q8
37 P—QB4         Resigns

The passed Pawn is decisive.

## 9.  LENINGRAD 1934

### Ruy Lopez

*Savitzky's conduct of the at-
tack is novel, imaginative, and
winning (in both senses). His
own King seems to be highly
exposed and vulnerable, but*

*Savitzky keeps his opponent too busy defending to think of counter-attack.*

| WHITE | BLACK |
|-------|-------|
| **F. Bogatyrchuk** | **L. Savitzky** |
| 1 P—K4 | P—K4 |
| 2 Kt—KB3 | Kt—QB3 |
| 3 B—Kt5 | P—QR3 |
| 4 B—R4 | Kt—B3 |
| 5 O—O | B—B4 |

and the position is shown on the diagram below:

**1.** Black's system of defense is now somewhat outmoded, as it generally leads to complications in White's favor.

        6 P—Q3        . . . .

Too tame to be considered an attempt at refutation. A good line is 6 Kt×P, Kt×Kt; 7 P—Q4, Kt×P; 8 Q—K2.

Reckless play is bad, but so is undue caution! A bad opening *becomes good if wrongly met.*

**2.** Black has a fairly easy game now that his Bishop is left undisturbed, and in possession of a good diagonal.

| 6 . . . . | P—Q3 |
|-----------|------|
| 7 P—Q4 | P×P |
| 8 Kt×P | B—Q2 |

Better than 8 . . . B×Kt; 9 B× Kt*ch*, P×B; 10 Q×B, and Black has lost his well-posted Bishop.

**3.**    9 Kt×Kt        P×Kt

White exchanged in order to avoid wasting a move.

*10 Kt—B3* . . . .

Overlooking Black's next move, or else he would have played 10 B—KKt5.

*10* . . . . **Kt—Kt5 !**

Presaging trouble for the King! White's pieces do not co-operate, and defense is thus doubly difficult.

**4.** Black threatens to win at once with 11 . . . Q—R5.

*11* **Q—B3** . . . .

White sees too late that 11 B×P fails on account of 11 . . . Q—R5; 12 P—KR3, Kt×P and Black wins the exchange. Or, if 11 P—KR3, Kt—K4 threatening 12 . . . Q—R5 followed by 13 . . . B×P.

*11* . . . . **O—O**
*12* **B—B4** **Q—K2 !**

This, and the next move are intended to discourage White from advancing his King Pawn.

**5.** Correct strategically (pressure in the center), Black's last move also involves a tactical maneuver. If White plays 13 B× BP, then comes 13 . . . Kt×BP; 14 B×R, B—KKt5; 15 Q—Kt3, Kt×P*ch* winning the Queen.

*13* **QR—K1** **QR—K1**
*14* **Q—Kt3** **P—B4 !**

**6.** White cannot reply 15 P×P, on account of 15 . . . Q×R.

*15* **P—KR3** **P—Kt4 !**

If 21 P×P, B×P*ch!* wins.

21 . . . .    P—Kt6

**7.**  If now 16 B×KtP, Q×B; 17 P×Kt, P—B5; 18 Q—Q3, P—B6; 19 P×P, B×P; 20 P×B, Q×P*ch;* 21 K—R1 (21 Q—Kt3, Q×Q*ch*), Q—R5*ch;* 22 K—Kt2, R—K2; 23 Q—Kt3*ch,* R—Kt2 and Black wins.

| 16 | P×Kt  | P×B   |
|----|-------|-------|
| 17 | Q×P   | P×KtP |
| 18 | Q—Kt3 | P—KR4! |

**9.**  22 Kt—Q1    P×P*ch*

22 . . . P—R6 also wins.

23 Kt×P    Q—Kt4

Intending 24 . . . P—R6.

24 K—R1    R×P

**8.**
| 19 | P—K5 | P—R5  |
|----|------|-------|
| 20 | Q—Q3 | B—B4  |
| 21 | Q—K2 | . . . . |

**10.**
| 25 | Q—B4*ch* | B—K3  |
|----|----------|-------|
| 26 | R×R      | Q×R   |
| 27 | Q×KRP    | . . . . |

Seems to protect the Knight, but—

27 . . . . B×Kt

**11.** Now if 28 R×B, Q—K8*ch*; 29 K—R2, Q×R leaves Black a Rook ahead.

28 Q—R6    R—B3
29 **Resigns,** as after 29 Q—R2 (to prevent a Queen check on the Rook file), Q×Q*ch*; 30 K×Q, R—R3 is mate.

## 10. LENINGRAD 1934

### Gruenfeld Defense

*The mid-game features ingenious attack and counter-attack on the Queen side, when suddenly Chekover shifts the scene of the fighting to the King side, and breaks through the defenses with a brilliant sacrifice to force the win.*

*The startling switch from one end of the board to the other was a characteristic of the pre-war Bogolyubov.*

| WHITE | BLACK |
|---|---|
| V. Chekover | V. Alatorzev |
| 1 P—Q4 | Kt—KB3 |
| 2 P—QB4 | P—KKt3 |
| 3 Kt—QB3 | P—Q4 |
| 4 P—K3 | P—K3 |

and the position is shown on the diagram below:

**1.** Black's last move weakens his black squares unnecessarily. More in the spirit of this defense would be 4 . . . B—Kt2 or 4 . . . P—B3.

| 5 Kt—B3 | B—Kt2 |
| 6 B—Q3 | O—O |
| 7 O—O | P—Kt3 |

A better plan might have been 7 . . . P—QR3, then 8 . . . P×P; 9 B×BP, P—QKt4.

**2.**  8 P×P          Kt×P

Naturally not 8 . . . P×P, as he wants to keep the long diagonal open for his Queen Bishop.

         9 Kt×Kt        Q×Kt

**4.**  13 P—QR4        Q—KR4
        14 P—R5         R—B1
        15 Kt—Q2        . . . .

Intending 16 Kt—B4 followed by 17 P×P. Then if 17 . . . P×P; 18 Kt×P wins the exchange, or if 17 . . . B×Kt; 18 P—Kt7 is a neat touch.

        15 . . . .      Q—QKt4

To prevent 16 Kt—B4—he thinks!

**3.**  10 Q—B2         . . . .

With two threats: 11 B—K4, and 11 Q×P.

        10 . . . .      B—QR3
        11 B—K4         Q—QKt4

Threat: 12 . . . Q×R mate.

        12 R—K1         P—QB3

**5.**  16 Kt—B4 !      . . . .

Now if 16 . . . Q×Kt; 17 Q×

Q, B×Q; 18 P×P (threatening 19 P—Kt7) B—QR3; 19 R×B! Kt×R; 20 P—Kt7, and the Pawn fork snags a Rook, leaving a won ending for White.

| 16 .... | Kt—Q2 |

Hoping for 17 Kt—Q6 when 17 . . . Q—Kt5 would win a piece.

**6.** | 17 P—QKt3 | .... |

An attack on White's Knight Pawn by 17 . . . Kt—B4 would be met by 18 Kt—R3, Q×KtP; 19 P×Kt, Q×Q; 20 Kt×Q, B×R; 21 Kt×B, and White wins.

| 17 .... | B—B1 |
| 18 B—Q3 | .... |

Threatening to win a piece by 19 Kt—K5, Q—Kt5; 20 B—R3, B× B; 21 Q×B, Q—Kt4; 22 Q×Q, P×Q; 23 Kt×Kt.

Alatorzev's pieces are awkwardly placed as a result of his deliberate flouting of principles in the opening—the combination of . . . P—KKt3 and . . . P—K3.

**7.** | 18 .... | Q—R4 |
| 19 B—K2 | Q—KKt4 |
| 20 P—K4 | Q—Q1 |

The threats against his Queen have made Black lose valuable time. White meanwhile has built up a powerful center.

| 21 B—Kt2 | .... |

**8.** | 21 .... | P—QKt4 |
| 22 Kt—K3 | P—QB4 |
| 23 P—Q5 | P—K4 |
| 24 Kt—Kt4 | P—B3 |

Saddles Black with an organic weakness, besides lessening the mobility of his Queen, Knight, and King Bishop.

**9.**  25 Q—Q2          P—R4

Black's best chance to make a fight of it was by 25 . . . B—Q3 and 26 . . . Q—K2.

|     |          |          |
| --- | -------- | -------- |
| 26  | Kt—K3    | B—Q3     |
| 27  | B×P !    | P×B      |
| 28  | Kt—B5    | . . . .  |

Establishing a beachhead.

**10.**  28 . . . .          B—B1
        29 R—K3          K—R2

|     |          |          |
| --- | -------- | -------- |
| 30  | Q—K2     | Q—K1     |
| 31  | R—KR3    | . . . .  |

Threatening to win by 32 R×P*ch*, K—Kt1; 33 Q—Kt4*ch*, K—B2; 34 R—R7*ch* and mate next move.

**11.**  31 . . . .          B—KKt2
        32 R×P*ch*          K—Kt1
        33 Q—Kt4          Resigns

Mate is threatened by 34 Q×B and if 33 . . . Q—B1 (33 . . . Q—B2; 34 Kt—R6*ch* wins the Queen); 34 Q—Kt6, and mate in three follows by 35 Kt—R6*ch*, K—R1; 36 Kt—B7*ch*, K—Kt1; 37 R—R8 mate.

## 11.  LENINGRAD 1934

### Bogolyubov Variation

*Chekover's clear-cut and logical opening play is the prelude to some sharp tactics, culminating in an original pinning maneuver. His opponent man-*

*ages to extricate himself from the pin, only to find himself the victim of a witty finale, carefully staged by Chekover. A beautiful game!*

| WHITE | BLACK |
|-------|-------|
| V. Chekover | I. Mazel |
| 1 P—Q4 | Kt—KB3 |
| 2 P—QB4 | P—K3 |
| 3 Kt—KB3 | B—Kt5*ch* |
| 4 B—Q2 | Q—K2 |
| 5 P—KKt3 | O—O |

and the position is shown on the diagram below:

**1.** Black's system of defense is an attempt to seize the initiative by force. White is content to keep his opening advantage by making simple developing moves—getting as many pieces into play as possible.

    6 B—Kt2    . . . .

Of course not 6 B×B, Q×B*ch*, and Black wins a Pawn.

**2.** Black is now practically forced to exchange Bishops, or run the risk of losing a piece. White's plan is to castle, then play B—K3, follow up with P—B5 (shutting the exit gate) and then win the Bishop by P—QR3 and P—QKt4.

| 6 . . . . | B×B*ch* |
|-----------|---------|
| 7 Q×B | P—Q3 |
| 8 Kt—B3 | QKt—Q2 |
| 9 O—O | P—K4 |

**3.** The exchange of Bishops developed White's Queen with his QKt on its best square.

| 10 P—K4 | Kt—Kt3 |
|---------|--------|
| 11 P—Kt3 | B—Kt5 |
| 12 KR—K1 | P—B3 |

**4.** White has a tiny positional advantage, but how does he proceed? If he plays 13 P×P, then the recapture 13 . . . P×P frees Black, besides giving him the open Queen file for his Rooks.

| 13 Q—K3 | QR—Q1 |
|---------|-------|
| 14 Kt—Q2 | . . . . |

**5.** White's last two moves cleared the way for the

KBP to come up, and attack the center.

14 . . . .        P×P

Black exchanges Pawns, in order to follow up with 15 . . . Q—K4 with the hope either of exchanging Queens, or giving his own Queen more mobility. Had he postponed 14 . . . P×P, then after 15 P—B4, his Queen could not get to K4.

**6.** 15 Q×P        Q—K4

That positional judgment outweighs the ability to concoct dazzling combinations, can be shown at this point. One ill-considered move can throw away all the previous gains. For example if 16 Q×Q, P×Q, and Black can double his Rooks on the Queen file with a good game.

| 16 Q—Q3 | Q—QB4 |
|---------|-------|
| 17 Kt—B1 | . . . . |

Can Black free himself?

**7.** White advances by re-treating. The Knight is headed for K3, from which point he will, together with five other White units, exert pressure on the important square Q5.

*17 . . . .*            **P—Q4**

If Black cannot free his game now, he will never be able to do it later.

*18* BP×P            P×P

**9.** Two more units have come off the board, and the position begins to clear up. Continuing the exchanges by 20 P×Kt, Kt×P; 21 B×Kt, R(or Q)×B, gives Black the best of it. The next two moves begin to reveal White's strategy.

*20* P×Kt            Kt×P
*21* R—K5 !!            . . . .

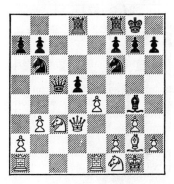

**8.** Again, White must make an important decision of policy.

**10.** A beautiful move! The Knight is pinned, and White threatens to win a piece at once by 22 R×Kt. Black must lose time in his effort to get out of the pin, and White will then disclose the real point of his combination.

    **21 . . . .**        **B—K3**

If Black tries a counter-attack on White's Queen by 21 . . . Kt—Kt5; 22 Q—K4 !, R—Q5; 23 R×Q, R×Q; 24 B×R wins.

**11.**    **22 R—Q1**        **Kt—Kt5**

This is forced, as the Knight was attacked four times, and only defended three times. Black could not bring up another defender, so he unpins himself by a double attack on White's Queen. White must be careful now as 23 Q×Pch, K×Q; 24 R×Q, R×R loses a Rook.

The pin is broken, but White is in full control of the Queen file—an important consideration in the coming combination.

    **23 Q×R !**        **. . . .**

**12.**  Another fine move! White offers his Queen, but Black does not dare take it. If 23 . . . R×Q; 24 R×Rch, Q—B1; 25 R×Qch, K×R, and White is a Rook up.

    **23 . . . .**        **Q×R**

Black must be content with recapturing the Rook, leaving pieces even, but with White in full control of the open Queen file.

    **24 Q—K7 !**        **. . . .**

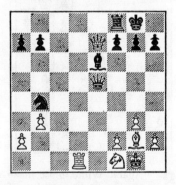

**13.**  Black has two things to worry about. One is 25

Q×Kt, and the other is 25 R—Q8 with 26 Q×R mate to follow. Once White's Rook reaches Q8, it's all over, as Black cannot exchange Rooks, nor can he protect his own Rook.

         **24 . . . .**        **Q—QR4**

On 24 . . . Kt—Q4 (to block the Rook) simply 25 R×Kt wins, or if 24 . . . Kt—B3; 25 B×Kt, P×B; 26 R—Q8 wins.

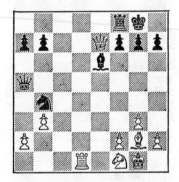

**14.** Black has succeeded in guarding against both threats.

         **25 P—QR3**      **. . . .**

Now White plans to chase the Knight, and then drive the Queen away from the defense of the square Q8.

         **25 . . . .**        **Kt—B7**

If 25 . . . Kt—B3; 26 Q×P wins a Pawn. Or if 25 . . . Kt—Q4; 26 B×Kt, B×B; 27 Q—K5 (the pin again) R—Q1; 28 P—QKt4, Q—Kt4; 29 Kt—K3 wins. The Knight is hors de combat.

**15.** White is now ready to put on the finishing touches.

         **26 P—QKt4**      **Q—Kt3**

The only square the Queen can go to, which still prevents 27 R—Q8. But now comes the knockout punch—

         **27 R—Q6 !**     **Resigns**

There is no way to stop White's Rook from reaching his goal.

## 12. MATCH, 1934

### Nimzoindian Defense

*Yudovich plays it in Capablanca style—simply, clearly, and logically. Apparently all he does is develop his pieces, and his opponent's game collapses. But—and this is in common with many of Capa's games— there are subtle finesses in the explanatory notes. A suitable motto for this game: The mailed fist in the velvet glove! Luckily, it is easier to appreciate such games than to play them.*

| WHITE | BLACK |
|-------|-------|
| I. Kan | M. Yudovich |

| | | |
|---|---|---|
| 1 | P—Q4 | Kt—KB3 |
| 2 | P—QB4 | P—K3 |
| 3 | Kt—QB3 | B—Kt5 |
| 4 | Q—B2 | P—Q4 |
| 5 | P×P | Q×P |

and the position is shown on the diagram below:

**1.** The recapture with the Queen followed by an early . . . P—B4 gives Black a fine free game.

| | | |
|---|---|---|
| 6 | Kt—B3 | P—B4 |
| 7 | P×P | . . . . |

More usual is 7 B—Q2 or 7 P—QR3 to force Black to exchange his Bishop for a Knight.

**2.** 7 . . . .    Q×BP
8 B—K3    . . . .

A strange move, to which may be attributed some of White's later difficulties. A better plan would have been 8 B—Q2, Kt—B3; 9 P—K3, O—O; 10 R—B1.

8 . . . .    B×Ktch !

**3.** 9 P×B    . . . .

Taking with the Queen leads to an end-game where White's weaknesses are further accentuated.

| | | |
|---|---|---|
| 9 .... | | **Q—K2** |
| 10 P—Kt3 | | .... |

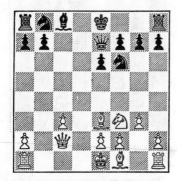

| | | |
|---|---|---|
| **4.** | 10 .... | **Kt—B3** |
| | 11 B—Kt2 | **O—O** |
| | 12 O—O | **P—K4 !** |

Getting his Bishop into action, and also preventing White from occupying the central square Q4.

| | | |
|---|---|---|
| **5.** | 13 QR—Kt1 | **R—Q1** |
| | 14 P—KR3 | **B—K3** |
| | 15 B—Kt5 | **P—QKt3** |

Not at once 15 . . . R—Q2 with

a view to doubling Rooks, as White's reply would be 16 Kt—Q2 threatening 17 Kt—K4, as well as 17 R×P, R×R; 18 B(Kt2)×Kt, winning a Pawn.

| | | |
|---|---|---|
| **6.** | 16 Kt—Q2 | **QR—B1** |
| | 17 Kt—K4 | **P—KR3 !** |

White must exchange, as the Bishop cannot retreat (18 B—K3, Kt×Kt wins a Pawn).

| | | |
|---|---|---|
| **7.** | 18 B×Kt | .... |

If instead 18 Kt×Kt*ch*, P×Kt;

19 B×RP, Kt—Q5!; 20 Q—Kt2, R×P; 21 KR—B1, (21 Q×R?, Kt×P*ch*), KR—QB1; 22 R×R, R×R; 23 R—B1, Q—B4! and Black wins the King Pawn.

18 .... P×B

**8.** Black plans to win by 19 ... P—B4; 20 Kt—Q2, Kt—Q5 followed by 21 ... R×P.

19 P—Kt4 ....

To stop 19 ... P—B4.

19 .... P—B4!

But it doesn't stop Black!

20 P×P B×BP

Black threatens 21 ... Kt—Q5; 22 Q—Q3 (if 22 Q—Kt2, B×Kt; 23 B×B, R×P), R×P!

Aside from this immediate tactical threat, Black intends to capitalize on the weakness of the pinned Knight and to initiate as well an attack on the King by way of the open Knight file.

**9.** 21 P—K3 R—Q3!

An extraordinary way to bring the Rook over to the Knight file.

22 K—R2 ....

Taking the Rook would be fatal: 22 Kt×R, B×Q; 23 Kt×R, Q—K3; 24 R—Kt2, B—R5! and White's Knight is lost, as after 25 B×Kt, B×B; 26 Kt×P, Q—Kt3*ch*; 27 K—R2, Q—Kt7 is mate!

22 .... R—Kt3

**10.** Black is preparing to mass his heavy pieces

against White's King side. If for example 23 R—Kt1, Q—R5; to be followed by 24 . . . K—R1 and 25 . . . R(B1)—KKt1.

| 23 P—KB4 | K—R1 |
|----------|------|
| 24 Q—B2  | .... |

To stop 24 . . . Q—R5, and free himself as well from the Bishop's embarrassing pin.

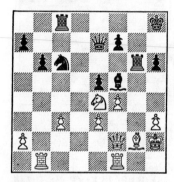

**11.**

| 24 .... | P×P |
|---------|-----|
| 25 Q×P  | R×B*ch*! |

Wins a piece.

| 26 K×R | Q×Kt*ch* |
|--------|----------|
| 27 **Resigns** | |

On 27 K—R2, Q×Q*ch*; 28 P×Q, B×R is convincing.

## 13. MOSCOW 1934

### French Defense

*A long time ago, the French Defense was considered dull and unenterprising. To-day, a census of brilliant and exciting*

*games would probably show that a goodly portion were produced by what one player called derisively, "the King's Pawn one sneak Opening."*

| WHITE | BLACK |
|-------|-------|
| **V. Panov** | **A. Poliak** |
| 1 P—K4 | P—K3 |
| 2 P—Q4 | P—Q4 |
| 3 Kt—QB3 | Kt—KB3 |
| 4 B—Kt5 | B—K2 |
| 5 P—K5 | KKt—Q2 |
| 6 P—KR4 | .... |

and the position is shown on the diagram below:

**1.** Accepting the offered Pawn leads to a difficult game to defend, for example: 6 . . . B×B; 7 P×B, Q×P; 8 Kt—R3, Q—K2; 9 Kt—B4, P—QR3 (9 . . . P—QB4; 10 Kt—Kt5); 10 Q—Kt4, P—KKt3; 11 O—O—O, P—QB4; 12 Q—Kt3, Kt—Kt3; 13 P×P, Q×P; 14 B—Q3, Q—B1; 15 B—K4!

6 . . . .                    P—KR3

9 . . . .                    P—KKt4
10 O—O—O                     P—R3

If 10 . . . P—QB4; 11 Kt—Kt5 !

**2.** Aside from Black's last move, he might have tried 6 . . . P—QR3 or 6 . . . O—O or 6 . . . P—KB3, of which the last is regarded as the best.

| 7 B×B | Q×B |
| 8 Q—Kt4 | P—KKt3 |
| 9 P—R5 ! | . . . . |

**4.**
| 11 P—B4 | P×P |
| 12 Kt—B3 | P—QB4 |
| 13 P×P | Kt—QB3 |

Black does not bite on 13 . . . Kt×BP; 14 Kt×P, P×Kt (14 . . . Q—B1; 15 Kt—B7*ch*, or 14 . . . Q—Q1; 15 Kt—B6*ch*); 15 Q×B*ch*, Q—Q1; 16 Q×Kt(B5).

**3.** If Black tries to break the attack by exchanging Queens, there is this pretty possibility: 9 . . . Q—Kt4; 10 Q×Q, P×Q; 11 P×P, R×R; 12 P—Kt7 !

**5.**
| 14 Q×BP | Kt×BP |

Black seems to have equalized, and if let alone will develop his Bishop at Q2, and then castle Queen side. But White intends to keep him busy!

|       |        |       |
|-------|--------|-------|
| 15 B—K2 | B—Q2 |
| 16 R—R4 | .... |

Preparing for 17 P—QKt4, which if played at once loses by 16 . . . Kt×KtP; 17 Q×Kt, Kt—Q6*ch* and White's Queen falls.

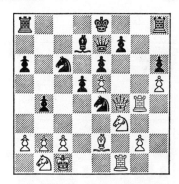

## 6. 16 .... P—Kt4

Black does not castle, as after 16 . . . O—O—O; 17 P—Kt4, Kt—K5 (17 . . . P—Q5; 18 P×Kt, P×Kt; 19 R—Q6); 18 Kt×Kt, P×Kt; 19 Q×KP he loses a Pawn.

|       |        |
|-------|--------|
| 17 R—Kt4 | P—Kt5 |
| 18 Kt—QKt1 | Kt—K5 |

Threatening 19 . . . Kt—B7.

|       |        |
|-------|--------|
| 19 R—B1 | .... |

The KBP is a target.

## 7. 19 .... Q—B4

Black gives up the idea of castling, and instead initiates a tricky counter-attack. If White now plays 20 B—Q3 (to displace the annoying Knight), Black wins by 20 . . . Kt—B7!

|       |        |
|-------|--------|
| 20 QKt—Q2 | Kt×Kt |
| 21 Kt×Kt | Kt—Q1 |

## 8.
The Knight's move not only defended the threatened Bishop Pawn; it also enhances the coming . . . QR—B1.

22 **Q—B6 !**     . . . .

After 22 Q×KtP, Q×Q; 23 R×Q, Black gets his Pawn back by 23 . . . Kt—B3.

| 22 . . . . | **R—KB1** |
| 23 **Q×P** | **R—B1** |

**9.**  Black threatens mate on the move.

| 24 **B—Q3** | **B—Kt4** |
| 25 **Kt—Kt3** | **Q—B2** |
| 26 **B×B**ch | **P×B** |

**10.**  27 **Q—Q2**     **Kt—B3**

If 27 . . . Q×P; 28 R—Kt5, Q—K5; 29 Kt—Q4 (but not 29 R—K1, R×Pch) with a decisive attack.

| 28 **R—K1** | **Kt×P** |
| 29 **R×P** | . . . . |

Tempting Black to play 29 . . . Q×Pch; 30 Q×Q, Kt—Q6ch; 31 K—Q2 ! (not 31 K—Kt1, R×Q; 32 K×R, Kt×R(5)ch), R×Qch; 32 K×Kt !

29 . . . .     **Kt—B5**

**11.**  30 **Q×P**     **Kt—R6**

Hoping for 31 Q—Q2, Kt×P catching a Rook.

31 **R×P**ch **!!**     . . . .

Forces the win. If 31 . . . P×R; 32 Q×KPch, Q—K2 (32 . . . K—Q1; 33 R—Q4ch); 33 Q× Rch, K—B2; 34 R—B4ch forcing a won ending.

31 . . . .     **Resigns**

Resourceful play by Panov.

### 14. TIFLIS 1934

### Colle System

*A charming miniature. Black whips up a combination as surprising as it is elegant, and tops it off with an artistic checkmate.*

| WHITE | BLACK |
|-------|-------|
| Sereda | Gambarashvilli |

| | |
|---|---|
| 1 P—Q4 | Kt—KB3 |
| 2 Kt—KB3 | P—K3 |
| 3 P—K3 | P—B4 |
| 4 B—Q3 | P—QKt3 |
| 5 QKt—Q2 | Kt—B3 |

and the position is shown on the diagram below:

**1.** Black's fianchetto is undoubtedly one of the best ways of taking the sting out of Colle's system.

6 P—QKt3          . . . .

Inferior to Colle's favorite procedure: 6 P—B3, 7 Q—K2; 8 O—O and an early P—K4.

**2.**
| | |
|---|---|
| 6 . . . . | P×P ! |
| 7 P×P | B—Kt2 |
| 8 O—O | Kt—Q4 |

Threatening to exchange White's attacking Bishop by 9 . . . Kt(3)—Kt5. If then 10 B—K2 ?, Kt—B6; 11 Q—K1, Kt×BP wins the Queen!

**3.**
| | |
|---|---|
| 9 P—B4 | Kt—B5 |
| 10 B—Kt1 | . . . . |

Much better was 10 Kt—K4, letting Black have his two Bishops.

**4.**        10 . . . .        Kt×QP !

Black's Knight cannot be taken as after 11 Kt×Kt, Q—Kt4 (threatening 12 . . . Q×P mate); 12 P—Kt3, Kt—R6 is mate!

         11 B—Kt2        Kt(Q5)—K7*ch*
         12 K—R1        Q—Kt4 !

**5.**        The intent is 13 . . . Q×P mate. Of course if 13 Kt× Q, B×P is mate.

13 R—Kt1        Q—Kt5

Threatens to win the exchange, to begin with.

        14 P—KR3        Q—R4

**6.**        Now the idea is 15 . . . Kt×RP; 16 P×Kt (otherwise 16 . . . Kt×P mate), Q×P mate.

        15 B—K4        B×B
        16 Kt×B        Kt×RP !

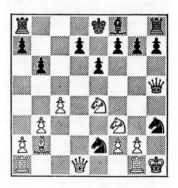

**7.**        Black finishes cleverly.

17 Kt—R2 ....

Or 17 P×Kt, Q×Ktch; 18 R—Kt2, Q×Pch; 19 R—R2, Q—B6ch; 20 R—Kt2, Q×Kt wins.

17 .... Kt×Pch !
18 Kt×Kt Kt—Kt6 mate

A beautiful smothered mate.

## 15. CORRESPONDENCE 1935

### French Defense

*Highlights in Baranov's masterly attack:*
*1. He induces the weakening 12 . . . P—KKt3.*
*2. He utilizes the weakness to force open the Rook file.*
*3. He climaxes the attack by a "quiet" move.*
*4. He simplifies the ending logically.*
*5. He garnishes his whole creation generously with some delightfully piquant surprise moves.*

| WHITE | BLACK |
|-------|-------|
| C. Baranov | Y. Rochlin |

| | | |
|---|---|---|
| 1 | P—K4 | P—K3 |
| 2 | P—Q4 | P—Q4 |
| 3 | Kt—QB3 | P×P |
| 4 | Kt×P | .... |

and the position is shown on the next diagram:

**1.** 4 .... Kt—KB3

More usual is 4 . . . Kt—Q2 and then 5 . . . KKt—B3, in order to reply to 6 Kt×Ktch by 6 . . . Kt×Kt.

5 B—Kt5 ....

Better is 5 Kt×Ktch, P×Kt (5 . . . Q×Kt brings the Queen out too soon) and Black's Pawn position is weakened.

**2.**

| | | |
|---|---|---|
| 5 | .... | QKt—Q2 |
| 6 | Kt—KB3 | B—K2 |
| 7 | Kt×Ktch | B×Kt |

| 8 B×B | Q×B |
|---|---|

8 . . . Kt×B is much safer.

**3.**  9 Q—Q2      O—O
    10 B—Q3·    P—B4

Black should have played 10 . . .
R—Q1, and if 11 Kt—Kt5, then
11 . . . Kt—B1, to avoid moving
any of the King side Pawns.

**4.**  11 O—O—O      . . . .

Indicating his intention of launch-
ing a King-side attack.

| 11 . . . . | P×P |
|---|---|
| 12 Kt—Kt5 ! | . . . . |

Stronger than the obvious 12
Kt×P. The threat of 13 Kt×RP
forces

    12 . . . .      P—KKt3

Now the weakened Pawn structure gives White a target to shoot
at.

**5.**  13 P—KR4      R—Q1
    14 P—R5      Kt—B1
    15 P×P      BP×P

No better was 15 . . . RP×P, and
White doubles his Rooks on the
open Rook file. Or 15 . . . Kt×
P; 16 R×P.

    16 R—R6      . . . .

Threatening 17 Kt×RP, Kt×Kt;
18 R×P*ch*, winning the Queen.
    The attack is to be built up
on the open King Rook file.
White's last move not only prepares for the doubling of the
Rooks, but also paralyzes Black's
King Rook Pawn.

**6.**
| 16 .... | R—Q2 |
|---|---|
| 17 QR—R1 | P—Kt3 |
| 18 Kt—K4 | Q—K4 |

Black must stop 19 Q—B4 (or Kt5) followed by 20 Kt—B6*ch*.

| 19 P—KB4 | Q—Kt2 |
|---|---|
| 20 P—B5 ! | KP×P |

**8.**
| 23 Q—B4 | P—R4 |
|---|---|

If 23 . . . B—Kt2 White wins by 24 Q—R4, Q—Kt2; 25 Kt×P, Kt×Kt; 26 R×Kt*ch*, Q×R; 27 Q—B6*ch*, R—Kt2; 28 R×Q*ch*, K×R; 29 Q—R4 mate! Black's last move is intended to meet 24 Q—R4 by 24 . . . QR—R2, adding another protector to his King Rook Pawn.

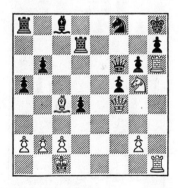

**7.**
| 21 B—B4*ch* | K—R1 |
|---|---|
| 22 Kt—Kt5 | .... |

Bearing down on Black's Rook Pawn and preparing to add more pressure by 23 Q—B4 and 24 Q—R4.

| 22 .... | Q—B3 |
|---|---|

**9.**
| 24 P—KKt4 ! | .... |
|---|---|

Now if 24 . . . QR—R2 White

wins by 25 Kt×P, R×Kt; 26 P—
Kt5, Q—Kt2 (if 26 . . . Q—K2;
27 Q×Pch wins); 27 Q—Q6!,
R—Q2; 28 R×Rch, Kt×R; 29
R×Ktch and mate in two moves.

        24 . . . .            P—Kt4
        25 Kt×P !            . . . .

**10.** White has started a far-
sighted combination.

        25 . . . .            R×Kt
        26 R×Rch            Kt×R
        27 R×Ktch            K×R

**11.**    28 P—Kt5 !        Q×P

Black must give up his Queen
to avoid mate. If for example 28
. . . Q—K2; 29 Q—R4ch, K—
Kt2; 30 Q—R6 is mate. Or if
28 . . . Q—R1; 29 Q—R2ch,
K—Kt2; 30 Q—B7ch, K—B1; 31
Q—B7 mate.

        29 Q×Q            P×B

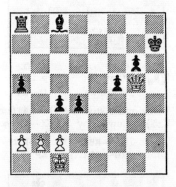

**12.** Black has enough material for his Queen, but
his forces are scattered and vulnerable.

        30 Q—Kt2 !        R—R2

Or    30 . . . R—R3    (30 . . .
R—Kt1; 31 Q—R2ch); 31 Q—
R2ch, K—Kt1; 32 Q—B7, R—R1;
33 Q—B6, R—Kt1; 34 Q×KtPch,
K—R1; 35 Q—Q6, R—R1; 36
Q—Q5 and White wins a piece!
    From this point to the end of
the game, Baranov demonstrates
in masterly manner the tremendous power of the Queen on an
open board. Unfortunately for
Rochlin, his forces are too scattered to offer more than token
resistance.

**13.** White proceeds to catch the Bishop.

| 31 | Q—R2*ch* | K—Kt2 |
| 32 | Q—Kt8 | R—KB2 |
| 33 | Q×B | P—B5 |

Black places his hopes on his two connected passed Pawns.

**14.**

| 34 | Q×P | P—B6 |
| 35 | Q×P*ch* | K—R3 |
| 36 | Q—R4*ch* | K—Kt2 |
| 37 | Q—B2 | . . . . |

Blockades the dangerous Pawn. White's problem is now to force advantageous simplification.

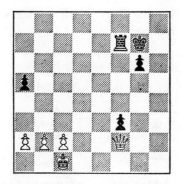

**15.**

| 37 | . . . . | P—Kt4 |
| 38 | K—Q2 | K—Kt3 |
| 39 | K—K3 | R—B5 |

If 39 . . . P—Kt5; 40 Q—R4, K—B4; 41 Q—R5*ch* followed by 42 Q×KtP winning.

| 40 | Q×P | **Resigns** |

After 40 . . . R×Q*ch;* 41 K×R, the Pawn ending is elementary.

## 16. MOSCOW 1935

### Reti Opening

*Alekhine once said that the longest combination he ever conceived was one of twenty moves. Botvinnik breaks Alekhine's record with a combination remarkable not only for its length, but also for its surpassing beauty. In the course of it Botvinnik gives away both Knights and a Rook, in order to start Black's King on a long journey from which he never returns.*

| WHITE | BLACK |
|-------|-------|
| M. Botvinnik | V. Chekover |

| | | |
|---|----------|----------|
| *1* | Kt—KB3 | P—Q4 |
| *2* | P—B4 | P—K3 |
| *3* | P—QKt3 | Kt—KB3 |
| *4* | B—Kt2 | B—K2 |
| *5* | P—K3 | O—O |

and the position is shown on the diagram below:

**1.** Modern masters rarely begin with turbulent openings such as Muzios, Danish or Evans Gambits. They start out quietly with a positional opening such as the Queen's Pawn, the Ruy Lopez, or the Reti—and yet they produce masterpieces that far outshine the old-time brilliancies.

*6* B—K2 . . . .

In the Reti, the Queen Pawn is held temporarily in leash.

**2.** *6* . . . . P—B3

This is meant to strengthen his Pawn center. A more vigorous defense was 6 . . . P—B4; 7 O—O, Kt—B3; 8 P—Q3, P—QKt3, followed by 9 . . . B—Kt2 and 10 . . . R—B1.

| | | |
|---|----------|----------|
| *7* | O—O | QKt—Q2 |
| *8* | Kt—B3 | P—QR3 |
| *9* | Kt—Q4 ! | . . . . |

**3.** White has adopted an original means of stopping Black from playing 9 . . . P—

K4. This would now be answered by 10 Kt—B5.

| 9 .... | P×P |
| 10 P×P | Kt—B4 |

| **4.** | 11 P—B4 | Q—B2 |
| | 12 Kt—B3 | R—Q1 |
| | 13 Q—B2 | .... |

If Black tries to develop by 13 ... B—Q2, then 14 P—Q4 wins a piece. This is a comment on Black's unsatisfactory opening play.

**5.**     13 ....     Kt(B4)—Q2

The fight to enforce ... P—K4 continues.

| 14 P—Q4 | .... |

This ends the argument. White is in full control of his K5.

| 14 .... | P—B4 |
| 15 Kt—K5 | .... |

**6.** A powerful outpost for the Knight! Black does not dare exchange Knights, as White would recapture with the Bishop Pawn, and open up a wonderful file for his King Rook.

| 15 .... | P—QKt3 |
| 16 B—Q3 | P×P |
| 17 P×P | B—Kt2 |

White has "hanging" center Pawns, but in return his pieces are excellently placed for attack.

Evidently Black has lost the battle of the opening. His efforts to enforce ... P—K4 have been thwarted, and in consequence his position is cramped. To add to his troubles his King needs tender care.

**7.**

| 18 Q—K2 | Kt—B1 |
|---|---|
| 19 Kt—Q1 | . . . . |

The Knight starts off on a long trip. Clearly he is headed for KKt5, but why go to all this trouble when Black can always play . . . P—R3?

**9.**

| 22 . . . . | P×Kt |
|---|---|

Black must take the Knight.

| 23 P×P | Kt(B1)—Q2 |
|---|---|

The other Knight must not move. If for example 23 . . . Kt(B3)—R2; 24 Kt×P, Kt×P; 25 Q—R5, Kt(Kt4)—R2; 26 P—Q5, P×P; 27 Kt—R6*ch*, K—R1; 28 Q—B7, Kt—B3; 29 Q—Kt8*ch!* Kt×Q; 30 Kt—B7 mate.

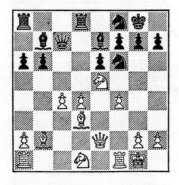

**8.**

| 19 . . . . | R—R2 |
|---|---|
| 20 Kt—B2 | Q—Kt1 |
| 21 Kt—R3 | P—R3 |

Confident that this will stop the Knight from landing at his Kt4.

22 Kt—Kt5 !! . . . .

**10.**

24 Kt×P !! . . . .

Beautiful! Instead of regaining his piece, he gives up another Knight.

24 .... **K×Kt**
25 **P—Kt6***ch* **K—Kt1**

If 25 . . . K—K1; 26 Q×P, Kt—B1; 27 Q—B7*ch*, K—Q2; 28 B—R3, R—K1; 29 R×Kt, P×R; 30 P—Kt7 wins neatly.

**11.** 26 **Q×P***ch* **K—R1**
27 **Q—R3***ch* **K—Kt1**
28 **B—B5** ....

Menacing mate in two by 29 B—K6*ch*, K—B1; 30 Q—R8 mate.

28 .... **Kt—B1**

On 28 . . . B—Q3 (to give the King more room) White forces mate by 29 B—K6*ch*, K—B1; 30 Q—R8*ch*, K—K2; 31 Q×P*ch*, K×B; 32 Q—B7 mate.

Or if 28 . . . B—Kt5; 29 B—K6*ch*, K—B1; 30 B×Kt, Q—Q3 (if 30 . . . R×B; 31 Q×R, Q—K1; 32 R×Kt*ch*, P×R; 33 P—Kt7*ch*); 31 Q—R8*ch*, K—K2; 32 Q×P mate.

**12.** 29 **B—K6***ch* **! Kt×B**
30 **Q×Kt***ch* **K—R1**

Of course not 30 . . . K—B1; 31 Q—B7 mate.

31 **Q—R3***ch* **K—Kt1**
32 **R×Kt !** ....

The third sacrifice!

**13.** 32 .... **B×R**

Naturally not 32 . . . P×R; 33 Q—R7*ch* and mate next move.

33 **Q—R7***ch* **K—B1**
34 **R—K1 !** **B—K4**

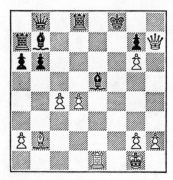

**14.** 　 35 **Q—R8**ch **!** . . . .

Much stronger and more brilliant than 35 R×B, Q×R; 36 P×Q, R—Q8ch. Black's King is now taken for a ride.

| 35 . . . . | **K—K2** |
|---|---|
| 36 **Q×P**ch | **K—Q3** |
| 37 **Q×B**ch | **K—Q2** |
| 38 **Q—B5**ch | **K—B3** |

On 38 . . . K—B2; 39 R—K7ch mates quickly.

**15.** 　| 39 **P—Q5**ch | **K—B4** |
|---|---|
| 40 **B—R3**ch | **K×P** |

41 **Q—K4**ch 　　 **K—B6**

There is no turning back (41 . . . K—Kt4; 42 Q—Kt4 mate). The King must go on.

42 **B—Kt4**ch 　　 **K—Kt7**
43 **Q—Kt1 mate**

An impressive achievement.

## 17.　EREVAN 1936

### King's Indian Defense

*White's King is separated from the rest of his army, and made to march all the way up the board to K8, there to be mated. A remarkable "King wandering," and a fine example of inspired imaginative chess by a great end-game composer.*

*The forced march of the King is a delightful motif. It must have given Kasparyan particular pleasure to have brought it about in actual play.*

| WHITE | BLACK |
|---|---|
| **V. Chekover** | **G. Kasparyan** |
| 1 **P—Q4** | **Kt—KB3** |
| 2 **P—QB4** | **P—Q3** |
| 3 **Kt—KB3** | **P—KKt3** |
| 4 **P—KKt3** | **B—Kt2** |
| 5 **B—Kt2** | **O—O** |
| 6 **O—O** | **QKt—Q2** |

and the position is shown on the next diagram:

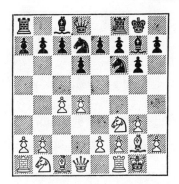

been 10 P—KR3, 11 B—K3, and 12 KR—Q1.

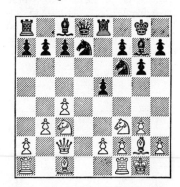

## 1.

Black's aim in this defense is an early . . . P—K4 with consequent counter-play.

| 7 Kt—B3 | P—K4 |
|---|---|
| 8 P×P | . . . . |

Better is 8 P—Kt3, R—K1; 9 Q—B2.

| 8 . . . . | P×P |
|---|---|

## 3.

| 10 . . . . | P—K5 ! |
|---|---|

Already the Bishop makes its power felt. For example, if 11 Kt—KKt5, P—KR3; 12 Kt(Kt5) ×KP, Kt×Kt; 13 B×Kt, B×Kt; 14 Q×B, R×B and Black has won a piece.

| 11 Kt—Q4 | . . . . |
|---|---|

## 2.

| 9 Q—B2 | R—K1 |
|---|---|
| 10 P—Kt3 | . . . . |

Now this move is out of place, as Black's pressure on the long diagonal is accentuated. A preferable development would have

## 4.

| 11 . . . . | P—K6 ! |
|---|---|

An unpleasant surprise.

*12 P—B4* . . . .

The reply to 12 B×KP would have been 12 . . . Kt—Kt5 followed by 13 . . . Kt×B, and Black has a won game in the positional sense.

12 . . . .      P—B3
13 B—Kt2     Q—R4 !

**5.** Black wants his Queen posted at KR4; chessically this is the shortest distance between two points.

*14 Kt—B3* . . . .

14 Kt—K4, Kt×Kt; 15 B×Kt, P—QB4; 16 B—QB3 (16 Kt—Kt5, B×B wins), permits Black to sacrifice his Queen for a powerful attack by 16 . . . Q×B; 17 Q×Q, R×B; 18 Q—Q3, R×Kt; 19 Q×KP, Kt—B3; 20 KR—Q1, B—R6 ! followed by 21 . . . Kt—Kt5.

Or if 14 B—B3 (to prevent 14 . . . Q—R4) then 14 . . . Kt—B1 followed by 15 . . . B—R6 is uncomfortable.

**6.** 14 . . . .      Q—R4
15 Kt—Q1     Kt—B4
16 B—K5      . . . .

Delightful complications ensue from White's attempt to win the King Pawn: 16 Q—B1, B—R6; 17 Kt×P, B×B; 18 K×B, Kt—Kt5; 19 Kt×Kt, R×Pch; 20 Kt—B2, Kt—Q6; 21 Q—Q1, Kt×Pch; 22 P×Kt, Q—Kt5ch; 23 K—R1, Q×Ktch; 24 K—Kt1, B×B and wins.

**7.** 16 . . . .      B—B4
17 Q—Kt2     R×B !
18 P×R       . . . .

Of course not 18 Q×R, Kt(B3)—
K5, and White's Rook falls. Or if
18 Kt×R, Kt—Kt5; 19 P—KR3,
Kt×Kt; 20 P×Kt, B×RP; 21
B×B, Q×B wins.

21 B×B would lose by 21 . . .
Q×B (stronger than 21 . . . B×
Kt; 22 R—B5); 22 R—B3, R—
K1; 23 Q—Q4, B×Kt; 24 Q×P,
Q—Q2! threatening 25 . . . B
—Q5 and 25 . . . B×R.

**8.** 18 . . . .      **Kt—Kt5**

Threatening 19 . . . B×P.

    19 **P—KR3**      . . . .

If 19 P—KR4, Kt—K5!

    19 . . . .      **Kt×KP!**

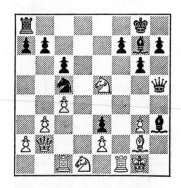

**10.** 21 . . . .      **B×Kt**
    22 **Q—B2**      **B×P**
    23 **Kt×P**      **B×B**
    24 **K×B**      . . . .

Not 24 Kt×B, Q—R7 mate.

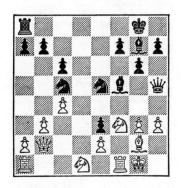

**9.** 20 **Kt×Kt**      **B×P**
    21 **R—B1**      . . . .

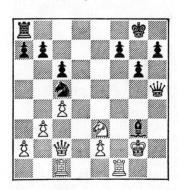

**11.** 24 . . . .      **Q—R7***ch*
    25 **K—B3**      **B—R5**

Intention: mate in one.

Now that retreat is impossible, White's King will be sent on a long trip. It is strange how helpless the other White pieces are to come to his aid!

26 R—KKt1    Q—R6ch
27 K—B4    ....

The King must go up.

27 ....    R—K1

Again menacing mate (by 28 ... Q×Kt).

**12.**    28 Kt—Kt4    ....

Protecting the Knight by 28 Q—Q2 permits 28 ... R—K5 mate.

28 ....    Kt—K3ch
29 K—K5    Kt—Kt4ch
30 K—Q6    ....

Going back to B4 would allow Black to spring a pretty Queen sacrifice: 30 K—B4, Q—B6ch!; 31 P×Q, Kt—R6 mate.

**13.**    30 ....    B—Kt6ch
31 R×B    Q×Rch
32 K—Q7    ....

There is no hope in 32 K—B5, Q×Kt. The King must go up!

32 ....    Q×Ktch
33 K×R    ....

**14.**    And still further up!

33 ....    Q—B1ch
34 K—K7    Q—B2ch
35 K—K8    ....

The King cannot escape by 35 K—B6. Black would reply by a

quiet little move 35 . . . P—KR3 protecting the Knight, and making room for the Knight to checkmate by 36 . . . Kt—R2!

## 15. 35 . . . . Kt—K3

The King is surrounded and Black threatens to finish him off with 36 . . . Q—Q1 mate.

**36 R—Q1    Kt—Kt2 mate**

An elegant termination, and in keeping with Kasparyan's reputation as player and end-game composer.

## 18. KIEV 1936

### Slav Defense

*This game satisfies the requirements for a masterpiece. It has an interesting opening (the sacrifice is reminiscent of Capablanca-Bogolyubov, Moscow 1925), fascinating mid-game complications, and a piquant*

*ending. Finally, Zhukovitzky's entire handling of it is in "the grand manner."*

| WHITE | BLACK |
|---|---|
| S. Zhukovitzky | A. Poliak |
| 1 P—Q4 | P—Q4 |
| 2 P—QB4 | P—QB3 |
| 3 Kt—KB3 | Kt—B3 |
| 4 Kt—B3 | P×P |
| 5 P—QR4 | B—B4 |

and the position is shown on the diagram below:

## 1. 6 P—K3 . . . .

White selects a quiet continuation. A good alternative, and one that keeps Black under pressure, is 6 Kt—K5, QKt—Q2; 7 Kt× P(B4), Q—B2; 8 P—KKt3, P—K4; 9 P×P, Kt×P; 10 B—B4, Kt(B3)—Q2; 11 B—Kt2.

| 6 . . . . | P—K3 |
|---|---|
| 7 B×P | . . . . |

# 2.
7 ....      **QKt—Q2**

More energetic is 7 . . . B—QKt5 preventing P—K4 for some time.

     8 O—O      **P—B4**

Premature.

     9 Q—K2      ....

# 3.
White threatens to advance his King Pawn.

     9 ....      **P×P**
     10 Kt×P      **B—KKt5**
     11 P—B3      **B—R4**

White's position is obviously much superior.

     *12* R—Q1      ....

# 4.
White's King Rook exerts tremendous pressure.

     *12* ....      **B—B4**

Now White begins a delightful combination, bristling with surprise moves.

     *13* B×P !      **P×B**
     *14* Kt×P      ....

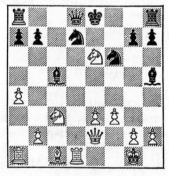

# 5.
*14* ....      **Q—B1**

On 14 . . . Q—K2, White would probably continue 15 Kt—B7*ch*, K—B2; 16 P—KKt4 (stronger than 16 Kt×R, Kt—K4!), B—KKt3; 17 Q—B4*ch*, with a winning game.

**15 Kt×P*ch*** . . . .

## 6. **15 . . . .** **K—B1**

If 15 . . . K—B2; 16 Kt×B, Kt×Kt; 17 R×Kt*ch!* (but not 17 Q—B4*ch*, K—B1; 18 R×Kt, B×P*ch* and White loses his Queen), Q×R; 18 Q—B4*ch* followed by 19 Q×B.

**16 Kt×B** **Kt×Kt**
**17 P—QKt4!** . . . .

A Pawn sacrifice which can hardly be refused.

If now 17 . . . B—K2; 18 B—Kt2 gives White a powerful attacking position.

If Black accepts the Pawn, White's Queen move in reply threatens everything on the board! Which is the lesser evil?

## 7. **17 . . . .** **B×P**
**18 Q—Kt5!** **Q×Kt**

On 18 . . . B×Kt White wins easily with 19 B—R3*ch*, K—Kt1; 20 Q—Q5*ch!* (better than 20 R×Kt, Q×R; 21 Q×Q, B×R), K—Kt2; 21 Q—Kt5*ch*, K—B2; 22 Q×Kt*ch*.

**19 B—Q2!** . . . .

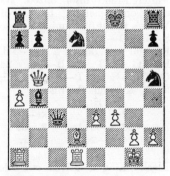

## 8. **19 . . . .** **Q×B**

Black must give up his Queen, as any other Queen move (including 19 . . . Q×R) loses by

20 B×Bch—Black's King being
so much exposed.

| | |
|---|---|
| 20 R×Q | B×R |
| 21 Q×Kt(Q7) | B×Pch |
| 22 K—B1 | .... |

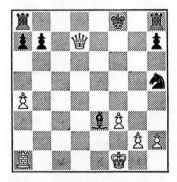

**9.** Black is actually ahead in
material, but his pieces are
scattered and disorganized. He
must do something too about
White's threat of winning a piece
by 23 Q—B5*ch*. 22 . . . Kt—
B3 will not do as 23 Q—K6,
B—Kt4 (23 . . . B—Q5; 24
Q—Q6*ch*); 24 P—B4, B—R5;
25 P—Kt3 wins the Bishop.

| | |
|---|---|
| 22 .... | Kt—Kt2 |
| 23 R—Kt1 ! | P—Kt3 |
| 24 Q—Q6*ch* | .... |

Black's King is driven out into
the open.

In contradistinction to the amateur's useless checks which drive
the King to safety and the spec-
tators to despair, are the well-
timed checks of the master.

**10.** 24 ....      K—B2

If 24 . . . K—Kt1; 25 Q—
Q5*ch* wins the Rook; if 24 . . .
K—K1; 25 Q—K5*ch* wins the
Bishop.

    25 **Q—Q5***ch*      **K—B3**

Again the only move. If 25 . . .
K—Kt3; 26 Q—K4*ch*, Kt—B4;
27 P—Kt4.

    26 **R—K1**      ....

**11.** The attacked Bishop
must not move. If 26

... B—B4; 27 R—K4 followed by 28 R—B4*ch* wins. If 26 ... B—Kt4; 27 P—R4, B×P; 28 Q—Q4*ch* and the King cannot protect both pieces. Finally, if 26 ... B—R3; 27 Q—Q6*ch*, K—Kt4; 28 P—R4*ch*, K—R4; 29 R—K5*ch* mates quickly.

| 26 .... | QR—K1 |
|---|---|

## 12.
| 27 R×B! | .... |
|---|---|

A pretty move, in keeping with the rest of White's fine play.

| 27 .... | R×R |
|---|---|
| 28 Q—Q4*ch* | R—K4 |
| 29 P—B4 | R—K1 |
| 30 P—Kt4! | .... |

Not 30 P×R*ch*, R×P; and White still has a difficult task.

| 30 .... | P—KR4 |
|---|---|
| 31 P—R3 | .... |

White's aim is to make Black run out of moves; the sad state where one is compelled to move, and can not. In one word—*Zugzwang!*

## 13.
| 31 .... | P×P |
|---|---|
| 32 P×P | R—K2 |
| 33 K—B2 | Kt—K1 |
| 34 K—B3 | .... |

Now we see White's plan. He intends 35 P×R*ch*, and if 35 ... R×P then 36 K—B4 wins the newly pinned Rook!

| 34 .... | Kt—B2! |
|---|---|

## 14.
Black has a clever counter-plan! If White plays hurriedly 35 P×R*ch*, R×P; 36 K—B4, then 36 ... Kt—K3*ch* and Black wins the Queen!

35 P—Kt5*ch* . . . .

The check is nicely timed, and there is no good reply.

**15.** If now 35 . . . K—B4; 36 P×R, R×P (36 . . . K×P; 37 Q—Kt4*ch*, K—R3; 38 Q—R4*ch* wins the Rook, or 36 . . . Kt—K3; 37 Q—K4*ch*, K× P; 38 Q—Kt4*ch*, K—R3; 39 Q— R4*ch* again wins the Rook); 37 Q—B4*ch*, K—K3; 38 P—Kt6!, R—KB4; 39 Q×R*ch* and White gets a new Queen.

| 35 . . . . | K—Kt3 |
| 36 P×R | Resigns |

## 19. LENINGRAD 1936

### Queen's Gambit Accepted

*Lively and enterprising tactics by both players make a 37 move game seem like a miniature! Interest is kept high all through, and we come to "Re-signs" rather regretfully. It has been a good fight.*

| WHITE | BLACK |
| I. Kan | V. Rauzer |
| 1 P—Q4 | P—Q4 |
| 2 P—QB4 | P×P |
| 3 Kt—KB3 | P—QB4 |
| 4 P—K3 | P×P |
| 5 B×P | . . . . |

and the position is shown on the diagram below:

**1.** Accepting the Queen's Gambit was at one time considered dangerous, but it seems to be coming back more and more into favor. It has been played with success by such diverse personalities as Reshevsky, Steinitz, Rubinstein and Janowsky.

5 . . . . P—K3

Of course not 5 . . . P×P?; 6 B×P*ch*—and sudden death! A useful trap to know.

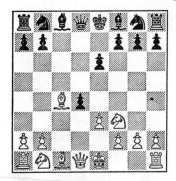

**2.** 6 P×P .....

White could have played 6
Q×P or 6 Kt×P. Instead, he
reconciles himself to an isolated
Queen Pawn, in order to give his
pieces more freedom.

6 .... Kt—KB3
7 O—O B—K2

7 ... Kt—B3 attacking the
Queen Pawn would have prevented 8 Q—K2.

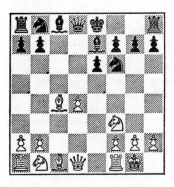

**3.** 8 Q—K2 O—O
9 Kt—B3 P—QR3

Preparing for 10 . . . P—QKt4,
and the development of his
Queen Bishop on the long diagonal.

10 B—B4 P—QKt4
11 B—QKt3 B—Kt2
12 QR—Q1 Kt—Q4

Gaining a tempo by the attack
on the Bishop.

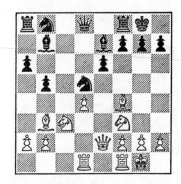

**4.** 13 B—K5 Kt×Kt
14 P×Kt Kt—Q2

Once more developing with gain
of time, as his opponent will
want to keep his Bishops for attack.

15 B—KB4 ....

Offhand 15 B—Kt3 seems more
natural, but White evidently
plans R—Q3, then B—Q2 (to
protect his weak Bishop Pawn)
and eventually R—KR3.

An inordinate fondness for the
"two Bishops" can turn wins into
losses. Kan gets a lesson similar
to the one Janowsky got from
Lasker in 1924.

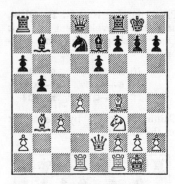

**5.** *15 ....*      **Kt—B3**

Black is ready for 16 R—Q3 to which he would reply 16 . . . B—K5. Then on 17 R—K3, B—KB4 threatens 18 . . . Kt—Kt5 as well as 18 . . . Kt—Q4.

    16 Kt—K5      Kt—Q4
    17 B—Q2      ....

Forced, but now the Rook will never get to Q3.

**6.** *17 ....*      **R—B1**
    *18 P—QB4*      ....

White exchanges, as he does not want to be tied down indefinitely to defending his weak Pawn.

    18 ....      P×P
    19 B×P      P—QR4

Intending 20 . . . B—Kt5, with consequent pressure on QB6.

**7.** *20 R—Kt1*      ....

Now if 20 . . . B—Kt5; 21 P—QR3, B×B; 22 R×B, with advantage to White.

**8.** *20 ....*      **B—R1**
    *21 R—Kt3*      **B—Kt5**

22 B—B1 ....

Much better was 22 R—KR3. White loses a great deal of time trying to keep his Bishops.

22 .... Kt—B6 !

A powerful move which assures Black the initiative.

23 Q—Kt4 ....

**9.** White seems to have found a good reply. He menaces 24 B—KR6, Q—B3; 25 B—KKt5, or 24 B—KKt5, Q moves; 25 B—B6, or simply 24 P—QR3 winning a piece. On 23 . . . Kt×P; 24 R—Kt3, P—Kt3; 25 B×Kt wins a piece.

23 .... R×B !

A brilliant reply which upsets all of White's calculations. Now on 24 B—R6, Q—B3; 25 B—Kt5, Q×Kt ! wins.

24 Kt×R B—Q4
25 B—R6 Q—B3
26 B—Kt5 ....

Black answers this with another surprise move.

**10.**
26 .... Q×P !
27 Q×Q Kt—K7*ch*
28 K—R1 Kt×Q
29 R×B ....

Of course not 29 R—Q3, B×Kt. As White must lose some material (his Rook and Knight are attacked) he decides to remove one of the dangerous Bishops.

**11.**
29 .... P×R
30 Kt—Kt6 ! ....

White plans this pretty combination: 30 . . . B×P; 31 B—K7, R—Kt1; 32 B×P!, R×Kt; 33 B—B5 with Bs of opposite color.

## 12.    30 . . . .       R—Kt1

Black does not bite!

    31 Kt×B        P×Kt
    32 R—Q1       . . . .

Despite Black's evident superiority, the ending still needs care.

## 13.    32 . . . .       Kt—K3

Endangers the win. Better would have been 32 . . . Kt—K7; 33 R×P, R—R1; 34 R—Kt5, P—R3; 35 B—K7, Kt—Q5!, 36 R×P (36 R—Kt7, R×P; 37 P—R3, P—Kt6), Kt—B3; 37 R—K4, R—K1 and wins.

    33 R×P        R—R1

Naturally Black does not exchange minor pieces.

## 14.    34 B—K7       . . . .

Here White misses his chance for a possible draw. He should have played 34 P—KR3, R×P; 35 B—K7, R×P (35 . . . R—Kt7; 36 R—QKt5!); 36 B×P, and now 36 . . . R×P? would lose by 37 R—QKt5!
After the text move, Black gives his opponent no more chances.

    34 . . . .       P—Kt6!

Threatening 35 . . . P×P.

White omitted P—KR3—and is victim of "whether you do or you don't, you'll be sorry!"

*final combination makes Black (as his best move!) give up his Queen.*

| WHITE | BLACK |
|-------|-------|
| A. Konstantinopolsky | V. Panov |

| | | |
|---|---|---|
| *1* | P—Q4 | Kt—KB3 |
| *2* | P—QB4 | P—Q3 |
| *3* | Kt—QB3 | QKt—Q2 |
| *4* | P—K4 | P—K4 |
| *5* | KKt—K2 | . . . . |

# 15.

35 P—QR3 . . . .

Of course not 35 P×P, R—R8*ch* and mate follows.

| 35 . . . . | P—Kt7 |
|---|---|
| 36 R—QKt5 | R—QB1 |

To which there is no answer. If 37 P—KR3, R—B8*ch* and 38 . . . P—Kt8(Q).

37 **Resigns**

## 20. LENINGRAD 1936

### Tchigorin's Defense

*The law of compensation rewards White for his subtle defense of the King Pawn. For it is this very Pawn which rips apart the center, and clears the way for his Rook to come through. There are some beautiful traps—see the notes to diagrams 6 and 7—and White's*

and the position is shown on the diagram below:

**1.** Tchigorin's Defense is quite popular with the Russian players, despite the fact that it gives Black a cramped game. One reason may be that it still lends itself to original ideas. White's last move is more elastic than 5 Kt—B3, as he intends to play (eventually) P—B4, attacking the center.

5 . . . . B—K2

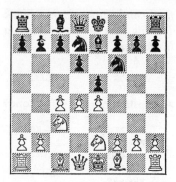

**2.** Developing the King Bishop at Kt2 would have given it more scope.

| 6 | P—KKt3 | O—O |
| --- | --- | --- |
| 7 | B—Kt2 | R—K1 |
| 8 | O—O | B—B1 |

Black's position is such that he can do nothing but sit tight.

**3.**
| 9 | P—Kt3 | P—B3 |
| --- | --- | --- |
| 10 | B—Kt2 | Q—B2 |
| 11 | P—KR3 | .... |

In order to play 12 P—B4 without being disturbed by a possible . . . Kt—Kt5 in reply.

11 . . . .        P—QR3

Black would like to free himself by following up with 12 . . . P—QKt4 and 13 . . . B—Kt2.

**4.** 12 P—QR4     ....

White of course puts a stop to that attempt.

| 12 | .... | P—QKt3 |
| --- | --- | --- |
| 13 | P—B4 | B—Kt2 |

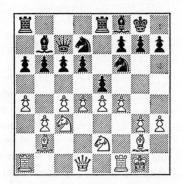

**5.** 14 R—B1 !     ....

But not 14 Q—B2, P—QKt4; 15 RP×P, RP×P; 16 P×KtP, P×KtP and White cannot take the Pawn, as his Knight is pinned.

*14 . . . .*     **P×QP**

Black is impatient, and he opens up the game. Better was the quiet 14 . . . QR—Q1.

*15 Kt×P*     **P—B4**

Simultaneously attacking the Knight and the King Pawn.

*16 Kt—B5 !*     . . . .

**7.** *17 Kt—K3*     **B—Kt2**

Again Black rejects the Pawn. If 17 . . . Kt×P; 18 Kt(K3) —Q5, B×Kt; 19 Kt×B, Q—Kt2; 20 Q—Q3, P—B4; 21 Kt—B7 winning the exchange as 21 . . . Q×Kt loses by 22 Q—Q5*ch* and mate next move.

**6.** White's defense of the Pawn is subtle and far-sighted. If now 16 . . . Kt×P; 17 Kt×Kt, B×Kt; 18 B×B, R×B; 19 Kt—R6*ch !*, K—R1 (or 19 . . . P×Kt; 20 Q—Kt4*ch,* and mate next move); 20 Kt×P*ch,* K—Kt1; 21 Q—Q5 ! and White threatens both Rooks, as well as mate in two moves.

*16 . . . .*     **P—Kt3**

Black sidesteps the trap, and drives the menacing Knight away.

**8.** *18 Q—B2*     **R—K2**

Preparing to double Rooks on the King file.

*19 P—KKt4*     **R(K2)—K1**

But he is quickly discouraged! If
19 . . . QR—K1; 20 P—Kt5,
Kt×P; 21 Kt(B3)—Q5, B×Kt;
22 Kt×B wins the exchange.

Kt(Kt4)—B6*ch*, Kt×Kt; 25 Kt×
Kt*ch*.

| 23 . . . . | B×Kt |
|---|---|
| 24 BP×B | R—R2 |
| 25 R(QB1)—K1 | . . . . |

**9.**
| 20 P—Kt5 | Kt—R4 |
|---|---|
| 21 Kt(B3)—Q5 | . . . . |

Taking advantage of Black's positional weakness.

| 21 . . . . | Q—Q1 |
|---|---|
| 22 B×B | Kt×B |
| 23 Kt—Kt4 | . . . . |

**11.**
| 25 . . . . | R—B1 |
|---|---|

Otherwise 26 Kt—R6*ch* forces
Black's King to B1, where he
would be even more exposed.

| 26 Kt—R6*ch* | K—R1 |
|---|---|

**10.** White threatens to win
the exchange by 24

**12.**
| 27 P—K5 ! | P×P |
|---|---|
| 28 P×P | . . . . |

Already threatening to win the exchange by 29 Kt×P*ch*.

| 28 | .... | Q—K2 |
| 29 | Q—B3 | P—Kt4 |
| 30 | P—K6 | .... |

Now White's Queen commands the important diagonal leading to Black's King.

## 13.

  30 ....    **BP×P**

On 30 ... Kt—Kt3 White wins by 31 R×P (threatening the Queen as well as 32 Q×Kt mate), R×R; 32 P×R, Q×KtP; 33 R—K8 mate.

| 31 | QP×P | R×R*ch* |
| 32 | R×R | .... |

The exchange of Rooks only increases the vigor of White's attack.

How does Black defend? If 32 ... Q×KtP; 33 Kt—B7*ch* wins the Queen. Or if 32 ... Q×KP; 33 R—B7 (threatening 34 Q×Kt mate), Q—K4; 34 Q×Q, Kt ×Q; 35 R—B8 mate.

## 14.

  32 ....    **P—Kt5**

Hoping for 33 Q—Kt2, Q×KP; 34 R—B7, Q—K6*ch;* 35 K—R1, Q—QB6.

## 15.

  33 Q—R1 !    **Q×KP**

Forced, in view of the threat of 34 R—B7.

  *34* **R—K1 !**    ....

Intending to crash through to K8 and force mate.

  *34* ....    **Q—Q3**

Now 35 R—K8*ch* would be met by 35 . . . Kt—B1, but—

35 Kt—B7*ch*     **Resigns**

## 21.  LENINGRAD 1936

### Dutch Defense

*Bondarevsky enriches the collections of "Brilliant Mating Combinations" by contributing a beautiful five-move mate.*

| WHITE | BLACK |
|-------|-------|
| A. Kotov | I. Bondarevsky |

| 1 | P—Q4 | P—K3 |
| 2 | Kt—KB3 | P—KB4 |
| 3 | P—KKt3 | Kt—KB3 |
| 4 | B—Kt2 | P—Q4 |

and the position is shown on the diagram below:

**1.** The Dutch Defense as Reinfeld points out, gives great scope for tactical play, and has therefore been favored by such strong attacking players as Tartakover, Mieses, Botvinnik and Torre. No wonder then that it enjoys such popularity with the Russians.

5 O—O     . . . .

**2.**     5 . . . .     B—Q3

Developing the Bishop to a more aggressive post than at K2, and also discouraging White from playing 6 B—B4, as the consequent exchange would break up White's Pawn position.

6 P—B4     P—B3

To support the Pawn center, and in the event of 7 P×P to recapture with the Bishop Pawn.

The strategy underlying Black's formation is based on complete control of K5—not only to post his Knight there strongly, but also to prevent P—K4 by White. Black makes a break through difficult.

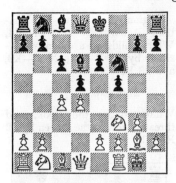

**3.** 7 QKt—Q2    O—O
8 P—Kt3    Q—K1

Black discloses his intention of attacking by . . . Q—R4, as soon as it is feasible.

9 Kt—K1    . . . .

More natural would seem to be 9 B—Kt2 followed by 10 Kt—K5.

**4.** 9 . . . .    QKt—Q2
10 Kt—Q3    Kt—K5

An annoying Knight which cannot be driven off by 11 P—B3, as

11 . . . Kt×P; 12 P×Kt, B×P followed by 13 . . . Q—R4 is too dangerous to risk.

11 Kt—B3    Q—R4

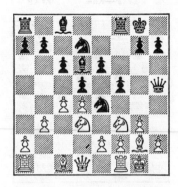

**5.** 12 Kt—B4    Q—B2
13 Q—B2    P—KKt4
14 Kt—Q3    Q—R4

Intending to continue with 15 . . . P—B5, to break up White's King-side Pawns.

**6.** 15 Kt(B3)—K5    R—B3
16 P—B3    R—R3 !

Offering a Knight for the attack resulting from 17 P×Kt, Q×Pch; 18 K—B2, R—R6 followed by 19 . . . Q×Pch.

| 17 P—KR4 | Kt×P |
|---|---|

**7.** 18 P×P . . . .

A better defense was 18 B×P, Kt×R; 19 R×Kt, Kt×Kt; 20 P× Kt.

| 18 . . . . | Q—R7ch |
|---|---|
| 19 K—B2 | R—R5 |

**8.** 20 R—KKt1 R×P !

Beginning a clever combination. Against 20 . . . Kt—R4, White builds up a defensive position by 21 P—B4, 22 P—K3, and 23 Kt—B3.

| 21 B—Kt2 | . . . . |
|---|---|

White attacks the Rook, and threatens to win the Queen by 22 R—R1.

**9.** White expects to force 21 . . . R—R5, after which he would win by 22 R—R1, Kt× Rch; 23 R×Kt, Q×R; 24 B×Q, R×B; 25 Kt×Kt, B×Kt; 26 Q— B3 !

| 21 . . . . | Q—R5 ! |
|---|---|
| 22 B×R | Kt—K5ch |

Once again, White must make a difficult choice. He must decide whether to try for a win by 23 K—K3 (and he is a Rook ahead!) or to play 23 K—B1 and give Black the opportunity of forcing a perpetual check. As he misjudges his chances, let us look at the alternative.

**10.** 23 K—B1 is correct, after which Black can force a draw by 23 . . . Kt—Kt6*ch;* 24 K—B2 (not 24 K—K1, Q×B winning) Kt—K5*ch,* etc. Or he can continue the attack by 23 . . . B×Kt; 24 Kt×B (if 24 B×B, Kt×B; 25 P×Kt, Kt—Kt5; 26 R—R1, Kt—K6*ch;* 27 K—Kt1, Q—Kt6, and Black wins the Queen), Kt—Kt6*ch;* 25 K—B2, Q×B*ch;* 26 K×Kt, Kt×Kt.

23 K—K3 . . . .

**11.** White has walked right into a beautiful mating

combination, allowing a remarkable finish.

| | | |
|---|---|---|
| 23 . . . . | | P—B5*ch* |
| 24 Kt×P | | Q—B7*ch* |
| 25 K—Q3 | | Q×B*ch* !! |

Including a startling Queen sacrifice!

| | | |
|---|---|---|
| 26 K×Q | | B—B4*ch* |
| 27 K—Q3 | | Kt×Kt **mate** |

## 22. MOSCOW 1936

### Queen's Indian Defense

*While "strategy" is concerned with positional chess—building up the structure of the game—"tactics" is the term for combinations which have as their object the gain of material, or the forcing of checkmate. White's dazzling play in this masterpiece is an excellent illustration of Fine's dictum that tactics is more than 90% of chess. Curiously enough, Tolush himself is a very fine tactician!*

| WHITE | BLACK |
|---|---|
| **A. Konstantinopolsky** | **A. Tolush** |
| *1* P—Q4 | Kt—KB3 |
| *2* Kt—KB3 | P—QKt3 |
| *3* B—Kt5 | Kt—K5 |
| *4* B—R4 | B—Kt2 |
| *5* QKt—Q2 | . . . . |

and the position is shown on the next diagram:

## 1. 5 ....    P—QB4

Better was 5 . . . Kt×Kt; 6 Q×Kt, P—Kt3. The same comment applies to his next move as well.

6 P—K3    P—Kt3

## 2. 7 Kt×Kt    B×Kt
8 B—B4 !    ....

The difference is that Black's Bishop is an exposed (unprotected) piece, against which attacks can be directed. White's immediate threat is 9 B×P*ch*, K×B; 10 Kt—Kt5*ch* and 11 Kt×B.

## 3. 8 ....    P—B3

An ugly move, but what can Black do? If 8 . . . B—KKt2; 9 B×P*ch*, or if 8 . . . B—QKt2; 9 Kt—K5 (threatening 10 B×P mate), P—Q4; 10 B—Kt5*ch* wins at once. Finally, if 8 . . . P—Q4; 9 B—Kt5*ch*, Kt—Q2; 10 Kt—K5 wins.

9 O—O    ....

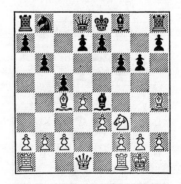

## 4. 9 ....    B—QKt2

Not 9 . . . P—Q4; 10 B—

Kt5*ch*, Kt—Q2; 11 Kt—Q2,
threatening 12 Kt×B, P×Kt; 13
B—B6, as well as 12 P—KB3, B
—B4; 13 P—K4.

    *10* **P—K4 !**     ....

A beautiful Pawn sacrifice.

    *10* ....      **B×P**

10 . . . B—Kt2 was safer.

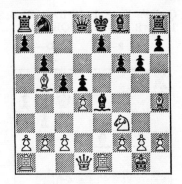

**5.**    *11* **R—K1**     ....

Sets Black a difficult problem.
If 11 . . . B×Kt; 12 Q×B, Kt—
B3; 13 Q×P wins or if 11 . . .
P—B4; 12 Kt—K5, Q—B1 (12
. . . P—Q4; 13 B—Kt5*ch* wins
the Queen); 13 P—KB3, B—
QKt2; 14 Kt—B7 threatening 15
Kt×R as well as 15 Kt—Q6*ch*
winning the Queen.

    *11* ....      **P—Q4**
    *12* **B—Kt5*ch***     ....

Black's King must move, as after
12 . . . Kt—Q2; 13 Kt—Q2
gives White a powerful attack.

**6.**    *12* ....      **K—B2**
    *13* **P×P**      **B—Kt2**

Of course not 13 . . . P×P; 14
R×B, and Black cannot recapture.

    *14* **P—B4 !**     ....

**7.**    White plays to open up
more lines, and to weaken
the position of Black's Bishop.

    *14* ....      **KtP×P**
    *15* **P×P**      **B×P**

On 15 . . . Q×P White wins
nicely by 16 Q—K2, B×Kt; 17

Q×P*ch*, K—Kt1; 18 B×P, B×B; 19 Q×B, B—K5; 20 QR—Q1.

| 16 | R—B1 | Q—Q3 |

| 17 | P—QKt4 ! | .... |

A brilliant surprise move! If in reply 17 . . . P—B5; 18 R×P, B×R; 19 Q×Q, P×Q; 20 B×B*ch*, K—B1; 21 B—Q5 wins a piece.

| 17 | .... | P×P |
| 18 | R—B7 ! | .... |

**9.** The Pawn sacrifice cleared the way for a Rook sacri-

fice! White threatens 19 R(K1) ×P*ch*, Q×R; 20 Q×B*ch* and mate in two more moves.

| 18 | .... | Q×R |

There is nothing better. If instead 18 . . . B—B1; 19 B—Kt3, Q—Q1; 20 B—QB4 wins a piece.

| 19 | Q×B*ch* | K—B1 |
| 20 | Q×R | P—Kt4 |
| 21 | B—Kt3 | P—K4 |
| 22 | Kt—Q4 | .... |

White threatens 23 Kt—K6*ch* winning the Queen.

**10.**
| 22 | .... | Q—Kt3 |
| 23 | Q—Q5 | Resigns |

Black has no defense to 24 Kt—K6*ch*. If 23 . . . P×Kt; 24 R—K8 mate, or if 23 . . . Q×Kt; 24 Q×Q, P×Q; 25 B×Kt, and White wins easily.

A masterpiece by Konstantin-opolsky, who attacks with the ferocity of a Tchigorin. His brilliant 10 P—K4, and the stabbing 17 P—QKt4 with its sequel of 18 R—B7 are reminiscent of Alekhine's alertness.

## 23. MOSCOW 1936

### French Defense

*Kotov demonstrates the tremendous potential power of Rooks on the center files. He shows that the adverse King facing a Rook is in constant danger,* no matter how many pieces stand between them.

| WHITE | BLACK |
|-------|-------|
| A. Kotov | Kalmanok |
| 1 P—Q4 | P—K3 |
| 2 P—K4 | P—Q4 |
| 3 Kt—QB3 | Kt—KB3 |
| 4 B—Kt5 | P×P |
| 5 Kt×P | B—K2 |

and the position is shown on the diagram below:

**1.** What started as a Queen's Pawn Opening has become, by a transposition of moves, a French Defense. Black chooses a simplifying variation.

| 6 B×Kt | P×B |
|--------|-----|

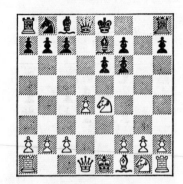

**2.** Black captured with the Pawn, as he wants to keep his two Bishops.

| 7 Kt—KB3 | .... |

A good alternative is 7 Q—Q2, followed by 8 O—O—O.

| 7 .... | Kt—Q2 |
| 8 B—B4 ! | .... |

**3.** White is prepared to reply to 8 ... P—QB4

with 9 P—Q5, Kt—Kt3; 10 B—Kt5ch, B—Q2; 11 B×Bch, Q×B; 12 P—Q6, Q—B3; 13 Q—K2, B×P; 14 Kt×Pch.

| 8 .... | P—B3 |
| 9 Q—Q2 | P—Kt3 |
| 10 Q—R6 ! | .... |

**4.** White intends 11 Q—Kt7, R—B1; 12 Q×RP.

| 10 .... | B—B1 |
| 11 Q—B4 | B—QKt2 |
| 12 O—O—O | P—KR4 |

**5.** Black's game is cramped, and he tries to free him-

self by driving White's Queen away from her commanding post. His immediate threat is 13 . . . B—KR3.

| 13 K—Kt1 | B—K2 |

If instead 13 . . . Q—Kt1; 14 Kt×P*ch*, or if 13 . . . Q—K2; 14 Q—B7 is uncomfortable for Black.

| 14 Q—Kt3 | .... |

Now threatening 15 Q—Kt7, R—KB1; 16 Q—R7, and Black's Rook Pawn falls.

**6.**

| 14 .... | Kt—B1 |

Slightly better was 14 . . . K—B1, but Black's game would still be difficult.

| 15 KR—K1 | P—KB4 |
| 16 P—Q5 ! | .... |

A brilliant move which leads to delightful combinative possibilities.

At the trifling cost of a Pawn, White's Bishop becomes a powerful factor in the attack.

Kt—Kt6*ch*, B—K2; 23 Q×R mate.

*18 . . . .*     **Q—B2**

**7.** If Black plays 16 . . . KP×P; 17 Kt—B6 is mate, or if 16 . . . P×Kt; 17 P×KP attacks the Queen, and also threatens 18 P×P mate.

*16 . . . .*     **BP×P**
*17* **B—Kt5***ch*     **Kt—Q2**
*18* **Kt—K5**     . . . .

**9.** Loses a piece, but Black hopes to regain it. The position is complicated, and White might miss his way.

*19* **B×Kt***ch*     **K—Q1**

If 19 . . . K—B1; 20 Kt—Kt6*ch* wins Black's Queen.

**8.** More troubles for Black! If 18 . . . B—QB1; 19 Kt—B6, B—R5; 20 Q—Kt7, B—B3; 21 Kt—Q6 mate. Another pretty win after 18 . . . B—QB1 is 19 Q—Kt7, R—B1; 20 R×P!, P×R; 21 Kt—B6*ch*, B×Kt; 22

**10.** 

*20* **Q—Kt7**     **R—KB1**
*21* **Kt—Kt5**     . . . .

Threatening among other things
22 Q×P, R×Q; 23 Kt×P mate.

21 . . . .          **Q—B4**

If 21 . . . P—B3; 22 Kt×P is
mate.

**11.**     22 B×P          . . . .

Rips up the defensive barrier
of Pawns surrounding Black's
King. As the Bishop cannot be
taken ( 22 . . . P×B; 23 Kt×P*ch*
winning the Queen), therefore

22 . . . .          **Resigns**

## 24. MOSCOW 1936

### Four Knights' Game

*The skill and ingenuity with
which the Russian players can
infuse such a drawish opening
as the Four Knights' with life
and sparkle is a tribute to their
wealth of imagination—and to
the writer a source of wonderment.*

*Every once in a while we
may think that we have seen
every idea possible on the
chessboard—and then along
comes a game like this one!*

| WHITE | BLACK |
|-------|-------|
| **V. Panov** | **M. Yudovich** |
| 1  P—K4 | P—K4 |
| 2  Kt—KB3 | Kt—KB3 |
| 3  Kt—B3 | Kt—B3 |
| 4  B—Kt5 | Kt—Q5 |

and the position is shown on the
diagram below:

**1.**     Black plays the Rubinstein
Defense, so named after
the great Polish master who discovered its strength and em-
ployed it with virtuosity. Even
though it violates the principle
which says that a piece must be
moved only once in the opening,
the move 4 . . . Kt—Q5 is both
sound and strong.

5  B—B4          . . . .

**2.** Black can now equalize by 5 . . . B—B4; 6 Kt×P, Q—K2; 7 Kt—B3, P—Q4.

    *5 . . . .*        **P—Q3**

Instead, he prefers to experiment with a quiet move.

    *6 Kt—KKt5*    **Kt—K3**
    *7 P—Q4*        . . . .

White wants quick action, and opens up the game.

**3.**   *7 . . . .*        **Kt×Kt**
    *8 B×Kt*        **B—K2**

    *9* **O—O**        **O—O**

At this point many a player would continue 10 P×P, P×P; 11 Q×Q, R×Q; 12 QR—Q1 to assure himself of the half-point.

    *10* **Q—Q3**        . . . .

But Panov wants to play chess! 10 Q—K2 was a bit more precise, to give the King Bishop more scope.

**4.**   *10 . . . .*        **P—B3**

An attempt to win a piece by the method used in the "Noah's Ark" trap: 11 . . . P—Kt4; 12 B—Kt3, P×P; 13 Q×QP, P—B4; 14 Q—Q2, P—B5.

    *11 P—QR4*    **Q—Kt3 !**

Black does not fear 12 P—Q5, as 12 . . . Kt×QP; 13 Kt×Kt, P× Kt; 14 B×B, P×B equalizes.

    *12* **B—K3**        . . . .

White protects his Queen Pawn, and in turn threatens to win a piece by 13 P×P.

Clearly expecting the immediate recapture of the Pawn.

**5.**
12 . . . .      Kt—Kt5
13 P—R5      Q—B2

Of course not 13 . . . Q×KtP?; 14 KR—Kt1, and the Queen is lost.

**7.**
14 . . . .      P—Q4 !!

A remarkable possibility is 15 B—Kt3, Q×KP; 16 P—B4, Q —R4; 17 P—R3, Kt×B; 18 Q× Kt, P—Q5 !, winning a piece as 19 Q×P is met by 19 . . . B— QB4 pinning the Queen.

**6.** White is now somewhat embarrassed for a suitable continuation. If he plays 14 B— Q2 (to keep both his Bishops) then 14 . . . P×P; 15 Q×P, P— Q4, wins a piece, as the threat of 16 . . . Q×P mate must be met.

14 P×P      . . . .

**8.**
15 P×P      Q×KP
16 P—KKt3      Q—R4

Again threatening mate on the move.

### 17 P—R4      B×P !

This is less surprising, but no less painful. On 18 P×B, Black intends 18 . . . Kt—K4; 19 Q—K4, Kt—B6*ch*; 20 K—R1, B—Kt5 with a decisive attack.

### 18 K—Kt2      . . . .

## 9.

### 18 . . . .      Kt—K4

Black may have missed a win here by 18 . . . Kt×B*ch;* 19 Q×Kt (19 P×Kt, Q—Kt5) B—Kt4 followed by 20 . . . B—R6*ch*.

### 19 Q—K4      Kt×B
### 20 Q×Kt      B—B3

Menacing 21 . . . B—R6*ch;* 22 K—Kt1 (22 K—R2 ?, B×R*ch* costs the Queen), B×Kt !, 23 Q×B, Q—B6.

### 21 R—R1      Q—Kt3

Now White sees the danger in 22 P×P, P×P; 23 Q×P, R—Kt1, and Black threatens 24 . . . B—Kt2, as well as 24 . . . R×P.

His next move aims to disrupt Black's Queen side.

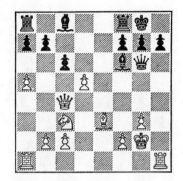

## 10.

### 22 P—R6      BP×P
### 23 Kt×P      . . . .

Black would have answered 23 Q×P with 23 . . . P×P, as White could not take the Rook on account of 24 . . . B—R6*ch* winning his Queen.

## 11.

### 23 . . . .      P×P

White can now play for a brilliant win by 24 B—Q4, Q—K5*ch;* 25 P—B3, Q×B; 26 Q×Q, B×Q; 27 Kt—K7*ch*, K—R1; 28 R×P*ch*, and mate follows. But he must resist temptation, as after 24 B—Q4, Black counters with the simple 24 . . . B—Kt2 and White is lost.

24 Q—B6        R—Kt1

**12.** Black intends to develop his Queen Bishop at Kt2, from where it will exert tremendous pressure on the long diagonal.

25 Kt×B*ch*    . . . .

White had better chances with 25 Q×KB !, P×Q; 26 Kt—K7*ch*, K—R1; 27 Kt×Q*ch*, P×Kt; 28 P—Kt3.

25 . . . .       P×Kt !
26 Q—QB3         B—Kt2*ch*
27 P—B3          QR—B1

Forcing White into a pin, as moving the Queen would lose quickly after 28 . . . R×P*ch*.

It is remarkable how Black utilizes the circumstance that the Bishop is pinned to force an exchange of Queens and Rooks—suddenly to emerge with a passed Pawn!

**13.** 28 B—B5        KR—K1
29 QR—K1       . . . .

He must not allow . . . R—K7*ch*.

29 . . . .       R×R
30 R×R          Q—B4

More pressure on the Bishop.

31 P—QKt4       P—QR4 !

**14.** Black hits at the supporter of the pinned piece. He now threatens 32 . . . P×P; 33 Q×KtP, Q×KBP*ch*; 34 K—R3, Q—R4*ch*, winning.

32 Q—Q3         Q×Q

| 33 | P×Q | P×P |
| 34 | B×RP | .... |

No better is 34 B×KtP, R—B7*ch;*
35 K—B1, B×P.

| 34 | .... | R—B7*ch* |
| 35 | B—B2 | P—Kt6 |

**15.** Black concludes incisively by utilizing the passed Pawn.

| 36 | R—K8*ch* | K—Kt2 |
| 37 | R—QKt8 | B—Q4 |
| 38 | P—Kt4 | P—Kt7 |
| 39 | P—Kt5 | B—R7 |
| 40 | P×P*ch* | K×P |
| 41 | **Resigns** | |

Unfortunately he cannot play 41 R×P, R×R; 42 B—Q4*ch,* as his Bishop is pinned.

## 25. MOSCOW 1936

### Gruenfeld Defense

*The action is fast and furious in this game. Black does not waste a single move in an at-*tack *that rises to a crescendo of power and energy.*

| WHITE | BLACK |
| E. Zagoryansky | S. Belavienetz |

| 1 | P—Q4 | Kt—KB3 |
| 2 | P—QB4 | P—KKt3 |
| 3 | Kt—QB3 | P—Q4 |
| 4 | Q—Kt3 | P—B3 |

and the position is shown on the diagram below:

**1.** 5 B—Kt5 ....

Intended to be aggressive, but in reality it permits Black to seize the initiative. Better would be 5 Kt—B3, B—Kt2; 6 P×P, P×P; 7 B—Kt5, Kt—B3; 8 P—K3 !

| 5 | .... | P×P |
| 6 | Q×BP | P—Kt4 |
| 7 | Q—Q3 | B—B4 ! |

White must make a difficult decision: he must either retreat ignominiously with his Queen, or go in for complications by 8 P—K4.

**2.** 8 Q—Q1 . . . .

The wrong choice. After 8 P—K4, Kt×P; 9 Kt×Kt, Q—Q4; 10 P—B3 (not 10 Kt—QB3, B×Q; 11 Kt×Q, B×B), B×Kt; 11 P×B, Q×B; 12 Kt—R3, he has a fair game.

**3.** 8 . . . .     P—Kt5
9 Kt—R4     . . . .

Not 9 B×Kt, P×Kt; 10 B×R, P×P; 11 P—Q5, P—K4 !! and Black wins.

9 . . . .     Kt—K5

10 Kt—KB3     B—Kt2

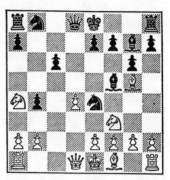

**4.** Black threatens to win a Pawn by 11 . . . Kt×B; 12 Kt×Kt, Q×P.

11 B—Q2     . . . .

Counter-attack on the KtP. If instead 11 P—K3, Q—R4 threatens 12 . . . P—Kt6ch; 13 Kt—B3, Kt×Kt; 14 Q—Q2, Q×P!

**5.** 11 . . . .     Q—R4
12 P—K3     P—B4 !

Gives White choice of two ways of capturing the Pawn—and losing. If 13 P×P, B—Q2; 14 P—

QKt3, B×R wins the exchange, or if 13 Kt×P, Kt×Kt; 14 P×Kt, B×P, and the Rook falls.

**6.**
| | 13 P—QR3 | Kt×B |
|---|---|---|
| | 14 Kt×Kt | P×QP |
| | 15 Q—B3 ? | .... |

White is intent on winning the Rook. Better would have been to head for the ending by 15 RP×P, Q—Q4; 16 Q—Kt3, Q×Q; 17 Kt×Q, P×P; 18 P×P, although Black's position is still superior.

**7.**
| | 15 .... | P×KP |
|---|---|---|
| | 16 Kt—B4 | P×Pch |

17 K×P          B—Q5*ch*

Black's handling of the attack is skilful and artistic.

**8.**
| | 18 K—K1 | Q×Kt |
|---|---|---|
| | 19 Q×R | .... |

White has no alternative but to take the Rook, as otherwise he is a piece down. He intends to get the Queen back into play next move, to help defend the King.

**9.**
| | 19 .... | O—O |
|---|---|---|

| 20 Q—B3 | P×P |
|---|---|
| 21 R×P | .... |

21 Q×P holds out a little longer.

| 21 .... | Q—Kt5*ch* |

**10.** 

| 22 K—Q1 | R—Q1 |
|---|---|
| 23 Kt—Q2 | .... |

If 23 B—Q3, B×B; 24 Q×B (24 R×B, Q×Kt), B—Kt3 wins the Queen. Or if 23 K—B1, B×P*ch*; 24 Kt×B, Q—Q7 is mate.

**11.** 

| 23 .... | B×P |
|---|---|
| 24 **Resigns** | |

For if 24 R—Q3, R×R; 25 B×R, B—Kt5 wins White's Queen.

## 26.  U.S.S.R. 1936

### Nimzoindian Defense

*Once again the perils of Queenside castling! Sokolsky's conduct of the attack is pleasing esthetically and irreproachable technically. Especially instructive is the manner in which he forces open lines for his Rooks.*

| WHITE | BLACK |
|---|---|
| A. Tolush | A. Sokolsky |
| 1 P—Q4 | Kt—KB3 |
| 2 P—QB4 | P—K3 |
| 3 Kt—QB3 | B—Kt5 |
| 4 Q—Kt3 | Kt—B3 |

and the position is shown on the diagram below:

**1.**  Black's last move is an interesting deviation from

the customary 4 . . . P—B4.

**5 P—K3** . . . .

P—Q5 is met by 5 . . . P×P; 6
P×P, Kt—Q5; 7 Q—Q1, Kt—B4.

**2.** 5 . . . . **P—Q4**
6 B—Q2 . . . .

If 6 Kt—B3, O—O; 7 B—Q3,
P×P; 8 B×P, B—Q3 followed by
9 . . . P—K4 *etc.*

6 . . . . o—o

**3.** 7 o—o—o . . . .
Tolush plays aggressively.

He reasons that with Black's
Queen Knight at B3 the Bishop
Pawn is blocked, and cannot
break up the center by . . . P—
B4.

7 . . . . **B—K2 !**

The Bishop retreats, so that the
Knight which protected it can be
free to move.

**4.** 8 P×P . . . .

Otherwise Black can get rid
of White's attacking Bishop by
8 . . . Kt—QR4; 9 Q—R4, Kt×
P; 10 B×Kt, P×B.

8 . . . . **P×P**
9 P—B3 . . . .

To support the contemplated advance of his King Knight Pawn.
Tolush is too aggressive for his
own health! He still had time
(as shown in the next note) to
change his mind—centralize his
King Knight at B4, and keep
Black busy defending his Queen
Pawn.

Pawn, but threatening also to re-move a Bishop by 14 . . . Kt—Kt5.

14 P—Kt5 . . . .

White stakes everything on a Pawn storm against the adverse King side, as passive defense (say by 14 Q—R4) will lose in the long run.

**5.** 9 . . . . B—K3
10 P—Kt4 . . . .

A less enterprising player would have been content with 10 KKt—K2, and then 11 Kt—B4.

10 . . . . Kt—QR4
11 Q—B2 P—B4 !

This will open the Bishop file against White's King whether he captures the Pawn or not.

**7.** 14 . . . . Kt—QKt5

Of course not 14 . . . Kt×P? 15 Q—R4 winning a piece.

15 Q—Kt1 . . . .

White gets the worst of it after 15 P×Kt, Kt×Q; 16 P×B, Q×P; 17 B×Kt, QR—B1. A possibility then would be 18 KKt—K2, P—QKt4; 19 Kt×KtP, R×Bch; 20 K×R, B—B4ch followed by 21 . . . Q×Kt.

After the actual move, Sokol-sky removes White's King Bishop (the poison in a King-side attack) and begins a profound re-group-ing, not only as a preventive measure, but also as a prelude to his own assault.

**6.** 12 B—Q3 P×P
13 P×P Kt—B3 !

Not only attacking the Queen

## 8.

| | |
|---|---|
| *15 ....* | Kt×B*ch* |
| *16* Q×Kt | Kt—K1 |

The correct maneuver, as the Knight is headed for B5.

| | |
|---|---|
| *17* P—B4 | Kt—Q3 |

Carrying out the plan, and meanwhile stopping 18 P—B5.

| | |
|---|---|
| *18* KKt—K2 | Q—Q2 |

## 9.

Black has made room for his King Rook to occupy QB1. His other Rook is to be posted on QKt1.

| | |
|---|---|
| *19* Kt—Kt3 | KR—B1 |
| *20* R(Q1)—K1 | P—Kt4 ! |

## 10.

If White tries to win a piece by 21 P—B5, Kt× P; 22 Kt×Kt, B×Kt; 23 R×B, Q×R; 24 Q×B, then 24 . . . P—Kt5 wins the pinned Knight.

| | |
|---|---|
| *21* K—Kt1 | P—Kt5 |
| *22* Kt—Q1 | Kt—B5 ! |

Black sets a diabolical trap!

## 11.

If White now plays 23 KR—B1 (to enforce 24

P—B5) Black replies 23 . . .
B—KB4!; 24 Kt×B, Q×Kt!; 25
Q×Q (25 R—B3, Kt×B*ch*),
Kt×B*ch*; 26 K—R1, R—B8*ch*;
27 Q—Kt1, R×Q mate.

**23 B—B1          Q—B2**

Threatening a quick mate by 24
. . . Kt—R6*ch* and 25 . . . Q×
B*ch*.

**12.** **24 Kt—B2          QR—Kt1**

Prepared to answer 25 P—B5
with 25 . . . Kt—R6*ch*; 26 P×
Kt (26 K—R1, Kt—B7*ch*), P×
P*ch*; 27 K—R1, Q—Kt3 with the
decisive threat 28 . . . R×B*ch*.

**25 P—Kt3          B—B1**
**26 P—B5           B—Q2**
**27 P×Kt           . . . .**

Otherwise Black breaks through
by 27 . . . Kt—R6*ch*; 28 B×Kt,
P×B and then 29 . . . B—Kt4.
On 27 Kt—Kt4, Kt—R6*ch*; 28
B×Kt, (28 K—Kt2, Q—B6*ch*),
P×B; 29 R—QB1, Q—KB5; 30
R×R, R×R; 31 Kt—K5, Q—B7;
32 Q—K2, B×P*ch*; 33 Kt—Q3,
B×Kt*ch* wins.

**13.** **27 . . . .          P×P**
**28 Q—K2          P—Kt6**

Forces the opening of the file, as
29 P—QR3 loses after 29 . . .
P—B6.

**29 Kt(B2)—K4     . . . .**

On 29 P×P, R×P*ch*; 30 K—B2,
B—R5 wins quickly.

**29 . . . .          P×P*ch***
**30 K—R1          . . . .**

**14.** The King tries to hide
behind the Pawn, but
Black roots him out.

30 . . . .  R—Kt8*ch* !
31 K×P   R—Kt6

Menacing mate in two.

32 K—R1  . . . .

Or 32 B—Kt2, Q—R4*ch;* 33 K—Kt1, B—R6.

32 . . . .  R(B1)—Kt1

The doubling of Rooks is deadly.

**15.** 33 Q—R2  Q—Kt3

Threatening annihilation by 34 . . . Q×P*ch,* as well as by 34 . . . R—Kt8*ch.*

34 B—K3  R—R6

Pins the Queen, and threatens 35 . . . Q—Kt7 mate.

35 R—QKt1  . . . .

Stops one mate, but there is another!

35 . . . .  R×Q*ch*
36 K×R   Q—R4 mate

Beautiful timing on the Queenside, and an enjoyable lesson on the dangers of premature attack.

## 27. CORRESPONDENCE 1937

### Sicilian Defense

*Had this game been played fifty years ago, Gergenreder would have lost it in a blaze of glory, thereby creating another "immortal gem."*

| WHITE | BLACK |
|---|---|
| V. Gergenreder | Moskaliev |
| 1 P—K4 | P—QB4 |
| 2 Kt—KB3 | Kt—QB3 |
| 3 P—Q4 | P×P |
| 4 Kt×P | Kt—B3 |
| 5 Kt—QB3 | P—Q3 |
| 6 B—KKt5 | . . . . |

and the position is shown on the diagram below:

**1.** White plays the Richter attack—an aggressive line

which for a time discouraged devotees of the Sicilian Defense.

| 6 . . . . | P—K3 |
| 7 Q—Q2 | . . . . |

**2.** White makes no secret of his intentions. He will castle Queen-side, and start an immediate King-side attack.

| 7 . . . . | B—K2 |
| 8 O—O—O | O—O |

White can win a Pawn, but after 9 B×Kt, B×B; 10 Kt×Kt, P×Kt; 11 Q×P, Q—Kt3 Black has a strong attack.

**3.**

| 9 Kt—Kt3 | Q—Kt3 |

Sets a subtle trap. If White wins a Pawn by 10 Kt—R4, Q—B2; 11 B×Kt, B×B; 12 Q×P, then Black wins by 12 . . . B—Kt4*ch;* 13 K—Kt1 (if 13 P—B4?, B×P*ch* or if 13 R—Q2?, Q×Q), R—Q1; 14 Q×Q, R×R*ch* and mate next move.

| 10 P—B3 | P—QR3 |

**4.** Black prevents any inroads by 11 Kt—Kt5.

| 11 P—Kt4 | Kt—QR4 |
| 12 Kt—Q4 | . . . . |

12 Kt×Kt is correct here, but White wants complications—and gets them!

| 12 . . . . | B—Q2 |
| 13 P—KR4 | KR—B1 |

Black plans to meet his opponent's attack not by defensive moves, but by a vigorous counterattack, using the open Bishop file as a base of operations. As in nearly all games featuring heterogeneous castling, the audience gets its money's worth.

**5.** 14 B—K3 . . . .

Not only threatening to win a Pawn by 15 Kt×P, but also to make room for P—Kt5.

**7.** 17 . . . . P—K4 !

Brilliant! Black intends to reply to 18 P×Kt with 18 . . . P×Kt and after 19 B×QP, to win by the pretty move 19 . . . P—Kt6 ! The threats would then be 20 . . . Q×P*ch* followed by mate, and 20 . . . P×RP Queening the Pawn!

18 Kt—Kt3 B—R5 !

**6.** 14 . . . . Q—B2
15 P—R5 P—QKt4
16 P—Kt5 P—Kt5

Both players have the same object in view—to drive away the other's powerful defensive Knight.

17 Kt—Kt1 . . . .

If 17 P×Kt, P×Kt followed by 18 . . . B×P favors Black.

**8.** Now 19 P×Kt loses by 19 . . . B×Kt (threatening mate in two); 20 B—Q3 (if

20 P×B, Kt×P mate), KB×P followed by 21 . . . B×RP. Another pretty variation is 19 Q—Q3, B×Kt; 20 P×B, Q×Pch; 21 Q×Q, Kt×P mate.

|        | 19 Kt—B5 | P×Kt     |
|--------|----------|----------|
|        | 20 P×Kt  | B(K2)×P  |

It is curious that Black's King is safer than White's, even with the Knight file open.

**10.**

|    | 23 P×R   | P—B5 !   |
|----|----------|----------|
|    | 24 Kt—B3 | . . . .  |

If 24 B×B, P×Pch; 25 Kt—B3, P×Kt; 26 Q—Kt5, P×Pch; 27 K—Q2, Q—B7ch; 28 K—K3, Q—K7 mate.

**9.**

|    | 21 B—KKt5 | . . . . |
|----|-----------|---------|

A better chance is offered by 21 P—Kt3, B—QKt4; 22 Q—B2.

|        | 21 . . . . | R—Q1 ! |
|--------|------------|--------|
|        | 22 B—Q3    | . . . . |

22 Q—K3 loses a piece by 22 . . . R×Rch; 23 K×R, Q—Q1ch followed by 24 . . . B×B.

|        | 22 . . . . | R×B !  |
|--------|------------|--------|

Now we see the brilliant reason for Black's previous move. The Rook sacrifice is a preliminary to 23 . . . P—B5 with which Black intends to pry open the Queen Bishop file.

**11.**

|    | 24 . . . . | P×Kt   |
|----|------------|--------|
|    | 25 KtP×P   | B×B !  |

White's last hope was for 25 . . . B×R; 26 B×B, P×B; 27 Q—R6, K—R1; 28 R—Kt1 and mate in three more moves.

|        | 26 Q×B | P—B3  |
|--------|--------|-------|

| 27 | Q—Kt4 | B×R |
|----|-------|-----|
| 28 | R×B | Q—B1 |
| 29 | **Resigns** | |

## 28.  LENINGRAD 1937

### Gruenfeld Defense

*A sprightly miniature! Volck plays with the effortless ease and grace of Morphy plucking combinations out of thin air.*

| WHITE | BLACK |
|-------|-------|
| Sokor | Volck |

| 1 | P—Q4 | Kt—KB3 |
|---|------|--------|
| 2 | P—QB4 | P—KKt3 |
| 3 | Kt—QB3 | P—Q4 |
| 4 | Q—Kt3 | P×P |
| 5 | Q×BP | B—K3 |

and the position is shown on the diagram below:

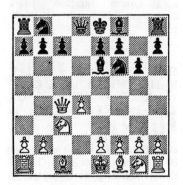

**1.** Black chooses a fighting defense—one which leads

to positions as wide-open as in an old-time King's Gambit.

There are critics who harp on the theme that 1 P—K4 is the only recipe for brilliant chess. If argument is needed this game may serve as one of countless refutations.

| 6 | Q—Kt5*ch* | Kt—B3 |
|---|-----------|-------|
| 7 | Kt—B3 | Kt—Q4 ! |

Stronger than the conservative 7 . . . R—QKt1.

**2.** White should refuse the Pawn offer.

| 8 | Q×P | . . . . |

Correct was 8 P—K4, Kt(Q4)—Kt5; 9 Q—R4, B—Q2; 10 B—QKt5, P—QR3; 11 B×Kt, Kt×B and White has a strong center as compensation for Black's two Bishops.

| 8 | . . . . | Kt(Q4)—Kt5 ! |

Black has two big threats: 9 . . . R—QKt1 winning the Queen, and 9 . . . Kt—B7*ch* winning the Rook.

**3.** 9 B—B4 !? . . . .

Intending to counter 9 . . . R
—QKt1 with 10 Q×BP, Q×Q; 11
B×Q, R—B1; 12 B—B4, Kt—
B7*ch;* 13 K—Q2, Kt×R; 14 P—
Q5, R—Q1; 15 P—K4 with ex-
cellent fighting chances.

**4.** 9 . . . . B—R3 !!

To lure White's Bishop away,
and get a magnificent diagonal
for his own Bishop.

*10* B×P . . . .

Of course not 10 B×B, R—QKt1
winning the Queen. And if 10
Q×BP, B×B; 11 Q×B, Kt—B7*ch.*

*10* . . . . Kt×QP !!

"A little bit of Morphy," as Black-
burne would say of this delightful
coup.

**5.** By means of the brilliant
Queen sacrifice, Black
threatens 11 . . . Kt(Q5)—B7
mate.

*11* B×Q . . . .

On 11 Kt×Kt, Black wins nicely
by 11 . . . Kt—B7*ch;* 12 K—Q1
(12 Kt×Kt, Q—Q7 mate), Q×
Kt*ch;* 13 K×Kt, Q—Q7*ch;* 14
K—Kt1, Q—B8 mate.

Black now forces the win by a
combination in which every one
of his pieces takes part. The finale is amusing. Black captures a
Bishop and two Knights, and
after that makes White return his
Queen—and resign!

## 29. MOSCOW 1937

### King's Indian Defense

*Some of the most remarkable brilliancies have been produced by little-known players —Hermann-Hussong, Adams-Torre, Hamppe-Meitner, Przepiorka-Patay, Langleben-Sobenheim and Kotz-Lebedev.*

**6.**

| | | |
|---|---|---|
| 11 .... | Kt(Q5)—B7*ch* |
| 12 K—Q1 | R×B*ch* |
| 13 Kt—Q5 | B×Kt |
| 14 Q—B7 | B×Kt*ch* |
| 15 Q×R*ch* | K×Q |
| 16 KP×B | K—B2 ! |

| WHITE | BLACK |
|---|---|
| **A. Kotz** | **P. Lebedev** |
| 1 Kt—KB3 | Kt—KB3 |
| 2 P—Q4 | P—KKt3 |
| 3 P—B4 | B—Kt2 |
| 4 P—KKt3 | O—O |
| 5 B—Kt2 | P—Q3 |
| 6 O—O | Kt—B3 |

and the position is shown on the diagram below:

**7.** Black has made room for the King Rook to do his bit. If White tries to save his Queen Rook by 17 QR—Kt1, then Black wins by 17 . . . R—Q1*ch;* 18 K—K2, R—Q7 mate. Therefore:

**17 Resigns**

**1.** Black chooses a defense favored by Tchigorin and

Yates, disparate personalities, but both protagonists of vigorous fighting chess.

| 7 Kt—B3 | P—K4 ! |

**2.** Black gets a grip on the center. If in reply 8 P—K4 then 8 . . . P×P; 9 Kt×P, Kt×P! and Black equalizes.

| 8 P—KR3 | Kt—Q2 |
| 9 B—K3 | P—KR3 |

**3.** Instead of this Black should have exchanged to free his cramped position, by 9 . . . P×P; 10 Kt×P, Kt×Kt; 11 B×Kt, Kt—K4.

| 10 Q—Q2 | K—R2 |
| 11 QR—Q1 | P—B4 |
| 12 P×P | . . . . |

A bit of psychology! With choice of four ways to recapture, Black was bound to select the wrong one!

**4.** 12 . . . .        P×P

But this capture is not in accordance with his own strategy in moving 8 . . . Kt—Q2. Black should have played 12 . . . Kt (Q2)×P, making room for the development of his Queen Bishop.

| 13 Q—B1 ! | . . . . |

Pins the Knight on Q7.

| 13 . . . . | R—K1 |
| 14 B—Kt5 !! | . . . . |

White's surprising last move has begun a wonderful combination!

## 5. 14 . . . .      Kt—K2

If 14 . . . P×B; 15 Kt×P*ch*, K—Kt1 (on 15 . . . K—R3, or 15 . . . K—R1; 16 Kt—B7*ch* wins the Queen); 16 B—Q5*ch*, K—B1; 17 Kt—R7*ch*, K—K2; 18 Q—Kt5*ch* wins.

          15 Kt—Q5 !      P—K5

Black must not take the Bishop, as then 16 Kt×P*ch*, K—Kt1; 17 Kt—K6 wins his Queen!

## 6. 16 Kt—Q4 !      . . . .

Threatens 17 Kt—K6, as well as 17 B×Kt.

    16 . . . .                B×Kt
    17 B×Kt              B×P*ch*

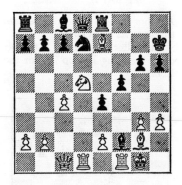

## 7. Black wants an extra Pawn but White's King Rook comes into play quickly.

    18 R×B              R×B
    19 Kt—B6*ch* !      K—Kt2
    20 Q—B3              . . . .

## 8. White plans to win the Queen by 21 Kt×Kt*ch*, K

moves (to a white square) 22 Kt
checks accordingly, followed by
23 R×Q.

| 20 .... | K—B2 |
| 21 B×P! | .... |

Another shock! The immediate
threat is 22 B—Q5ch.

The ulterior purpose is to tear
open the King Bishop file for the
Rook.

**9.** 21 ....          P—B3

Black saw that 21 . . . P×B;
22 Kt×Ktch, K—Kt1 (otherwise
Rook mates); 23 Kt—B6ch was
fatal and that 21 . . . R×B; 22
Kt×R would lose the exchange,
as he could not recapture.

22 B×KBP!          ....

White insists on giving up his
Bishop.

| 22 .... | P×B |
| 23 R×P | .... |

But now both Rooks have open
files on which to work.

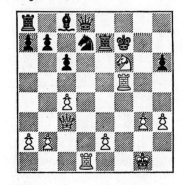

**10.** 23 ....          K—Kt3

23 . . . Q—Kt3ch; 24 P
—B5 does not help Black any.

24 R—Q6!          ....

Black dare not take the Rook. If
24 . . . K×R; 25 Q—Q3ch, K—
K4 (or 25 . . . K—Kt4, 26 P—
R4 mate); 26 Kt—Kt4 mate.

24 ....          R—K3!

**11.** Black's clever counter-
offer gives him his best
chances of resistance.

25 R×R      K×R
26 R—Q6      ....

Forces Black to give up his Queen.
If 26 . . . K—Kt3, 27 Q—Q3*ch*,
K—Kt2 (27 . . . K—Kt4; 28
P—R4 mate); 28 Q—R7*ch*, K—
B1; 29 Q—Kt8*ch*, K—K2; 30
R—K6 mate.

    26 ....      Q×Kt
    27 Q—Q3*ch* !    ....

More elegant than 27 R×Q*ch*
which might not even win! There
are more "problem" moves coming, and the Queen does not run
away.

**13.** Black has another opportunity of going wrong: If
28 . . . K—Kt5; 29 R×Q, Kt×R;
30 Q—Kt6*ch*, and White wins the
Knight.

    28 ....      K—R4
    29 P—Kt4*ch*    K×RP
    30 R×Q      Kt×R
    31 Q—Q8      ....

**12.** White was in no hurry to
take the Queen. His in-
tention is to get his own Queen to
Q8, where it will paralyze all of
Black's pieces.

    27 ....      K—Kt4

If 27 . . . K—K4, White wins
delightfully by 28 Q—Q4*ch*, K—
B4; 29 Q—Kt4*ch*, K—K4; 30 R—
K6*ch* !, Q×R; 31 Q—B4 mate.

    28 P—R4*ch*      ....

**14.** The Knight is pinned;
nor can Black's Bishop
and Rook come into play.

    31 ....      K—Kt4

The Knight must be protected.

    32 P—K4 !    . . . .

Threatens 33 P—K5 winning the pinned Knight.

    32 . . . .    K—Kt3
    33 P—K5    . . . .

**15.** The Pawn means to march on, and cost Black a piece. If for instance 33 . . . Kt×P; 34 P—K6, Kt—B3; 35 P—K7, K—B2; 36 Q—B8*ch*.

    33 . . . .    Kt—Q2

Loses gracefully, by permitting White to mate neatly.

    34 Q—Kt8 mate

### 30. TIFLIS 1937

### Philidor Defense

*An unexpected pin by Ilyin-Genevsky is utilized cleverly— not as a weapon in itself, but as the basis of a pretty combination to win the Queen. The*

*first World War took Ilyin-Genevsky's memory away, and he had to learn everything all over again—including the moves of chess. The second War (more cruel) took his life.*

| WHITE | BLACK |
| --- | --- |
| V. Rauzer | A. Ilyin-Genevsky |
| *1* P—K4 | P—K4 |
| *2* Kt—KB3 | P—Q3 |
| *3* P—Q4 | P×P |
| *4* Kt×P | Kt—KB3 |
| *5* P—KB3 | . . . . |

and the position is shown on the diagram below:

**1.** White's last move, instead of the more natural 5 Kt—QB3, is based on a similar idea in the Sicilian Defense. White anticipates controlling the center with 6 P—QB4 etc.

    5 . . . .    P—Q4 !

Counter-attack in the center!

**2.**    6 P—K5        KKt—Q2
         7 P—KB4     ....

On 7 P—K6, Kt—KB3; 8 P×P*ch*, K×P; 9 Kt—QB3, B—K2 and Black continues 10 ... R—K1, castling "by hand."

         7 ....        Kt—QB3

A simple developing move.

**3.**   If now 8 B—K2 ? Kt(Q2) ×P; 9 P×Kt, Q—R5*ch* followed by 10 ... Q×Kt wins a Pawn! A simple refutation of White's advance of the King's Bishop Pawn.

         8 Kt×Kt        P×Kt
         9 B—Q3     ....

Better would have been 9 Q—B3.

**4.**   Alert Ilyin-Genevsky immediately takes advantage of White's error.

         9 ....        Q—R5*ch* !
        10 P—Kt3     Q—R6

To prevent White from castling.

       11 Q—B3     ....

White must not permit 11 ... Q—Kt7.

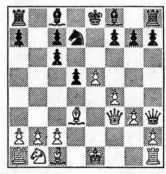

**5.**   11 ....        B—B4
       12 B—K3     O—O

Mobilizes the King Rook, which will play an important part in the attack.

    *13* Kt—Q2          P—B3 !

A powerful move which threatens to win at once by 14 . . . P×P.

White's best line is probably 14 B×B, Kt×B; 15 B—B1, Q—K3; 16 Q—K3, Kt—Q2; 17 Kt—B3. His King Pawn would fall, but there would still be some fight left in the position.

**6.**   *14* P×P          . . . .

Expecting in reply 14 . . . Kt×P, or 14 . . . R×P; but he gets a shock!

    *14* . . . .        R—K1 !

Pinning the Bishop, which is now attacked twice.

    *15* Kt—B1          Kt×P

Simpler than 15 . . . B×B; 16 Kt×B, P—Q5; 17 B—B4*ch*, K—R1; 18 P×P*ch*, K×P; 19 O—O—O, R×Kt; 20 Q×P.

**7.**   *16* K—Q2          . . . .

If 16 O—O—O, B—KKt5 wins.

    *16* . . . .        B—KKt5
    *17* Q—B2          P—Q5
    *18* B×P            R—K7*ch* !
    *19* B×R            Kt—K5*ch*

    20 **Resigns**, as his Queen is lost.

### 31.  KIEV 1938

#### Queen's Gambit Declined

*This variation of the Queen's has occurred thousands of times between all grades of players from beginner to World's Champion, its ramifications have been explored by hundreds of annotators and analysts, and yet—Dus-Choti-mirsky gives it new life and spirit.*

*To those who consider the Queen's as the last refuge of mediocrity, we recommend this game.*

| WHITE | BLACK |
|---|---|
| F. Dus-Chotimirsky | A. Kotov |

| | |
|---|---|
| *1* P—Q4 | Kt—KB3 |
| *2* Kt—KB3 | P—Q4 |
| *3* P—B4 | P—K3 |
| *4* Kt—B3 | QKt—Q2 |
| *5* B—Kt5 | B—K2 |
| *6* P—K3 | O—O |

and the position is shown on the diagram below:

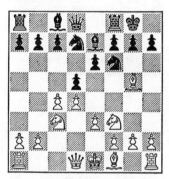

**7.**   *7* R—B1          ....

The Rook move discourages Black from freeing his game by 7 . . . P—B4 as then White gets the best of it by 8 QP×P !, Kt×P; 9 P×P, P×P; due to Black's isolated Queen Pawn.

|  |  |
|---|---|
| *7* .... | P—B3 |
| *8* P—QR3 | .... |

Stronger is 8 B—Q3.

**2.**   *8* ....          P—QR3

Black misses the chance to free his game by 8 . . . Kt—K5; 9 B×B, Q×B; 10 Q—B2, Kt×Kt; 11 Q×Kt, R—K1 with equality.

          *9* P×P          ....

Else Black continues with 9 . . . P×P; 10 B×P, P—QKt4 followed by . . . B—Kt2 and . . . P—B4.

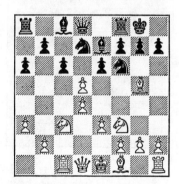

**3.**
| | |
|---|---|
| *9* .... | BP×P |
| *10* B—Q3 | P—Kt4 |
| *11* O—O | B—Kt2 |
| *12* P—QR4 ! | .... |

To weaken Black's grip on his QB5.

**4.**  12 ....        P—Kt5
       13 Kt—Kt1       R—K1

He should dispute control of the Bishop file by 13 . . . R—B1.

       14 Kt(Kt1)—Q2   ....

**5.**  White's Knight is headed for Kt3 from where he will exert pressure on R5 and B5.

       14 ....         Q—R4

Again 14 . . . R—B1 was strong-

er. The Queen move is meant to prevent 15 Kt—Kt3, as then the Rook Pawn is unprotected.

**6.**  15 Kt—Kt3 !     ....

Practically forcing Black to take the Pawn, for, after 15 . . . Q—Q1; 16 P—R5 gives White a tremendous positional advantage.

       15 ....         Q×P
       16 R—B7 !       ....

**7.**  16 ....         QR—Kt1

Forced. If 16 . . . B—B3; 17 Q—B2, B—Kt4; 18 R—R1, B× B; 19 Q×B, Q—Kt4; 20 Q×Q, P×Q; 21 R×R, R×R; 22 B×Kt and White wins a piece.

**17 Kt—K5 !** · . . . .

The winning move. If 17 . . . B—Q3; 18 R×Kt, Kt×R ( . . . B×Kt; 19 R×B !); 19 B×P*ch*, K×B; 20 Q—R5*ch*, K—Kt1; 21 Q×P*ch*, K—R1; 22 Kt×Kt, Q× Kt(Kt6); Kt—B6 ! forces mate.

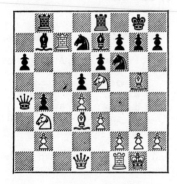

**8.** Black has no defense: if 17 . . . Kt×Kt; 18 P×Kt, Kt—Q2; 19 B×B, R×B; 20 Q— B2 threatens the unanswerable 21 R—R1. Or if 17 . . . B—R1; 18 R×Kt !, Kt×R; 19 B×P*ch*, K—B1; 20 Kt—B5 !, Kt×Kt(B4); 21 Q×Q, Kt×Q; 22 Kt—Q7 mate!

**17 . . . .**     **Kt—B1**
**18 B×Kt !**     . . . .

White switches to a sharp King-side attack, hardly to be foreseen from his early Queen-side maneuvers.

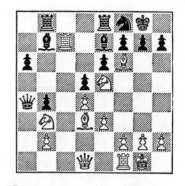

**9.** *18 . . . .*     **B×B**

If 18 . . . P×B; 19 Q— Kt4*ch*, Kt—Kt3; 20 B×Kt !, RP ×B; 21 Kt×KtP !, P×Kt; 22 Q× KtP*ch*, K—R1; 23 Kt—B5, Q— Kt4; 24 Kt×KP wins for White.

**19 Q—R5**     . . . .

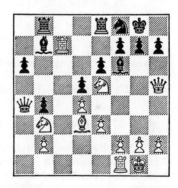

**10.** *19 . . . .*     **Kt—Kt3**

If 19 . . . P—Kt3; 20 Q—B3 wins. Or if 19 . . . KR—B1; 20 B×P*ch*, Kt×B; 21 Q×P*ch*, K— R1; 22 Kt—Kt6 mate!

*20 Kt—Q7 !*     *Q×Kt(Kt6)*

If the Bishop moves instead, to K2 or Q1, then 21 Kt(Kt3)—B5 wins.

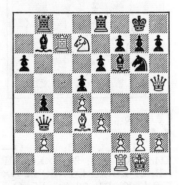

**11.** White concludes with a pretty Rook sacrifice.

    *21 Kt×Bch*     *P×Kt*
    *22 R×P !*     *R—K2*

Bewildered by all he has gone through, Black overlooks the threatened mate; but if instead 22 . . . K×R; 23 Q×Pch, K—B1; 24 B×Kt, R—K2; 25 Q—R8 mate.

    *23 Q×P mate*

Clever play by the man who beat Lasker and Rubinstein in one tournament! Chess playing must certainly sharpen the wits for here we have a beautiful game by Dus-Chotimirsky whose vivid imagination and talent for attack are even greater now than at the start of his tournament career—thirty years earlier.

## 32. KIEV 1938

### Catalan Opening

*Panov ties up his opponent hand and foot, in the style made famous by Tarrasch. Not even the worthy Doctor, however, could have improved in his palmiest days on the cold-blooded methodical efficiency of Panov.*

| WHITE | BLACK |
|-------|-------|
| V. Panov | V. Makogonov |
| *1* P—Q4 | Kt—KB3 |
| *2* P—QB4 | P—K3 |
| *3* P—KKt3 | P—Q4 |
| *4* Kt—KB3 | QKt—Q2 |
| *5* B—Kt2 | . . . . |

and the position is shown on the diagram below:

**1.**     *5 . . . .*     *P—B3*

Too cautious. A good continuation would be 5 . . . P×P; 6 Q—R4, P—QR3; 7 Kt—B3, R—QKt1 !; 8 Q×BP, P—QKt4; 9 Q—Q3, B—Kt2; 10 O—O, P—B4.

|     |            |             |
| --- | ---------- | ----------- |
| 6   | Q—B2       | B—Q3        |
| 7   | QKt—Q2     | O—O         |
| 8   | O—O        | P—K4        |

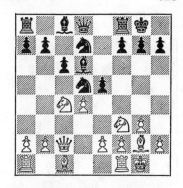

**3.** 

|     |            |             |
| --- | ---------- | ----------- |
| 10  | . . . .    | Q—K2        |
| 11  | P—K4 !     | KKt—Kt3     |

If 11 . . . Kt—Kt5; 12 Q—Kt3, P×P; 13 B—Kt5, Q—K3; 14 Kt×P, Q—Kt3; 15 Kt×B, Q×Kt; 16 Kt—B5, Q—B4; 17 B—K7 and White wins.

|     |            |             |
| --- | ---------- | ----------- |
| 12  | Kt×B       | Q×Kt        |
| 13  | R—Q1       | P×P         |

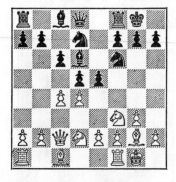

**2.** Black is attempting to free his cramped game, but his last move should have been prefaced by 8 . . . R—K1. If then 9 P—K4, Kt×P; 10 Kt×Kt, P×Kt; 11 Q×P, P—K4; 12 R—K1, Kt—B3; 13 Q—B2, P—K5.

|     |            |             |
| --- | ---------- | ----------- |
| 9   | BP×P       | Kt×P        |

9 . . . BP×P was much better. After the move actually made, White gets a grip on the position —and tightens his grip with every move!

|     |            |             |
| --- | ---------- | ----------- |
| 10  | Kt—B4 !    | . . . .     |

Not only is Black's Bishop threatened, but his King Pawn is also attacked three times.

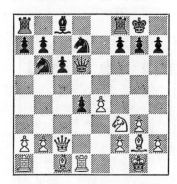

**4.** 

|     |            |             |
| --- | ---------- | ----------- |
| 14  | B—B4 !     | Q—K2        |

Now 14 . . . Q—B4 would lose by 15 Q×Q, Kt×Q; 16 B—Q6.

15 R×P     . . . .

**5.** White threatens to win the exchange by 16 B—Q6.

15 . . . .     R—K1
16 B—Q6     Q—K3
17 P—QR4 !     Kt—B1

Else P—R5 wins a piece.

18 P—R5     Kt(Kt3)—Q2
19 QR—Q1     . . . .

**6.** White is in complete command of the center. Strate-

gically, he has a won game. The technique by which he "wins a won game" is extremely instructive.

19 . . . .     P—B3

Black fears the possibility of Kt—Kt5 coming in at some time.

20 B—B1     . . . .

The Bishop is to be given a more active role. Black's Queenside pieces are still asleep.

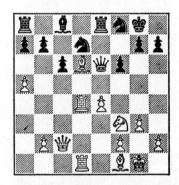

**7.** Tactically the threat is 20 B—QB4 winning the Queen. Strategically, the threat is 20 B—QB4 not to win material, but to control an important diagonal which has been weakened by Black's last move.

20 . . . .     Q—B2
21 B—QB4     Kt—K3
22 P—K5 !     . . . .

The tactical threats commence; but only now when White's strategical aims have been carried out—every one of his pieces effectively posted.

**8.** Now the Rook can swing over to attack Black's King-side.

22 ....         **K—R1**

22 . . . P—KB4 loses at once by 23 Kt—Kt5, and if 22 . . . Kt× P; 23 QB×Kt, P×B; 24 Kt—Kt5, Q—Kt3; 25 Q×Q, P×Q; 26 R— Q8 and Black has no defense.

**9.**     23 R—Kt4 !      ....

Not 23 R—B4, Q—Kt3; nor 23 R—R4, P—KKt4; 24 R—R6, Q— Kt2 and Black can still fight a bit.

23 ....         **Kt(Q2)—B1**
24 P×P        **Q×P**

On 24 . . . P×P; 25 Kt—K5 !, P×Kt (25 . . . Q—R4; 26 R— R4, Q—Kt4; 27 Kt—B7*ch* wins) 26 B×P*ch* wins at once.

25 Kt—K5        ....

**10.** The Knight controls Kt6, an important preparatory step for the attack by R—R4.

25 ....        **P—QKt4**
26 B—R2       **P—B4**
27 B—Q5       ....

Not in order to win the exchange, but to keep the Bishop from being shut out by 27 . . . P—B5.

27 ....        **B—R3**
28 R—KR4     **P—Kt4**

If 28 . . . P—Kt3; 29 Kt—Kt4, Q—Q1; 30 B—K5*ch*, K—Kt1; 31 Kt—R6 mate.

Or if 28 . . . QR—B1; 29 QB ×Kt, Kt×B; 30 Kt—B7*ch*, K— Kt1; 31 Kt—Kt5*ch*, K—R1; 32 Q×P*ch*, Kt×Q; 33 R×Kt mate.

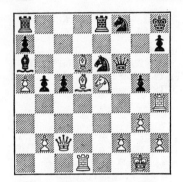

## 11.

29 R—R6 !　　Q—Kt2

If 29 . . . Q×R; 30 Kt—B7*ch* wins the Queen.

30 QB×Kt　　Kt×B
31 Kt—B7*ch*　　Resigns

On 31 . . . K—Kt1, White wins as he pleases, the simplest being 32 R×B with additional material gain to follow.

### 33. MOSCOW 1938

#### French Defense

*Riumin plays this game as though he were giving a lesson in the art of attack. He follows the maxim of developing every one of his pieces before making a single aggressive move. Then he adds some piquant touches by his clever tactics on the King's Knight file.*

*Riumin's vigorous attacking style and his fund of bold origi-* nal ideas were responsible for many a high place in Russian tournaments. So bewildering were his conceptions that they once caused even the great Capablanca to lose his bearings and forfeit a game to him on time limit!

| WHITE | BLACK |
|---|---|
| **N. Riumin** | **V. Alatorzev** |
| 1 P—K4 | P—K3 |
| 2 P—Q4 | P—Q4 |
| 3 Kt—Q2 | . . . . |

and the position is shown on the diagram below:

## 1.

No routine, mechanical chess for Riumin! The usual move is 3 Kt—QB3, but developing the Knight at Q2 has certain advantages, as we shall see from the subsequent play.

3 . . . .　　Kt—KB3

Inferior to the simpler alternative 3 . . . P—QB4.

Presaging a King-side attack.

8 . . . .   P—B4

**2.** 4 P—K5   KKt—Q2
   5 P—KB4  . . . .

Another good line is 5 B—Q3,
P—QB4; 6 P—QB3, Kt—QB3;
7 Kt—K2.

   5 . . . .   P—QB4
   6 KKt—B3  P×P

**3.** If White recaptures me-
chanically by 7 Kt×P,
then Black wins a Pawn by 7
. . . Kt×P; 8 P×Kt, Q—R5*ch*
followed by 9 . . . Q×Kt.

   7 Kt—Kt3  Kt—QB3
   8 B—Q3  . . . .

**4.** Black has cut down the
scope of White's King
Bishop.

   9 O—O   Kt—B4
  10 QKt×P  Kt—K5
  11 B—K3  B—B4
  12 P—B3  O—O
  13 Q—K2  . . . .

**5.** Before breaking through
on the King side, White
mobilizes all his pieces.

| 13 .... | B—Q2 |
| 14 QR—Q1 | R—B1 |
| 15 K—R1 | Q—Kt3 |
| 16 R—KKt1 | B—K1 |

A better defense was 16 . . .
K—R1; 17 P—KKt4, P—Kt3.

| 17 P—KKt4 | .... |

If 17 . . . B—Kt3; 18 P×P, B×
P; 19 Kt×B, P×Kt; 20 B×B, Q
×B; 21 R—Kt2 followed by
bringing the Bishop to Kt3.

**7.** White has various threats:
19 Kt(Kt5)×KP or 19
Q×P or 19 Kt(Kt5)×Kt, P×Kt;
20 B×P.

| 18 .... | B×Kt |
| 19 P×B | Kt×Kt |

If 19 . . . Kt—Kt5; 20 B×Kt,
P×B; 21 P—Q5, Q—Kt4; 22 Q×
P and White has a winning at-
tack.

| 20 Q×P! | .... |

Another important interpolation.

**6.** White's idea is of course
to open the Knight file for
his Rook.

| 17 .... | P×P |

Black expects 18 R×P, to which
his reply would be 18 . . . B—
R4. But White does not oblige.

| 18 Kt—KKt5 ! | .... |

An important interpolation. Aside
from keeping the King Knight
file open, White is concerned with
undermining Black's powerfully
posted Knight at K5.

**8.** Black's Knight will not run
away!

20 ....        Q—Q1

The Knight must not move, as 21 Q×P mate would follow. Black's move is made with the intention of exchanging Queens on 21 Q×Kt.

21 P×Kt       ....

If 21 ... P—KKt3 (to stop the Bishop sacrifice); 22 Q×P*ch* wins.

**9.** White has blocked the Knight file, but he will find a way to open it.

21 ....        Q—Q2
22 B×P*ch* !   ....

A sacrifice which is as logical as it is brilliant.

22 ....        K×B
23 P—Kt6*ch*   K—Kt1

If 23 ... B×P; 24 Q—R3*ch*, K—Kt1; 25 R×B winning as in the game. White's kind gift of the Bishop will have to be returned quickly, as the advanced Knight Pawn must be removed.

**10.** 24 Q—R5       B×P

If instead 24 ... R—B4; White wins nicely by 25 Q—R7*ch*, K—B1; 26 Q—R8*ch*, K—K2; 27 B—Kt5*ch* !, R×B; 28 Q×P*ch*, K—Q1; 29 Q—B6*ch*, Q—K2; 30 R×R.

25 R×B       ....

**11.** Now White can double his Rooks on the newly opened Knight file.

25 ....        R—KB2
26 QR—KKt1     Kt—K2

27 R—R6     **Resigns**

There was no hope in 27 . . . K—B1; 28 R—R8*ch*, Kt—Kt1; 29 Q—R7, and White wins easily.

### 34. TULSK 1938

#### Slav Defense

*White's vigorous attack leads to an exciting battle, with many surprising touches.*

| WHITE | BLACK |
|-------|-------|
| **P. Lebedev** | **Gonak** |
| 1 Kt—KB3 | P—Q4 |
| 2 P—Q4 | Kt—KB3 |
| 3 P—B4 | P—B3 |
| 4 Kt—B3 | . . . . |

and the position is shown on the diagram below:

**1.** Black plays the Slav Defense, a great favorite of

Dr. Euwe, former World Champion.

| 4 . . . . | P×P |
|-----------|-----|
| 5 Kt—K5 | P—K3 |

**2.** Black made no attempt to keep his extra Pawn by 5 . . . P—QKt4, as experience has shown it to be risky policy.

| 6 P—K3 | QKt—Q2 |
|--------|--------|
| 7 P—B4 | B—Kt5 |

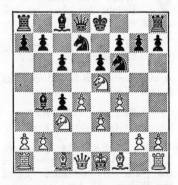

**3.** Black pins the Knight, intending to pile up pressure

on it by . . . Kt—K5 and . . . Q—R4. Somewhat better would have been the less aggressive 7 . . . B—K2. White's position at this stage would fill an attacking player's heart with joy. His Knight is planted at K5 like a Colossus bestriding the chessboard.

8 B×P        Kt—K5

**4.** Black sees visions of a mating attack! He threatens 9 . . . Q—R5*ch;* 10 K—K2, Q—B7*ch;* 11 K—Q3, Kt(Q2)—B4*ch;* 12 P×Kt, Kt×P*ch;* 13 K—Q4, O—O, followed by 14 . . . R—Q1*ch,* either mating or winning the Queen. White meets this threat by simply going about his business—which is to complete his development.

9 O—O        Kt(K5)×Kt

Black has decided that he might just as well win a Pawn, as some sort of compensation for his inferior position.

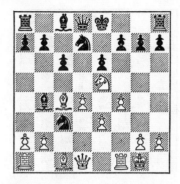

**5.** White, on the other hand, is strongly centralized; he does not mind the loss of a Pawn.

10 P×Kt        B×P

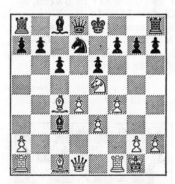

**6.** Let us see what White has for his Pawn. His Queen can be posted menacingly at KR5, KKt4 or QKt3, his QR (after 11 R—Kt1) will control an open file, his KR can get to Kt3 or R3 via B3, his QB will occupy the beautiful square R3, while his Knight stands firmly on K5.

11 R—Kt1        Kt—B3

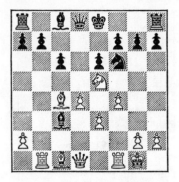

**7.**    Now comes a powerful thrust at the King Pawn.

*12 P—B5 !    . . . .*

If 12 . . . P×P; 13 B×Pch, K—K2 (or B1); 14 B—R3ch, and Black must interpose his Queen. Or if 12 . . . O—O; 13 Q—Kt3, B—R4; 14 P×P, P×P; 15 B×Pch, B×B; 16 Q×Bch.

*12 . . . .    Kt—Q4*
*13 P×P    . . . .*

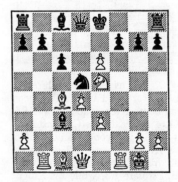

**8.**    Rips right into Black's position, giving him no time to consolidate his forces. Notice how White's last move opened up a splendid file for his King Rook.

*13 . . . .    B×KP*

On 13 . . . P×P, White has the pleasant task of deciding whether to win by 14 Kt—B7, or by 14 Q—R5ch.

*14 R×KtP    O—O*

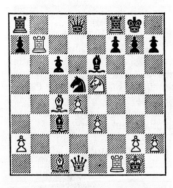

**9.**    Black has returned the Pawn, and thankfully castled into apparent security. White must hatch new schemes to keep his opponent on the run. It would be an error to play 15 Kt×QBP as after 15 . . . Q—B1; 16 B×Kt (hoping for 16 . . . B×B; 17 Kt—K7ch), Q×R, and 17 Kt—K7ch fails on account of 17 . . . Q×Kt.

*15 Q—Kt3    Q—B1*
*16 B—R3    R—K1*

White's last two moves have given him complete control of the board.

**10.** Every White piece is placed about as well as it possibly can be. The question now is: how is he to derive the benefits of his superiority? Can he gain material, or will he get the opportunity to bring off a mating combination?

*17 Kt×KBP !* . . . .

**11.** The beginning of the winning maneuver. White's previous move drove Black's Rook away from the protection of the

KBP, and now the capture of the Pawn will enable White's pieces to crash through.

*17 . . . . Kt×P*

But not 17 . . . B×Kt, as after 18 R(B1)×B with both Rooks on the seventh rank, White wins on the spot.

*18 B×B* . . . .

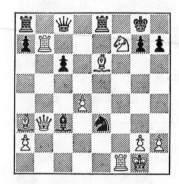

**12.** Leaves no choice for Black. If 18 . . . R×B; 19 Kt—Q6 drives the Queen away, so that the Rook is unprotected. Then on 19 . . . Q—Q1; 20 Q×R*ch* forces mate quickly.

*18 . . . . Q×B*

Will Black's game hold? He threatens to exchange Queens, and beat off the attack.

*19 Kt—R6ch !* . . . .

A little surprise! But it is all part of a brilliantly conceived and accurately executed attack.

## 13. 19 ....     K—R1

If 19 . . . P×Kt; 20 R—B8*ch*, R×R; 21 Q×Q*ch* wins.

20 R—B8*ch* !     R×R

## 14. White's last was another "surprise" move, but has he miscalculated? If he plays 21 Q×Q, he gets mated by 21 . . . R—B8.

21 B×R !     ....

Now if 21 . . . Q×Q; 22 B×P is mate. Or if 21 . . . Q×Kt; 22

B×P*ch*, Q×B; 23 R×Q, K×R; 24 Q—Kt7*ch*, and Black's Rook falls.

21 ....     R×B

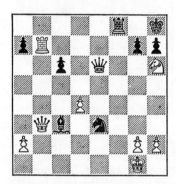

## 15. Black still hopes for 22 Q×Q, when 22 . . . R —B8 mates White.

22 Kt—B7*ch* !     ....

But this last brilliant move puts an end to that hope, as well as to the game. If 22 . . . K—Kt1; 23 Q×Q wins (Black's Rook is blocked) while 22 . . . R×Kt loses by 23 R—Kt8*ch* forcing mate. Finally, if 22 . . . Q×Kt; 23 Q×Q, R×Q; 24 R—Kt8*ch*, and mate next move. Therefore:

22 ....     **Resigns**

A game studded with surprise moves. Strange how often surprise moves occur in the games of the masters! One reason for this is that the master posts his pieces where they enjoy the greatest freedom of movement; "surprise" moves then fit in as part of the plan.

### 35. U.S.S.R. 1938

### Sicilian Defense

*Kopayev brings about a remarkable ending where he twice threatens to win by promoting a Pawn to a Knight! The actual continuation is more conventional, featuring a "mere" sacrifice of the Queen.*

| WHITE | BLACK |
|-------|-------|
| N. Kopayev | V. Alatorzev |
| 1 P—K4 | P—QB4 |
| 2 Kt—KB3 | P—Q3 |
| 3 P—Q4 | Kt—KB3 |
| 4 Kt—B3 | P×P |
| 5 Kt×P | P—QR3 |
| 6 B—K2 | P—K3 |

and the position is shown on the diagram below:

**1.** Black plays the Scheveningen Variation. This branch

of the Sicilian Defense, though difficult, is extremely popular.

7 O—O          Q—B2

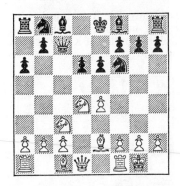

**2.** Black's Queen is posted on its best square. One of Black's objectives in this variation is to control the QB file.

8 P—QR4      . . . .

To prevent 8 . . . P—QKt4.

8 . . . .      P—QKt3

**3.** Black prepares to develop his Bishop at Kt2, from

where it will bear down on the long diagonal.

9 P—B4          QKt—Q2

Evidently the Knight is headed for B4, and there in conjunction with the Bishop at Kt2, will exert pressure on the center.

**4.**  10 B—B3          B—Kt2
        11 P—KKt4         Kt—B4

Black counterattacks in the center.

**5.**  12 Q—K2          B—K2
        13 Q—Kt2 !       . . . .

Still guarding the KP and preparing for the coming attack.

**6.**  13 . . . .        O—O
        14 P—Kt5          Kt—K1

14 . . . KKt—Q2 would be met by 15 B—Q2, threatening 16 P—Kt4; but not at once 15 P—Kt4, Kt—Kt6 !

15 B—K3          P—K4

**7.**  Black has lost patience, and tries to seize the initiative by force.

*16 Kt(Q4)—K2 !* . . . .

Much stronger than the instinctive 16 Kt—B5. Now if 16 . . . P×P; 17 Kt×P, and White is in full control of Q5.

Black insists on opening up the game, and as usual the prospects favor the better developed player.

| | | |
|---|---|---|
| 20 | P×P | P×P |
| 21 | R×R | B×R |
| 22 | B×Kt | . . . . |

**8.**

| | | |
|---|---|---|
| 16 | . . . . | B—QB3 |
| 17 | P—B5 | B—Q1 |
| 18 | Q—Kt4 | . . . . |

Probably planning to continue with 19 B—Kt2, and 20 R—B3.

**10.** Now White wins a Pawn —with delightful complications.

| | | |
|---|---|---|
| 22 | . . . . | P×B |
| 23 | R—Q1 | Kt—Q3 |

**9.**

| | | |
|---|---|---|
| 18 | . . . . | Q—Q2 |
| 19 | P—Kt3 | P—Kt4 |

**11.**

| | | |
|---|---|---|
| 24 | Kt×P | Q×Kt |
| 25 | R×Kt | P—B5 |

*26 K—Kt2          K—R1*

It would have been dangerous to regain the Pawn, as after 26 . . . P×P; 27 P×P, Q×P; 28 P—B6, White has a vigorous attack.

## 12.   *27 Q—R5          . . . .*

Threatening Q×P!

*27 . . . .          B—K2*
*28 R—Q1          P×P*
*29 P×P          Q×P*

## 13.   *30 R—Q7          . . . .*

The Rook has reached the seventh rank, but how does White break through?

*30 . . . .          B—Q1*

Against 30 . . . R—K1, White wins a Pawn by 31 P—Kt6, P×P; 32 P×P, P—R3; 33 Q×P.

*31 P—B6          Q—K3*

Of course not 31 . . . P—Kt3; 32 Q—R6, R—Kt1; 33 R×B, and White wins. The move actually made leads to an exquisite ending.

## 14.   *32 P—Kt6 !!          . . . .*

Threatening 33 Q×P mate. If 32 . . . BP×P; 33 P×P*ch*, K—Kt1; 34 Q×P*ch !*, K×Q; 35 P×R(Kt)*ch !* followed by 36 Kt×Q wins.

*32 . . . .          P—R3*
*33 Q×P*ch *!          . . . .*

A spectacular sacrifice. The Knight Pawn will now advance with fatal effect.

**15.**

| 33 | .... | P×Q |
|----|------|-----|
| 34 | P—Kt7*ch* | .... |

On the reply 34 . . . K—R2 the pretty underpromotion 35 P×R (Kt)*ch*, followed by 36 Kt×Q wins artistically.

| 34 | .... | K—Kt1 |
|----|------|-------|
| 35 | P×R(Q)*ch* | K×Q |
| 36 | R×B*ch* | Q—K1 |

Black must give up his Queen.

| 37 | R×Q*ch* | **Resigns** |
|----|---------|-------------|

## 36. LENINGRAD 1939

### Caro-Kann Defense

*One can feel the impress of a powerful personality in Makogonov's original treatment of this fascinating game. The bizarre effects he produces in the ending border on the surrealistic in chess.*

*Makogonov keeps his Queen side pieces at home for the first*

*fifteen moves. He knows that chess is a fight—and that it is sometimes more important to interfere with the opponent's development than to continue your own.*

| WHITE | BLACK |
|-------|-------|
| **I. Kan** | **V. Makogonov** |
| 1 P—K4 | P—QB3 |
| 2 P—Q4 | P—Q4 |
| 3 P×P | P×P |
| 4 P—QB4 | .... |

and the position is shown on the diagram below:

**1.** Known as the Panov-Botvinnik attack, this as Fine says "almost demolished the whole defense in 1931–35." Indicative of its bewildering complexities is the fact that Spielmann was bowled over by it in twelve moves against Botvinnik!

| 4 | .... | Kt—KB3 |
|---|------|--------|
| 5 | Kt—QB3 | .... |

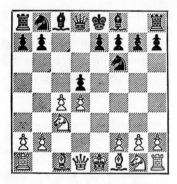

**2.**  5 . . . .        **P—K3**

Objectively the better move
may be 5 . . . Kt—B3 but Black
wants to avoid the difficulties
arising from 6 B—Kt5, P×P; 7
P—Q5.

|   |          |          |
|---|----------|----------|
| 6 | Kt—B3    | B—K2     |
| 7 | B—Kt5    | O—O      |
| 8 | P—B5     | . . . .  |

**3.**  If it can be maintained,
this is a strong Pawn formation. But if it can be under-
mined by . . . P—K4 or . . .
P—QKt3, Black gets the edge.

|   |          |            |
|---|----------|------------|
| 8 | . . . .  | P—QKt3 !   |
| 9 | P—QKt4   | P—QR4 !    |

**4.**  10 P—QR3        . . . .

10 Kt—QR4 is answered by
10 . . . KKt—Q2; 11 B×B, Q×
B. Then if 12 Kt×P, Black wins
a Pawn by 12 . . . Kt×Kt; 13
P×Kt, Q×Pch etc.

|    |         |        |
|----|---------|--------|
| 10 | . . . . | Kt—K5  |
| 11 | B×B     | Q×B    |

**5.**  An exchange of Knights
now would benefit Black,

*e.g.* 12 Kt×Kt, P×Kt; 13 Kt—Q2, Kt—B3 threatening 14 . . . Kt× QP, as well as 14 . . . RP×P.

| 12 Kt—QR4 | RP×P |
|---|---|
| 13 RP×P | P×P |

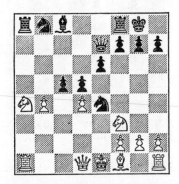

**6.** If 14 QP×P, Q—B3, and Black's Queen has tremendous scope. Or if 14 Kt×P, R×R; 15 Q×R, Kt—QB3; 16 Q—Kt2, P—K4 !

| 14 KtP×P | Q—R2 ! |
|---|---|

**7.** Black pins the Knight, and threatens to win it by 15

. . . B—Q2. If White plays 15 R—R2, in order to unpin himself by 16 Kt—B3, then Black wins by 15 . . . Q—R4*ch;* 16 Kt— Q2, Q—Kt5, threatening 17 . . . Kt×Kt and 18 . . . R×Kt.

| 15 B—Q3 | . . . . |
|---|---|

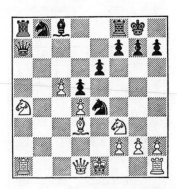

**8.** White has brought out his Bishop in order to protect his Knight by B—B2.

| 15 . . . . | Q—R4*ch* |
|---|---|

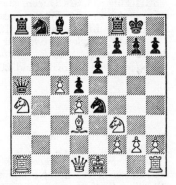

**9.** White cannot answer the check by 16 K—K2 on ac-

count of the reply 16 . . . B—
Q2, menacing 17 . . . B×Kt followed by the Knight fork at B6.

> *16* Kt—Q2     B—Q2
> *17* B—B2     B—Kt4 !

Much stronger than 17 . . . Kt
—B6. First, White must be prevented from castling.

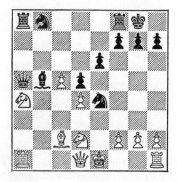

**10.**   *18* P—B3     Kt—B6 !

Attacking White's Queen, and
the pinned Knight. White must
not play 19 Kt×Kt, as after 19
. . . Q×Kt, Black has two mur-
derous threats: 20 . . . Q—
K6*ch*, followed by mate, and 20
. . . R×R.

> *19* Kt—Kt3     Kt×Q
> *20* Kt×Q     Kt—K6

Black's chief threats are 21 . . .
Kt×B*ch*, and 21 . . . R×Kt.

White must lose a piece. The
next dozen moves devolve about
White's efforts to regain, and
Black's efforts to retain the
piece.

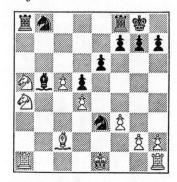

**11.**   *21* K—Q2     Kt×B
      *22* Kt—Kt6     . . . .

22 K×Kt, R×Kt loses at once.

**12.**   *22* . . . .     Kt×R
      *23* Kt×R     . . . .

The position of the Knights is
such as has never been seen on
land or sea!

> *23* . . . .     Kt—B3

24 Kt—B7     . . . .

24 R×Kt is met by 24 . . . R×
Kt, as is 24 Kt×Kt.

**13.**  24 . . . .     Kt×Kt
25 Kt×B     . . . .

Certainly not 25 R×Kt, Kt—
Kt6*ch.*

25 . . . .     R—Kt1
26 Kt—Q6     R—Kt7*ch*
27 K—B3     . . . .

**14.**  27 . . . .     R—Kt6*ch*
28 K—Q2     R—R6

29 R—QKt1 Kt(R8)—Kt6*ch*
30 K—B3     Kt×BP*ch* !
31 K—Kt4     . . . .

And where in chess literature is
there a position where a King in
the end-game attacks three
pieces?

**15.**  31 . . . .     R—Kt6*ch*
32 K×Kt(R5) Kt—Kt2*ch* !

A nice point. If at once 32 . . .
R×R, then 33 P×Kt gives White
a passed Pawn, and a semblance
of a fight. Black does not intend
to give his opponent even the
ghost of a chance.

### 33 Resigns

After 33 Kt×Kt, R×R, the win is
elementary.

Primarily noted as a "position" player, Makogonov's games
abound in sparkling tactical maneuvers. In this connection it is
noteworthy that such masters of
position play as Botvinnik, Euwe,
Lasker, and Capablanca always
took intricate combinations in
their stride.

### 37. LENINGRAD-MOSCOW 1939

#### Queen's Gambit Declined

*Keres is undoubtedly the most brilliant player in the world to-day. The game against Smyslov which follows is a dazzling exhibition of his attacking skill.*

| WHITE | BLACK |
|-------|-------|
| P. Keres | V. Smyslov |

| | | |
|---|---------|---------|
| 1 | P—Q4 | Kt—KB3 |
| 2 | P—QB4 | P—K3 |
| 3 | Kt—QB3 | P—Q4 |
| 4 | B—Kt5 | B—K2 |
| 5 | P—K3 | O—O |
| 6 | Kt—B3 | P—QKt3 |

and the position is shown on the diagram below:

**1.** Black's system of defense was at one time considered

the best way to meet the Queen's Gambit. But that was a long time ago.

| 7 | P×P | P×P |
|---|-----|-----|

**2.** White exchanges Pawns in order to block the diagonal of Black's Queen Bishop after . . . B—Kt2.

| 8 | B—Q3 | B—Kt2 |
|---|------|-------|
| 9 | Q—B2 | QKt—Q2 |
| 10 | O—O | . . . . |

**3.** White could also have safely castled Queen Rook,

as Black's Queen Knight Pawn prevents his Queen from reaching QR4 or QKt3.

|       |       |        |
|-------|-------|--------|
| 10 . . . . | | P—KR3 |
| 11 B—KB4 ! | | . . . . |

**4.**
| 11 . . . . | P—R3 |
|-------|------|
| 12 KR—Q1 | . . . . |

Brings pressure on the Queen file, discouraging 12 . . . P—B4.

| 12 . . . . | Kt—K1 |
|-------|------|
| 13 QR—B1 | B—Q3 |

**5.**   14 Kt—K2   . . . .

The Knight uncovers an attack on the Queen Bishop file. There is another object too, as we shall see.

| 14 . . . . | | Q—K2 |
|-------|------|------|
| 15 B×B | | Q×B |

Black could have recaptured by 15 . . . Kt×B, as 16 Q×P is impossible on account of 16 . . . QR—B1 winning the Queen. The Knight would have been centralized, and the Rooks mobile.

**6.**   16 Kt—Kt3   . . . .

The purpose of the Knight's tour is now clear. He threatens to dominate the board by occupying B5.

16 . . . .   P—Kt3

To meet the threat, Black is forced to make this weakening move.

17 P—KR4   . . . .

White intends to push on with the Pawn, and hit out at the vulnerable Knight Pawn.

**7.** *17 . . . .*    **P—KR4**

This threat too is met, but a new weakness is created.

*18 Kt—Kt5 !*    *. . . .*

The Knight plants himself firmly on enemy territory.

**8.** *18 . . . .*    **P—QB4**
*19 B—B5 !*    *. . . .*

Brilliant and unexpected! The intention is 20 B×Kt, Q×B; 21 Kt ×RP and if 21 . . . P×Kt?; 22 Q—R7 mate.

*19 . . . .*    **P×P**

If 19 . . . P×B; 20 Kt×P(B5), Q—B2 (20 . . . Q—Kt3; 21 Kt —K7*ch* wins the Queen, or if 20 . . . Q—KB3; 21 Kt—K7*ch*, followed by 22 Q—R7 mate); 21 Kt—K7*ch*, K—Kt2; 22 Q—R7*ch*, K—B3; 23 Kt—Kt8*ch*, R×Kt; 24 Q×P mate.

**9.** *20 B—K6 !*    *. . . .*

Another beautiful surprise! The threat is 21 Q×P*ch*, and 22 Q— R7 mate.

*20 . . . .*    **P—Q6 !**

A *Zwischenzug* which wins a tempo by attacking the Queen. If at once 20 . . . Kt—K4; 21 P×P, P×B; 22 P×Kt, Q×P; 23 Q×P*ch* wins. Or if 20 . . . K—Kt2; 21 Kt×P*ch*, K—R3 (if 21 . . . K— R1; 22 B×BP); 22 Kt—B4 !

*21 Q×P*    **Kt—K4**

The point of the previous move. The Knight not only guards the Knight Pawn, but gains time by attacking the Queen.

## 10. 22 Q—Kt1 ....

Threatening 23 P—B4, as well as 23 B×P, B×B; 24 P—K4.

22 .... P×B

The alternative 22 ... Kt—B2 would be met by some pretty Knight play: 23 Kt—B5! Q—Q1; 24 Kt—R6ch, K—Kt2; 25 Kt(R6) ×P, Kt×Kt; 26 B×Kt, R×B; 27 R×Kt!, R(or Q)×R; 28 Kt—K6ch, winning the Queen.

## 11. 23 P—B4 K—Kt2

The Knight must not move, as 24 Q×Pch would force mate.

24 P×Kt Q×P
25 R—B1! ....

Keres' fund of ideas is inexhaustible! His immediate threat is 25 Kt×RPch. If Black plays 25 ... Q×Kt(Kt6); 26 Kt×Pch wins, or if 25 ... Kt—B3; 26 R—B7ch! K—R3; 27 R×Kt! with two threats of mate.

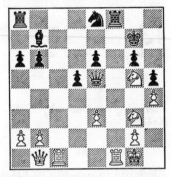

## 12. 25 .... R×Rch
26 R×R ....

Now 26 ... Q×Kt(Kt6) loses by 27 R—B7ch, and quick mate.

26 .... Kt—Q3

Prevents the Rook check, but White has some trumps left.

Correct was 26 ... Kt—B3! Then if 27 R×Kt, K×R (not 27 ... Q×R; 28 Kt×RPch, P×Kt; 29 Q—R7ch, K—B1; 30 Q×B and the threats 21 Q×Rch and 21 Kt—R7ch win); 28 Q—B1ch, K—K2; 29 Q—B7ch, K—Q3; 30 Q×B, Q×Kt(Kt6)!

27 Kt×RPch! ....

**13.** Black must not take the Knight, as the reply would be 28 Q—R7 mate.

| | |
|---|---|
| 27 . . . . | K—R3 |
| 28 Kt—B6 | . . . . |

Menacing the Queen by 29 Kt—Kt4*ch*.

| | |
|---|---|
| 28 . . . . | Q×P*ch* |
| 29 K—R1 | Q—Q5 |

Black had to stop 30 Kt—Kt4*ch*.

**14.** 30 Kt×KP . . . .

Looks risky as White's King seems to be exposed, but Keres has everything under control.

| | |
|---|---|
| 30 . . . . | Q×P*ch* |
| 31 K—Kt1 | . . . . |

Now he has various winning ideas. If 31 . . . R—QB1 (to stop 32 Q—B1*ch*) then 32 R—B4, Q—Kt6; 33 R—B3 followed by 34 R—R3*ch* is decisive.

**15.** 31 . . . . P—Q5

At last the Bishop has some scope, and prevents White's Rook from occupying B3—but it's too late!

| | |
|---|---|
| 32 Q—B1*ch* | P—Kt4 |
| 33 Q—B7 | Resigns |

Mate by the Queen at Kt7 or R7 cannot be stopped.

A scintillating display of the magical art of Keres. He dazzles his opponent (one of the strongest players in the world) with a bewildering assortment of surprise moves, sacrifices, and Knight forks both threatened and actual.

### 38. U.S.S.R. 1939

#### Ruy Lopez

*An amusing gamelet! Black's superior development enables him to toy with his adversary in this delightful encounter.*

| WHITE | BLACK |
|---|---|
| F. Bogatyrchuk | Dzagurov |
| 1 P—K4 | P—K4 |
| 2 Kt—KB3 | Kt—QB3 |
| 3 B—Kt5 | P—QR3 |
| 4 B—R4 | Kt—B3 |
| 5 O—O | P—QKt4 |
| 6 B—Kt3 | P—Q3 |

and the position is shown on the diagram below:

**1.** Black's last move aims to remove White's attacking Bishop by 7 . . . Kt—QR4.

**7 Kt—Kt5** . . . .

Winning a Pawn, but losing valuable time.

| 7 . . . . | P—Q4 |
|---|---|
| 8 P×P | Kt—Q5 ! |

**2.** The point of Black's Pawn sacrifice. Much inferior is 8 . . . Kt×P; 9 Kt×BP, K×Kt; 10 Q—B3*ch*, K—K3; 11 Kt—B3 with a powerful attack.

**9 Q—K1** . . . .

On 9 Kt—QB3, Kt×B; 10 RP× Kt, P—Kt5; 11 QKt—K4, Kt×Kt; 12 Kt×Kt, Q×P equalizes for Black.

**3.** 9 . . . . B—QB4 !

Black does not waste time saving Pawns, when he can get more pieces into play.

    **10 Q×Pch**     . . . .

Better than this obvious move was getting rid of Black's powerfully centralized Knight first by 10 P—QB3, Kt×B; 11 Q×Pch, B—K2; 12 P×Kt.

    *10* . . . .     **K—B1**

The only move, but good enough. Now comes the reaction which follows a premature attack.

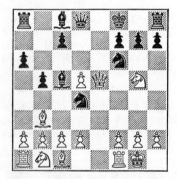

**4.** Black threatens to win a piece by 11 . . . Kt—Kt5 attacking Queen and Knight. White could not then protect his Knight by 12 Q—B4, as 12 . . . Kt—K7*ch* would cost his Queen.

    **11 P—QB3**     . . . .

White avoids the loss by 11 Kt—KB3, Kt—Kt5; 12 Q—K1, Kt×Kt*ch;* 13 P×Kt, Q—R5; 14 P×Kt, Q×Kt*Pch;* 15 K—R1, Q—B6*ch;* 16 K—Kt1, B—KR6, followed by . . . Q—Kt7 mate.

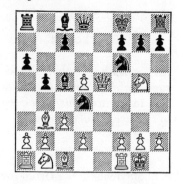

**5.** *11* . . . .     **Kt—Kt5**

A vigorous move which gives White no time for defensive moves. If White retreats his threatened Queen by 12 Q—K1 then comes 12 . . . Kt×B; 13 P ×Kt, Q×Kt; 14 P—Q4, Q—R5; 15 P—R3, B—Q3 and wins.

    **12 Kt×BP**     . . . .

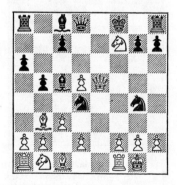

**6.** White is forced to play "brilliantly."

    *12* . . . .     **Q—R5 !**

Certainly not 12 . . . Kt×Q; 13

Kt×Q, and much superior to 12 . . . K×Kt; 13 Q—B4*ch* etc.

Black's attack must be successful. But the manner in which he forces the win is highly entertaining.

14 K—R1      Q×P!

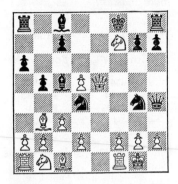

**7.**    13 Q×P      . . . .

White's Queen must stay on the diagonal in line with his King Rook Pawn to avoid being mated. He cannot do it by moving 13 Q—B4 or 13 Q—Kt3 as 13 . . . Kt—K7*ch* wins his Queen.

13 . . . .      Kt—K7*ch*

**9.**   White cannot reply 15 R× Q as 15 . . . Kt×R is mate.

15 Q×KB*ch*      . . . .

Desperation—if 15 R—Q1, Q—Kt8*ch;* 16 R×Q, Kt—B7 mate.

15 . . . .      Q×Q

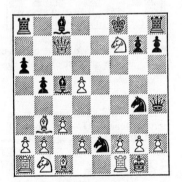

**8.**   With so many pieces trained on the King,

**10.**   16 P—Q4      . . . .

White blocks the Queen's path, as he sees that 16 Kt×R*ch* at once loses by 16 . . . Kt—B7*ch;* 17 R×Kt*ch*, Q×R followed by . . . Q—Kt8 mate.

|   16 . . . .   | Q—K2   |
| 17 Kt×R*ch* | . . . . |

A last faint hope: if 17 . . . K—Kt1 ?; 18 P—Q6*ch* wins Black's Queen.

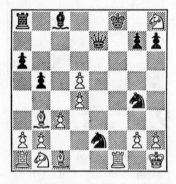

**11.**

| 17 . . . .     | K—K1   |
| 18 Kt—Q2       | Q—R5   |
| 19 P—KR3       | Q—Kt6  |

20 **Resigns,** as 20 P×Kt permits 20 . . . Q—R5 mate.

## 39. MOSCOW 1940

### Gruenfeld Defense

*Chess seems an easy game when the pieces co-ordinate as they do here in Bogatyrchuk's capable hands. He solves the technical problem of convert-ing a positional advantage into an absolute win with consummate mastery.*

| WHITE | BLACK |
| --- | --- |
| G. Safonov | F. Bogatyrchuk |
| 1 P—Q4 | Kt—KB3 |
| 2 P—QB4 | P—KKt3 |
| 3 Kt—QB3 | P—Q4 |
| 4 B—B4 | B—Kt2 |
| 5 P—K3 | O—O |

and the position is shown on the diagram below:

**1.** Black has offered a Pawn in the interest of rapid development.

    6 P×P    . . . .

White should shun the offer, and play instead 6 Q—Kt3 (on 6 Kt—B3, P—B4 is very strong), P—B3; 7 Kt—B3, P×P; 8 B×P, QKt—Q2; 9 O—O.

| 6 . . . . | Kt×P |
| 7 Kt×Kt | Q×Kt |
| 8 B×P | . . . . |

Bishop, but he has removed all the protective Pawns which surrounded White's King.

**2.** Black's best strategy to refute White's win of a Pawn is to develop more pieces.

| 8 . . . . | Kt—B3 |
| 9 Kt—K2 | B—Kt5 |
| 10 P—B3 | . . . . |

A natural move to get out of the pin, but it is met by a vicious sacrificial attack.

**4.** 
| 14 B—Kt2 | Q—B4 |
| 15 Q—Q2 | . . . . |

Hoping to castle into safety.

| 15 . . . . | P—K4 ! |
| 16 B×Kt | . . . . |

No better is 16 P×P, QR—Q1.

**3.** 
| 10 . . . . | B×BP ! |
| 11 P×B | Q×BP |
| 12 R—KKt1 | Q×P |
| 13 B—B4 | Q—K5 |

Black has only two Pawns for his

**5.** 16 . . . . KP×B

Now Black's Rooks have open files on which to operate.

**17 B—B3      KR—K1 !**

A clever move which prevents White from castling.

**6.**   *18* **K—B2     . . . .**

If instead 18 O—O—O, Black replies 18 . . . R×Kt!; 19 Q×R (19 B×R, R—B1*ch;* wins the Queen), R—B1*ch;* 20 K—Q2, R—B7*ch* and wins the Queen.

*18* . . . .     **R—K6 !**

**7.**   Black has two threats— one is to double Rooks on

the King file, the other is to play 19 . . . Q—R6.

**19 R—Kt4      . . . .**

To prevent the Queen from penetrating. If instead 19 Kt×P, Q× Kt; 20 Q×R, B×P pins the Queen.

White hopes to remove the advanced Bishop Pawn which is so terribly constricting.

**8.**   *19* . . . .     **QR—K1**

Positionally a powerful move, it involves also a tactical threat: 20 . . . R×B*ch;* 21 K×R, R— K6*ch* followed by 22 . . . Q×R.

**20 QR—KKt1      . . . .**

The Pawn is immune to capture: if 20 R×BP, Q—R6 or if 20 Kt× P, P—KR4; 21 R—R4, B—B3.

The critical stage of the game is reached. Black must evolve something at once, as White seems to be wriggling out of his cramped position. His next two moves initiate a fine combination.

If 22 Q—K1 (to protect the minor pieces), R×B*ch!*; 23 K×R, Q—K5*ch*; 24 K—B2, Q—K6*ch* followed by 25 . . . P—B6 wins.

22 . . . .　　　　R×B*ch!*

## 9. 20 . . . . 　　　B—R3

With a concealed attack against the Queen. The threat is 21 . . . R×Kt*ch*; 22 B×R, P—B6; 23 Q×B (23 B—Q3, Q—R4; 24 Q moves, Q×P*ch* wins), R×B*ch*; 24 K—Kt3, Q—Q6 and White has no good defense against 25 . . . P—B7*ch*.

21 R—R4　　　R—Q6 !

## 11. Black plays it anyway!

23 K—K1　　　. . . .

If 23 K×R, Q—Q6*ch*; 24 K—Kt2 (24 K—Kt4, P—B4 mate, or 24 K—B2, Q×Kt mate), R×Kt*ch* forces mate.

| 23 . . . . | R×Kt*ch* ! |
|---|---|
| 24 K×R | Q—Q6*ch* |
| 25 K—K1 | R—K6*ch* |
| 26 K—B2 | Q—K7 mate |

## 40. MOSCOW 1940
### Catalan Opening

*Bondarevsky evolves a pretty combination, the main theme of which is a sacrifice of the Queen followed by a Knight fork. Rendered desperate by*

## 10. "Puts the question" to Black's Queen.

22 Q—Kt4　　　. . . .

*his inability to prevent the execution of the threat, Lissitzin commits chessic suicide.*

| WHITE | BLACK |
|---|---|
| I. Bondarevsky | G. Lissitzin |
| 1 P—Q4 | Kt—KB3 |
| 2 P—QB4 | P—K3 |
| 3 P—KKt3 | P—Q4 |
| 4 B—Kt2 | . . . . |

and the position is shown on the diagram below:

**1.** 4 . . . .        B—K2

Better is 4 . . . P×P and if 5 Q—R4*ch*, QKt—Q2; 6 Kt—QB3, P—B4; 7 Kt—B3, P—QR3; 8 O—O, B—K2; 9 P×P, B×P etc.

| 5 Kt—KB3 | QKt—Q2 |
| 6 O—O | P—B3 |

Black should still have played 6 . . . P×P. In recapturing, White's Queen would be exposed.

**2.** Now Black gets a cramped game.

7 QKt—Q2        . . . .

In order to recapture with the Knight if 7 . . . P×P.

| 7 . . . . | O—O |
| 8 Q—B2 | P—QKt3 |
| 9 P—K4 | . . . . |

With the powerful threat of 10 P—K5 driving Black's King Knight out of play.

**3.** 9 . . . .        Kt×P
10 Kt×Kt        P×Kt

11 Q×P      B—Kt2

12 R—K1      . . . .

Out of the Catalan opening, White has achieved an attacking position akin to the Colle—and with similar means: advance of the King Pawn and an exchange of his QKt for the KKt. White has a beautifully centralized position, and it is difficult to suggest a satisfactory continuation for Black.

**5.**    13 . . . .      **P—Kt3 ?**

There was no reason to weaken the black squares with this move. Black should have played 13 . . . P—QB4, which he evidently avoids because he fears the possibility of surprise threats on the long diagonal (such as 14 Kt —Kt5).

14 B—B4      P—QB4

Just one move too late.

**4.** If now 12 . . . Q—B2; 13 B—B4, B—Q3; 14 Kt —Kt5, Kt—B3 (14 . . . P—Kt3; 15 Kt×KP, P×Kt; 16 Q×KP*ch* followed by 17 B×B and wins); 15 Kt×KP, Kt×Q; 16 Kt×Q wins for White.

12 . . . .      R—K1

13 Q—B2      . . . .

The Queen was too exposed at K4.

While there was no immediate threat, the Queen would be driven away sooner or later by . . . Kt—B3 or . . . P—QB4. At B2, the Queen is tremendously effective.

**6.** Now White has a fine reply.

| 15 P—Q5 ! | P×P |
|---|---|
| 16 P×P | B—KB3 |

Taking the Pawn loses: 16 . . .
B×P; 17 QR—Q1, B×Kt; 18
B×B, QR—B1; 19 B—Kt7, and
White wins the exchange!

| 17 R×R*ch* | . . . . |
|---|---|

White intends to control the only
open file.

**7.**

| 17 . . . . | Q×R |
|---|---|
| 18 R—K1 | Q—KB1 |

Making room for . . . R—K1
disputing the open file.

| 19 Q—R4 ! | . . . . |
|---|---|

But White gives him no time!

| 19 . . . . | Q—Q1 |
|---|---|

Deplorable, but there is nothing
else. If 19 . . . R—Q1; 20 B—
B7 wins, and if 19 . . . Kt—Kt1;
20 R—K8 pins the Queen!

Now we see the subtle purpose
of White's last move. Black's
Rook is shut off from K1 by his
own Queen, and cannot challenge
the file.

**8.**

| 20 Kt—Q2 ! | P—KKt4 |
|---|---|
| 21 Kt—K4 !! | . . . . |

White menaces all sorts of combinations in which a Knight fork
is the motif. Black cannot reply
21 . . . P×B as White would
win by 22 Q×Kt !, Q×Q; 23 Kt×
B*ch* followed by 24 Kt×Q.

| 21 . . . . | B×QP |
|---|---|

Stopping 22 Q×Kt, as after 22
. . . B×Kt there is no Knight
fork.

**9.**

| 22 R—Q1 | B—Q5 |
|---|---|

If instead 22 . . . B—K3, White wins neatly by 23 R×Kt!, B×R; 24 Q×B, Q×Q; 25 Kt× B*ch*, K—Kt2; 26 Kt×Q, R—Q1; 27 B—K5*ch*.

With the text move, Black blocks the Rook's path, and threatens to remove the annoying Knight.

**23 B×P!**      . . . .

There is no rest for the weary!

**11.** If now 24 . . . Kt×B; 25 Kt×Kt*ch*, Q(or B)× Kt; 26 B×B*ch* wins the exchange. Or if 24 . . . B×B; 25 R×B and White wins the pinned Knight. Finally, if 24 . . . Q—B2; 25 B×B, P×B; 26 Q×Kt!, Q×Q; 27 Kt—B6*ch* wins. Black, probably bewildered by this time, throws himself on the sword.

24 . . . .      **Q×B**
25 Kt×Q*ch*      **Resigns**

**10.** 23 . . . .      **P—B3**

Running away with the Queen does not help: if 23 . . . Q—B2; 24 B—B4, Q—Q1 (24 . . . Kt —K4; 25 Kt—B6*ch*); 25 R×B, P×R; 26 Q×Kt, Q×Q; 27 Kt— B6*ch* wins.

**24 B×P!**      . . . .

A pretty capture which wins against any defense.

Black has three ways to remove the Bishop, and they all lose— as shown in the following analysis.

## 41. SVERDLOVSK 1942

### Sicilian Defense

*A King-side attack is always exciting, and Sokolsky packs a lot of action into this one. He keeps slugging without a let- up, and wins the fight by a technical knock-out.*

*More impressive than the surge and sweep of the assault (soul stirring though it is) is the sense of rhythm which pervades the game. The moves are not just moves by themselves —they are each an integral part of one grand all-embracing symphony of attack.*

| WHITE | BLACK |
|-------|-------|
| A. Sokolsky | G. Bastrikov |
| 1 P—K4 | P—QB4 |
| 2 Kt—KB3 | P—K3 |
| 3 P—Q4 | P×P |
| 4 Kt×P | Kt—KB3 |
| 5 Kt—QB3 | P—Q3 |

and the position is shown on the diagram below:

**1.** The Scheveningen variation which Black is playing exercises a strange fascination. The analysts agree in condemning it, and yet it continues to be popular. Psychologically the reason may lie in the thrill it provides of flirting with danger.

    6 P—KKt3 !    . . . .

**2.** White's last move is an interesting departure from the usual development of the King Bishop to K2 and B3.

| 6 . . . . | P—QR3 |
|-----------|-------|
| 7 B—Kt2 | Q—B2 |

Black's chief weapon is his domination of the Queen Bishop file, and he mobilizes accordingly.

**3.**  
| 8 O—O | Kt—B3 |
|-------|-------|
| 9 K—R1 | . . . . |

In order to play 10 P—B4 without fear of a check, or a pin on the diagonal. For example, if 9 P—B4, Kt×Kt; 10 Q×Kt, P—Q4, Black already threatens to win the Queen by 11 . . . B—B4.

**4.**
| 9 . . . . | B—Q2 |
| 10 P—B4 | B—K2 |
| 11 Kt—Kt3 | . . . . |

White's last two moves prevent Black's Queen Knight from getting to B5 by way of K4 or QR4.

| 11 . . . . | P—QKt4 |
| 12 B—K3 | O—O |

**5.** Black's King-side position seems to be well barri-

caded. White's method of breaking through is to advance his Knight Pawn and Bishop Pawn, driving away the defenders.

| 13 P—QR3 | . . . . |

If at once 13 P—Kt4, then Black plays 13 . . . P—Kt5, and the Knight cannot get to the King side by 14 Kt—K2 on account of 14 . . . Kt×KtP.

White keeps an eye on the Queen-side, as that is where Black's counterchances lie.

**6.**
| 13 . . . . | QR—Kt1 |
| 14 P—Kt4 | P—Kt5 |

A better plan might have been 14 . . . P—QR4 with . . . P—R5 to follow, with the idea of enforcing . . . Kt—QR4 and . . . Kt—B5.

| 15 P×P | QKt×P |
| 16 P—Kt5 | Kt—K1 |

One Pawn push by White, and Black's Knight is useless, his King Rook shut off, his King Bishop restrained, and—

**7.** The most important defender has been driven off.

**17 Kt—Q4        P—B3**

Black tries to free himself by exchanging Pawns. Better chances were offered by 17 . . . Kt—QB3, with the idea of exchanging *pieces*.

**18 B—R3 !        . . . .**

He is alert to the opportunity.

**8.** White hits at the King Pawn, weakened by Black's last move.

**18 . . . .        Q—B1**

If 18 . . . P—K4; 19 Kt—K6, B×Kt; 20 B×B*ch*, K—R1; 21 P—Kt6, P—R3 (21 . . . RP×P; 22 Q—Kt4); 22 P—B5 followed by 23 Q—R5 and 24 B×P wins.

**19 P—B5        P—K4**

Better chances were offered by 19 . . . KP×P; 20 Kt×P, B—Q1.

**9.** Now Sokolsky is inspired!

**20 P—Kt6 !!        P×P**

20 . . . P×Kt loses by 21 Q—R5, P—R3; 22 B×RP.

**21 P×P        . . . .**

Again threatening 22 Q—R5.

**21 . . . .        P—B4**
**22 Kt×P        R×Kt**

The Knight must be removed. On 22 . . . B×Kt; 23 B×B, Q—B2; 24 B—K6*ch* wins.

Or if 22 . . . B—Q1; 23 Q—R5, Kt—KB3; 24 Kt—K7*ch* !, B×Kt; 25 R×Kt !, R×R; 26 Q—R7*ch*, and mate next move.

On 26 . . . B×B; 27 Q—R5, B—R3 (27 . . . Q×R permits mate in two); 28 Kt—K7*ch* wins the Queen.

|       |         |
|-------|---------|
| 27 R×Kt | Q—Kt2 |
| 28 Q—R5 ! | Resigns |

He sees that 28 . . . Q×Kt*ch*; 29 K—Kt1, B—B3 loses by 30 Q—R7*ch*, K—B1; 31 R×B*ch*, P× R; 32 P—Kt7*ch*—so he gives up the struggle.

## 10.

|       |         |
|-------|---------|
| 23 B×R | B×B |
| 24 R×B | Kt—KB3 |

Black seems to have consolidated but Sokolsky finds a brilliant continuation.

|       |         |
|-------|---------|
| 25 B—Kt5 ! | Kt×KP |
| 26 Kt—Q5 ! | . . . . |

A beautiful move! If 26 . . . Q× R; 27 Kt×B*ch*, K—B1; 28 Kt× Q, Kt—B7*ch*; 29 K—Kt2, Kt×Q; 30 R×Kt, with a piece up.

## 11.

| 26 . . . . | Kt—B7*ch* |

## 42.  MOSCOW 1944

### Slav Defense

*Flohr once said "Soviet players always aim at winning their games with speed and artistry. This has impressed me very much, and I hope I am playing with more energy, and not chasing after material." The classic game which follows, has its full share of "speed and artistry." It is a beautiful specimen of sustained attack.*

| WHITE | BLACK |
|-------|-------|
| S. Flohr | G. Ravinsky |
| 1 P—Q4 | P—Q4 |
| 2 P—QB4 | P—QB3 |
| 3 Kt—KB3 | Kt—B3 |
| 4 Kt—B3 | P×P |

and the position is shown on the next diagram.

**1.** Black plays the Slav, a defense favored by two former World Champions—Euwe and Alekhine.

　　　**5 P—K3**　　　　....

A good alternative is 5 P—QR4 to prevent 5 . . . P—QKt4.

**2.**　　**5 ....**　　　　**P—QKt4**
　　　　**6 P—QR4**　　　**P—Kt5**

On 6 . . . P—QR3, White recovers his Pawn at once by 7 P× P, BP×P; 8 Kt×P.

　　　**7 Kt—R2**　　　　**P—K3**
　　　**8 B×P**　　　　　**QKt—Q2**

　　　**9 O—O**　　　　　**B—Kt2**

**3.** Black will evidently try to free his game by 10 . . . P—B4. The positions are fairly equal, White's displaced Queen Knight being balanced by Black's weakened Queen-side.

　　　**10 Q—K2**　　　　....

**4.**　　**10 ....**　　　**P—B4**
　　　　**11 R—Q1**　　　....

White gets a grip on the important center file.

　　　**11 ....**　　　　**Q—B2**

Black knows that the Queen must not stay on the same file as the adverse Rook.

### 5.    12 B—R6 !    ....

Flohr varies from the usual 12 P—K4, P×P; 13 KKt×P, B—B4; 14 B—K3. His idea is not only to exchange Black's Queen Bishop (his best piece) but also to prevent Black from supporting his weak QKtP by . . . P—QR4.

### 6.    12 ....        B—Q4

Better than evading the exchange was simple development by 12 . . . B—K2.

### 13 B—Q2    ....

Threatening 14 P×P, B×P; 15 Kt×P winning a Pawn.

   13 ....        QR—Kt1
   14 KR—QB1      Q—Kt3

Once more the Queen must flee from the Rook's pressure.

Black also had to guard against 15 Kt×P.

### 7.    15 B—Kt5    ....

Again threatening to win a Pawn by 16 P×P, B×P; 17 Kt ×P.

   15 ....        P—QR4
   16 Kt—K5       B—Q3

On 16 . . . P×P; 17 P—K4 ! followed by 18 B—Kt5 wins.

   17 P×P        B×BP

Flohr's aim now is to get his Queen Bishop into play quickly. He begins with a pseudo-sacrifice of a Pawn.

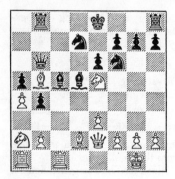

## 8.    18 P—K4 !    . . . .

Black is given no time to breathe. Naturally he cannot take the Pawn, as after 18 . . . B×P; 19 Kt×Kt, Kt×Kt; 20 Q×B, B× P*ch,* his position is hopeless.

18 . . . .    B—Kt2

## 9.    19 B—Kt5    . . . .

Threatening 20 B×Kt, P×B; 21 Kt×Kt and wins.

19 . . . .    B—QB1
20 B—KB4    . . . .

Menacing the exchange by 21 Kt ×Kt followed by 22 B×R.

20 . . . .    R—R1

## 10.    21 Q—B2    . . . .

Now, Black must guard against 22 Q×B, as his QKt is pinned.

21 . . . .    B—K2
22 Q×B*ch* !    . . . .

The quickest way to win.

## 11.    22 . . . .    R×Q
23 R×R*ch*    B—Q1

24 Kt—B4 ....

Black's replies are greatly limited. If 24 . . . Q—R2; 25 B—K3, Q—Kt2; 26 Kt—Q6*ch* wins the Queen nicely.

24 .... Q—Q5

Now Flohr deploys his QB to a powerful post, incidentally preventing Black from castling.

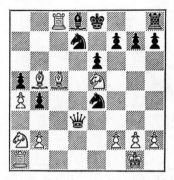

## 12.

25 B—K3 Q—Q6

The only square left to the Queen. Of course if 25 . . . Q×KP; 26 Kt—Q6*ch* catches the Queen.

26 B—B5 ....

Intending to win the Queen by 27 Kt—Q6*ch*.

In spite of his superiority in material, Black is astonishingly helpless in the face of the many threats. Flohr's attack has been rising to a crescendo of power and fury.

26 .... Kt×P
27 Kt—K5 ....

## 13.

Not only attacking the Queen but also with this in mind: (say after 27 . . . Q—Q7) 28 Kt×Kt, Q×Kt; 29 R—Q1, Kt×B; 30 R×Kt !

27 .... Q×B
28 P×Q Kt×Kt
29 R—Q1 ....

The Queens are off the board but White's attack does not let up.

## 14.

29 .... Kt—Q2
30 B—Kt6 K—K2

If 30 . . . Kt×B; 31 R(B8)×B*ch*, K—K2; 32 R×R wins easily.

| 31 B×P | Kt×P |
|--------|------|
| 32 R×B | Kt×R |

**15.**
| 33 R×R | P—Kt6 |
|--------|-------|
| 34 Kt—B1 | Resigns |

## 43. MOSCOW 1944

### Queen's Gambit Declined

*One hardly knows which to admire more—Ragozin's pretty finesse 13 Q—B2 followed by 14 Q—K2, or the assault on the King side which he conducts with classic simplicity.*

| WHITE | BLACK |
|-------|-------|
| V. Ragozin | A. Kotov |

| 1 | P—Q4 | P—Q4 |
|---|------|------|
| 2 | P—QB4 | P—K3 |
| 3 | Kt—QB3 | Kt—KB3 |
| 4 | B—Kt5 | B—K2 |
| 5 | Kt—B3 | O—O |

| 6 P—K3 | QKt—Q2 |
|---------|--------|

and the position is shown on the diagram below:

**1.** Black's system of play, known as the Orthodox Defense, is supposed to give him equality against any White attack. Theoretically, this may be true—but in practice Black usually has a difficult time of it.

| 7 R—B1 | P—B3 |
|--------|------|

The best reply.

**2.**
| 8 B—Q3 | P—KR3 |
|--------|-------|
| 9 B—R4 | . . . . |

Another good line is 9 B—B4, Kt —R4; 10 B—K5 !, Kt×B; 11 P× Kt with a superior game.

       *9 . . . .*         **P—R3**

A better continuation is 9 . . . P×P; 10 B×P, P—QKt4 etc.

**3.**    *10* P×P !      BP×P
          *11* P—R4      P—QKt3
          *12* O—O       B—Kt2

The Bishop has no future on the diagonal.

**4.**    *13* Q—B2 !      . . . .

A shrewd move. White tempts his opponent to make what looks like a strong reply.

       *13 . . . .*         **R—B1**

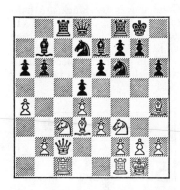

**5.**    *14* Q—K2 !      . . . .

The point of White's previous move. The attack on Black's QRP gains a tempo.

       *14 . . . .*         **Kt—Kt1**

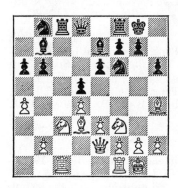

**6.**    *15* B—Kt3      . . . .

Planning to win a Pawn by 16 B×Kt, R×B; 17 B×P.

| 15 . . . . | B—Q3 |
| 16 Kt—K5 | . . . . |

Good moves for Black are hard to find. If 16 . . . KKt—Q2 (to get rid of White's Knight) then 17 Kt×BP wins at least a Pawn.

White groups his pieces for attack in the style made famous by Pillsbury.

## 7.
| 16 . . . . | Q—K2 |

16 . . . Q—B2, facing White's Rook, does not look inviting.

| 17 B—R4 | . . . . |

Threatening 18 Kt—Kt4 followed by 19 B×Kt, P×B; 20 Kt×RPch.

| 17 . . . . | Q—Q1 |
| 18 P—B4 | . . . . |

Intending 19 P—B5, or 19 P—KKt4 and 20 P—Kt5.

White is now strongly centralized—a prerequisite to action on either wing.

## 8.
| 18 . . . . | B—K2 |

In order to break the pin on his Knight. Naturally not 18 . . . B×Kt; 19 BP×B, P—KKt4; 20 R×Kt and if 20 . . . P×B White mates in two.

| 19 P—B5 | P×P |

If 19 . . . Kt—K5; 20 B×B, Kt× Kt (20 . . . Q×B also loses); 21 Q—Kt4, Q×B; 22 P—B6 wins.

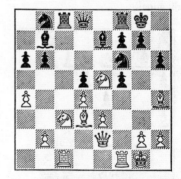

## 9.
| 20 B×BP | R—B2 |
| 21 B—Kt3 | . . . . |

Potentially threatening the Rook.

21 ....      B—Q3
22 B—Kt1      R—K1
23 Q—Q3      ....

The Queen will penetrate at R7.

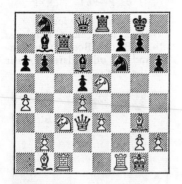

**10.**   23 ....      K—B1

On 23 . . . P—Kt3, 24 Kt×KtP
is decisive.

24 R×Kt!      ....

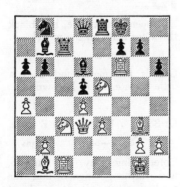

**11.**   24 . . .      Q×R

Or 24 . . . P×R; 25 Q—R7
(threatening 26 Q×RP*ch*) wins.

25 R—B1      Q—K3

If 25 . . . Q—Kt4; 26 B—R4,
Q—R4 (26 . . . Q×B; 27 Kt—
Kt6*ch*); 27 P—KKt4 winning the
Queen.

White's Queen will now invade
the enemy lines, and root the
King out.

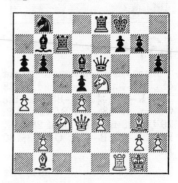

**12.**   26 Q—R7      ....

Cuts off the King and menaces
the Queen by 27 Kt—Kt6*ch*.

26 ....      K—K2
27 Q×KtP      ...

Now the intention is mate in three
beginning with 28 B—R4*ch*.

27 ....      K—Q1

On 27 . . . R—KB1; 28 B—R4*ch*,
K—K1; 29 B—B5 wins the
Queen.

The King seems to be escaping!
White's next move, obvious but
withal very fine, remedies that.
Black's pieces stand in each other's way.

## 13.    28 B—R4*ch*    ....

Black has *seven* ways to get out of check—all of them bad! If 28 ... K—B1; 29 B—B5 pins the Queen. If 28 ... R(K1)—K2; 29 Q—B8 is mate. Or if 28 ... B—K2; 29 B—B5, Q—Q3; 30 Kt×P mate!

        28 ....        R(B2)—K2

## 14.    29 B—B5        B×Kt
          30 P×B         ....

Naturally not 30 B×Q, as White's Queen was attacked.

        30 ....        Q—QB3

Of course if 30 ... Q×P; 31 Q×Q and the Rook cannot recapture.

        31 P—K6 !      P×P

Otherwise 32 P×P wins.

White's next move paralyzes both of Black's Rooks. One cannot, and the other dares not stir from the spot.

## 15.    32 B—Kt6        P—Q5

It seems incredible, but Black threatens mate on the move!

        33 B×R         ....

Guards the mate, and does a little threatening of his own.

        33 ....        Q×B

Or 33 ... K×B; 34 Q×R mate.

        34 R—B8        Resigns

Entertaining play by Ragozin, and further evidence that the modern master is as much at home in positional maneuvering as in violent onslaughts.

### 44. OMSK 1944

#### French Defense

*Ufimtsev's play fairly scintil-
lates—what with his lavish offers of Queen, Rook, and
Knight. Boleslavsky, dreading
to be the victim of a brilliancy,
gives up his own Queen, but
cannot stave off disaster.*

| WHITE | BLACK |
|---|---|
| I. Boleslavsky | A. Ufimtsev |

| | |
|---|---|
| 1 P—K4 | P—K3 |
| 2 P—Q4 | P—Q4 |
| 3 Kt—QB3 | P×P |
| 4 Kt×P | Kt—KB3 |

and the position is shown on the
diagram below:

**1.** As early as this, Black
looks for original situa-
tions, and the opportunity to
create complications. Usually 4
. . . QKt—Q2 is played first.

**5 Kt×Ktch        P×Kt**

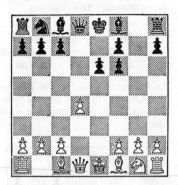

**2.** Black has accepted a bro-
ken-up Pawn position, in
return for attacking chances for
his Rooks on the open Kt file.

| | |
|---|---|
| 6 Kt—B3 | P—Kt3 |
| 7 B—Kt5ch | P—B3 |
| 8 B—QB4 | B—QR3 |
| 9 B—Kt3 | . . . . |

Better 9 B×B and 10 Q—K2.

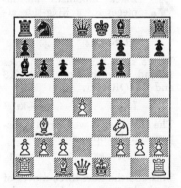

**3.** White's retreat turns out
to be weak, but he could

hardly have foreseen danger in
his apparently safe position.

| | | |
|---|---|---|
| '9 . . . . | | Q—B2 |
| 10 | P—B4 | Kt—Q2 |
| 11 | O—O | O—O—O |
| 12 | Q—K2 | B—Q3 |

An excellent post for the Bishop.
The Queen Rook is now in position to seize the attractive open
file.

**4.** Black mobilizes all his
pieces for a King-side attack.

| | | |
|---|---|---|
| 13 | P—QR4 | . . . . |

White should develop his pieces
instead by means of 13 B—K3
and 14 QR—B1.

| | | |
|---|---|---|
| 13 | . . . . | QR—Kt1 |

The Rook has wonderful prospects on this open file.

| | | |
|---|---|---|
| 14 | P—R5 | P—QB4 ! |

This and the next three moves of
Black, though made on the
Queen-side, directly affect the
King-side attack.

**5.** Black has two ideas behind his Pawn move. One
is to give his Bishop (now locked
in at R3) a long diagonal on
which to operate. The other is to
exchange Pawns, and then bring
his Knight to B4 where it will
exert pressure on the center.

| | | |
|---|---|---|
| 15 | RP×P | Q×P |
| 16 | B—K3 | B—Kt2 |

Not 16 . . . Q×B; 17 R×B and
the attack changes hands.

**6.**
| | | |
|---|---|---|
| 17 | P×P | Kt×P |
| 18 | B—Q1 | R—Kt5 |

Black prepares to double Rooks. He does not do so by 18 . . . R—Kt3 because of 19 Kt—R4.

More fireworks! Now if 21 B× Q, R×P*ch;* 22 K—R1, Kt×P*ch;* 23 B×Kt (or 23 R×Kt, R—Kt8 mate), R×P mate.

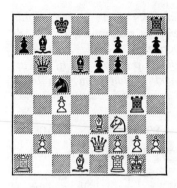

**7.** *19 Q—Q2* **Kt—K5 !**

Beautiful and unexpected! If 20 B×Q, Kt×Q; 21 Kt×Kt (Black threatens 22 . . . Kt×R as well as 22 . . . Kt×Kt*ch;* 23 B×Kt, B×B), R×P*ch;* 22 K—R1, R× RP*ch;* 23 K—Kt1, R—R8 mate.

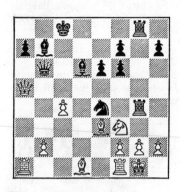

**9.** *21 Kt—K1* **. . . .**

Or 21 P—KKt3, Kt×KtP !; 22 RP×Kt, R×P*ch;* 23 P×R, Q× B*ch;* 24 K—R2, R×P with an easy win for Black.

*21 . . . .* **R×P*ch* !!**

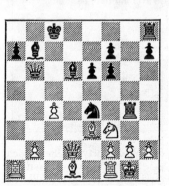

**8.** *20 Q—R5* **KR—Kt1 !**

**10.** *22 Kt×R* **Kt—Q7 !!**

The final blow! On 23 B×Q, Black wins by 23 . . . R×Kt*ch;* 24 K—R1, R×RP*ch;* 25 K—Kt1, R—R8 mate. Nor can White block the Bishop's diagonal by 23 P—B3, as 23 . . . Q×B*ch* wins.

**23 Q—Q5        . . . .**

White is at a loss as to what to do—but he does not want to be mated!

**11.**  
| | | |
|---|---|---|
| 23 . . . . | B×Q |
| 24 P×B | Q×P |
| 25 B×Kt | Q×R |
| 26 B—KB3 | B×P*ch* |

27 **Resigns,** as he is convinced that there is no hope after 27 K×B, Q×R.

Black's utilization of the open King Knight file was classic.

A brilliant victory over a top-flight master. It is an interesting commentary on the strength of Russia's "unknown" chess stars that Ufimtsev was not a master, but a "first-category" player.

## 45.  OMSK 1944

### Gruenfeld Defense

*Sokolsky finds a remarkable way to rid himself of Black's powerful King Bishop—he gives up a Rook for it! His attacking play from then on is a model of beautiful timing.*

| WHITE | BLACK |
|---|---|
| A. Sokolsky | A. Tolush |
| 1 P—Q4 | Kt—KB3 |
| 2 P—QB4 | P—KKt3 |
| 3 Kt—QB3 | P—Q4 |
| 4 P×P | . . . . |

and the position is shown on the diagram below:

**1.**  White plays a line which for a time was out of favor. In the mid-game White's center Pawns are bombarded strongly, the result very often being an inferior end-game.

| 4 .... | Kt×P |
|---|---|
| 5 P—K4 | Kt×Kt |
| 6 P×Kt | P—QB4 |

two Pawns to one on the Queen side.

| 11 .... | Kt—R4 |
|---|---|

**2.** Black intends to hammer away at the Queen Pawn by . . . B—Kt2 and . . . Kt—B3.

| 7 B—QB4 | B—Kt2 |
|---|---|
| 8 Kt—K2 | Kt—B3 |
| 9 B—K3 | O—O |
| 10 O—O | P×P |
| 11 P×P | .... |

**4.** Black could hardly have foreseen that 11 . . . B—Kt5 first forcing 12 P—B3, would interfere with White's coming combination.

| 12 B—Q3 | B—K3 |
|---|---|
| 13 P—Q5 ! | .... |

**3.** Black has attained his end-game objective: he has

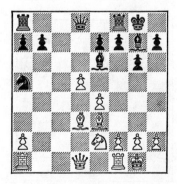

**5.** Black can hardly refuse this sacrifice as otherwise

his Knight will have difficulty
getting back into play.

13 . . . .          B×R
14 Q×B          P—B3

If 14 . . . B—Q2; 15 B—KR6
regains the exchange.

**6.** 15 B—KR6          R—K1

Of course not 15 . . . R—B2?
16 P×B, Q×B; 17 P×R*ch*.

16 Kt—B4          B—Q2

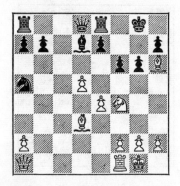

**7.** 17 P—K5 !          . . . .

To which Black cannot reply
17 . . . P×P? as after 18 Q×P
White forces mate at Kt7.

17 . . . .          P—K3
18 QP×P          . . . ,.

The decisive break-through.

The exchange of Pawns has
the double purpose of exposing
Black's King, and opening lines
for White.

**8.** 18 . . . .          B×P

The Pawn must be taken. If
18 . . . B—B3; 19 P×P wins at
once.

19 B—QKt5          . . . .

White's inventiveness in finding
one threat after another is an instructive lesson in the art of main-
taining an attack. It is important to lure the Bishop away from
K3. If at once the tempting 19
P×P, threatening 20 P—B7*ch*
followed by 21 Q—Kt7 mate,
then 19 . . . B—B2 blockades
the Pawn—and the attack.

**9.** *19 . . . .* **B—Q2**

Black has no choice as after 19 . . . R—K2; 20 P×P wins, and if 19 . . . Kt—B3; 20 Kt×B, R×Kt; 21 B—QB4, K—B2 (21 . . . Q—K2; 22 P×P); 22 R—Q1 followed by 23 R—Q6 wins.

*20 P×P !* . . . .

**10.** Now White has the pretty threat of 21 P—B7*ch*, K×P; 22 Q—Kt7 mate.

*20 . . . .* **K—B2**
*21 B×B* . . . .

Faster than 21 R—Q1, B×B (not 21 . . . Kt—B3; 22 B—B4*ch*) 22 R×Q, QR×Q and Black still puts up a bit of resistance.

*21 . . . .* **Q×B**
*22 Kt—R3 !* . . . .

White intends to drive the King away, and then advance the passed Pawn with terrific effect.

**11.** Black is faced with the terrific threat of 23 Kt—Kt5*ch*, K—Kt1; 24 P—B7*ch* winning the Queen.

*22 . . . .* **K—K3**
*23 P—B7 !* **Resigns**

Black has no defense; if 23 . . . Q×P; 24 Kt—Kt5*ch* wins the Queen; or if 23 . . . K×P; 24 Q—Kt7*ch*, K—K3; 25 Kt—Kt5 *ch*, K—Q3; 26 R—Q1*ch* followed by 27 Q×Q wins.

Black's usual objective in the Gruenfeld is to reach the ending with a Queen side Pawn majority. But as Sokolsky played it, there was no ending.

## 46. U.S.S.R. CHAMPIONSHIP 1944

### Nimzovich Opening

*A game to fill one with admiration and amazement. Admiration at the ease with which the powerful Tolush is subdued, and amazement at the extraordinary number of pretty Knight forks at Smyslov's disposal.*

| WHITE | BLACK |
|-------|-------|
| A. Tolush | V. Smyslov |
| 1 Kt—KB3 | P—Q4 |
| 2 P—QKt3 | Kt—KB3 |
| 3 B—Kt2 | B—B4 |
| 4 P—K3 | P—K3 |
| 5 B—K2 | P—KR3 |

and the position is shown on the diagram below:

**1.** After only a few moves, the players are in unfamiliar territory. White's original opening is met by a development reminiscent of a famous Reti-Lasker game.

| 6 O—O | QKt—Q2 |
|-------|--------|

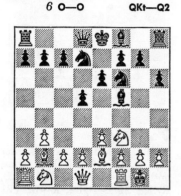

**2.** The Knight has not gone to B3, as the Bishop Pawn must be free to advance.

| 7 P—Q3 | B—K2 |
|--------|------|
| 8 QKt—Q2 | O—O |
| 9 R—K1 | B—R2 |
| 10 B—KB1 | P—QR4 |

**3.** The Rook Pawn intends to push on to R5 and R6.

*11* P—QR4 . . . .

A better measure was 11 P—QR3, to avoid weakening QKt4.

    *11* . . . .     P—B3

    *12* P—K4     . . . .

**4.** The advance of the King Pawn is certainly plausible but Black refutes it.

    *12* . . . .     P×P

    *13* P×P     B—Kt5

**5.**   *14* Q—K2     Q—K2

      *15* KR—Q1     KR—Q1

*16* P—Kt3 . . . .

To give his KB more scope.

**6.**   *16* . . . .     Kt—B4

Threatening the King Pawn.

    *17* P—K5     . . . .

A better alternative was 17 P—B3, Kt—Q6; 18 P×B, Kt×B; 19 KR—Kt1, Kt—Q6.

    *17* . . . .     Kt—Q4

**7.** Aside from the immediate threat of 18 . . . B×P,

Black's pieces look menacing in the center.

**18 Kt—B4** . . . .

18 P—B4 allows this pretty win of the exchange: 18 . . . Kt—B6; 19 B×Kt, B×B; 20 R—R3 (20 QR—B1, B—Kt7), B—B7; 21 R—B1, B—Kt7.

White decides to fight on, and that gives Smyslov a chance to display his tactical abilities.

| 20 . . . . | Kt—KKt4 |
|---|---|
| 21 Q—Kt4 | R×Kt ! |

**10.** Instead of capturing the Rook, Smyslov sacrifices!

**22 R×R** **B—KB4 !**

An embarrassing move to meet, as the Queen has no good flight square.

**8.**
| 18 . . . . | Kt—K5 |
|---|---|
| 19 Kt—Q4 | Kt(Q4)—B6 |

This wins the exchange.

**9.** 20 Q—B3 . . . .

**11.** If now 23 Q—B4, Kt—K7*ch;* 24 B×Kt, Kt—R6

*ch* wins the Queen (Black's Knight checks can be reversed with equal effect). On 23 Q—R4, Kt—B6 is a "family check," while 23 Q—R5 loses by 23 . . . P—KKt3; 24 Q×P, Kt—B6*ch*.

**23 B×Kt**     . . . .

| 26 | P—B3 | B×BP |
| 27 | R—Q7 | B×P ! |

More "brilliancies."

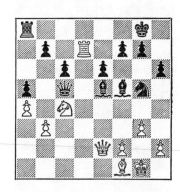

**14.** If now 28 Q×B, Kt—B6*ch*, while 28 Kt×B is answered by 28 . . . Q×Kt !

| 28 | P—R4 | Kt—K5 |
| 29 | Kt×B | Q×Kt |
| 30 | P—KKt4 | B—Kt3 |
| 31 | P—R5 | B—R2 |
| 32 | B—Kt2 | . . . . |

**12.** If now 23 . . . B×Q; 24 B×B holds out for a while.

| 23 | . . . . | B×B ! |
| 24 | Q—K2 | . . . . |

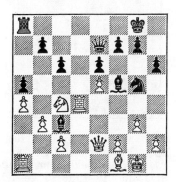

**13.** 
| 24 | . . . . | B×R(Q5) |
| 25 | R—Q1 | Q—B4 |

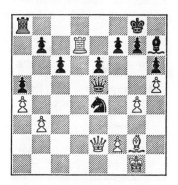

**15.** The pinned Knight is in no danger.

| 32 . . . . | Q—B5 |
| 33 R—Q4 | . . . . |

Black can now play 33 . . . Q—B8*ch*, and if 34 R—Q1, Kt—B6 wins a Rook.

| 33 . . . . | Kt—B6 ! |

But this is prettier. If 34 R×Q, Kt×Q*ch* wins the Rook, and if 34 Q—B4, Q×R; 35 Q×Q, Kt—K7*ch* wins.

**34 Resigns**

### 47. MATCH, 1945

### Vienna Game

*Kamyshov creates a master-piece with such attractive ele-gance as one can only hope to emulate in some rare inspired moment—and secretly envy!*

*Quite as pretty as the game itself are the ideas which Kamyshov had in mind—the variations which never oc-curred!*

| WHITE | BLACK |
| M. Kamyshov | V. Panov |
| 1 P—K4 | P—K4 |
| 2 Kt—QB3 | Kt—QB3 |
| 3 B—B4 | Kt—B3 |
| 4 P—Q3 | B—B4 |
| 5 P—B4 | P—Q3 |
| 6 Kt—B3 | . . . . |

and the position is shown on the next diagram:

**1.** The players have reached a familiar position in the King's Gambit Declined.

| 6 . . . . | Kt—KKt5 |

An interesting deviation from the usual 6 . . . B—K3 or 6 . . . B—KKt5.

| 7 Kt—KKt5 ! | . . . . |

**2.** White's aggressive reply has prevented 7 . . . Kt—B7, as White could continue with 8 Q—R5, P—KKt3; 9 Q—R6, Kt×R; 10 Q—Kt7, R—B1; 11 B×P*ch* winning.

| 7 .... | O—O |
|---|---|
| 8 P—B5 | .... |

Now on 8 . . . Kt—B7; 9 Q—R5, P—KR3; 10 Kt×P (threatening mate in three) wins.

| 8 .... | B—B7*ch* |
|---|---|

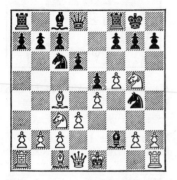

**3.** Black plays to remove one of White's Bishops.

| 9 K—B1 | Kt—K6*ch* |
|---|---|
| 10 B×Kt | B×B |
| 11 P—KR4 ! | .... |

| 11 .... | B×Kt |
|---|---|

Or if 11 . . . P—KKt3; 12 Kt× BP, R×Kt; 13 Q—B3, B—B5 (if 13 . . . B—Kt3; 14 P×P wins); 14 P×P, P×P; 15 B×R*ch*, K×B; 16 P—KKt3 winning the Bishop.

| 12 P×B | Q×P |
|---|---|
| 13 R—R5 | .... |

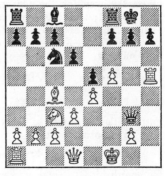

**5.** White has an open file to work on.

| 13 .... | Q—Kt6 |
|---|---|

**4.** The Knight stays!

**6.** 14 Kt—Q5    P—KKt3

Black cannot imitate the centralizing maneuver, as after 14 . . . Kt—Q5 ? White forces mate by 15 Kt—K7*ch*, K—R1; 16 R×P*ch*, K×R; 17 Q—R5 mate.

| 15 R—R3 | Q—Kt4 |
|---------|-------|
| 16 K—B2 ! | . . . . |

A quiet King move in the midst of complications—as in the famous Breyer-Esser game.

**7.** White's last was a fine move strategically, as it clears the way for the Queen's move to R1; and excellent tactically as it prevents 16 . . . P× P, when 17 R—Kt3 would win the Queen.

| 16 . . . . | Kt—Q5 |
|-----------|-------|
| 17 P—B3 | . . . . |

White has no intention of permitting Black's Knight to occupy such an important post.

| 17 . . . . | Kt—K3 |

He guards his QBP, and prepares to drive off the enemy Knight by . . . P—B3.

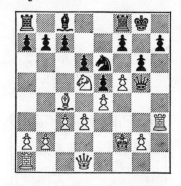

**8.** Now Black's Knight aims for B5.

| 18 Q—R1 | . . . . |

Naturally not 18 P×Kt, P×P*ch*; followed by 19 . . . P×Kt.

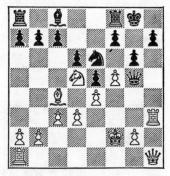

**9.** 18 . . . .     Q—Q7*ch*

Black avoids 18 . . . Kt—B5 as he sees this combination: 18 . . . Kt—B5; 19 R×P, Kt—R4 (19 . . . Q×P*ch* ? 20 Q×Q, Kt× Q; 21 Kt—B6 mate); 20 P×P, P×P*ch*; 21 Kt—B6 mate!!

| 19 K—Kt1 | . . . . |

## 10.

19 . . . .       Kt—Kt4

Thereby depriving White of the pleasure of bringing about a beautiful problem-like finish: 19 . . . Kt—B5; 20 Kt—K7*ch*, K—Kt2; 21 R×P*ch*, K—B3; 22 Q—R4*ch*, P—Kt4; 23 Kt—Kt8*ch!*, R×Kt; 24 R×P mate.

    20 R—Kt3       K—Kt2
    21 P—B6*ch*       K—R1

## 11.

22 Kt—K3       . . . .

White plays to win the Queen.

Had he played instead 22 Q—R4 (not 22 Q—R6, Kt—B6*ch* followed by 23 . . . Q×Q), Black's defense would be 22 . . . Kt—K3; 23 R—R3, Kt—Kt4 (but not 23 . . . P—KR4; 24 Q×P*ch*, P×Q; 25 R×P*ch*, K—Kt1; 26 Kt—K7 mate).

    22 . . . .       P—KR4

## 12.

White was planning to win by 23 Q—R6, Kt—K3; 24 B×Kt.

    23 R—Q1       Q—K7
    24 P—Q4       . . . .

Attacking the Queen which cannot run away (24 . . . Q×P; 25 R×Kt).

    24 . . . .       Kt×P
    25 B×Q       Kt×R
    26 Q—R4       Kt×B*ch*
    27 K—B1       Kt—B5

Black has saved himself from material loss, but his position is hopeless, as White forcefully demonstrates. He begins by opening up a file for his Rook.

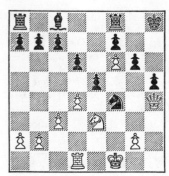

**13.**

| 28 P×P | P×P |
|---|---|
| 29 Q—Kt5 | .... |

Menaces mate in two.

| 29 .... | K—R2 |
|---|---|
| 30 Q×P | Kt—K3 |
| 31 P—KKt4 | .... |

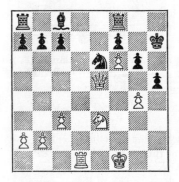

**14.** White threatens to break through the defensive barrier of Pawns.

| 31 .... | P—R5 |
|---|---|
| 32 P—Kt5 | P—Kt3 |
| 33 Q—K4 | R—Q1 |

Hoping for 34 Q×R, B—R3*ch;* followed by 35 . . . R×Q.

*34* Q×RP*ch* ....

Simple and strong!

**15.**

| 34 .... | K—Kt1 |
|---|---|
| 35 R×R*ch* | Kt×R |
| 36 Kt—Q5 | **Resigns** |

There is no defense against White's mating threats. If 36 . . . Kt—K3; 37 Kt—K7*ch,* K—B1; 38 Q—R8 mate, and if 36 . . . Kt—B3; 37 Q—R6 followed by Q—Kt7 mate.

### 48. MOSCOW 1945

### Scotch Game

*Lilienthal just seems to toy with his adversary in this attractive little game. But then, do we not expect sparkling play from Lilienthal who once sacrificed his Queen against the mighty Capablanca, beating him in 26 moves?*

*Lilienthal quickly wrests the initiative from his opponent with an unexpectedly early sortie of the Queen. In no time at all Koblentz finds himself facing a host of vicious mating threats.*

| WHITE | BLACK |
|-------|-------|
| A. Koblentz | A. Lilienthal |

| 1 | P—K4 | P—K4 |
| 2 | Kt—KB3 | Kt—QB3 |
| 3 | P—Q4 | P×P |
| 4 | Kt×P | B—B4 |

and the position is shown on the diagram below:

**1.** White chooses one of the oldest known openings— possibly with the idea of surprising his opponent, who might not be familiar with its fine points.

    **5 Kt—Kt3**    . . . .

But this move, which weakens the King-side, is no improvement on the customary 5 B—K3.

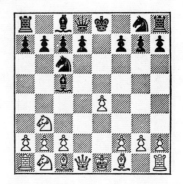

**2.**
| 5 | . . . . | B—Kt3 |
| 6 | Kt—B3 | P—Q3 |
| 7 | B—K2 | . . . . |

Somewhat better was 7 Kt—Q5, and if 7 . . . Q—R5, then 8 Q—B3.

    7 . . . .     Q—R5

**3.**
| 8 | O—O | Kt—B3 |
| 9 | P—Kt3 | . . . . |

Hoping to drive away the annoying Queen.

    9 . . . .     Q—R6

But she only comes closer!

## 4.

**10 K—R1** . . . .

To evade the threat of **10 . . . Kt—KKt5; 11 B×Kt, B×B; 12 Kt—K2, B—B6; 13 Kt—B4, Q—Kt5; 14 Q—Q5** (if **14 P—KR3, Q×Pch**), **P—Kt4**, followed by **15 . . . Q—R6** and Black wins.

**10 . . . .** **P—KR4 !**

## 5.

Again Black menaces **11 . . . Kt—KKt5**, and if then **12 B×Kt, P×B** wins, as **. . . Q×P** mate cannot be stopped.

**11 B—KKt5** . . . .

**11 P—B3** would also have been answered by **11 . . . Kt—KKt5.**

**11 . . . .** **Kt—KKt5**

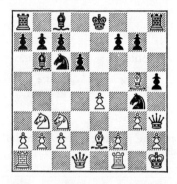

## 6.

**12 B×Kt** **P×B**
**13 B—R4** . . . .

White breaks the line of communication between Queen and Rook—and also sets a little trap.

## 7.

**13 . . . .** **Kt—K4 !**

But not the plausible **13 . . .**

P—Kt4, as White plays 14 Kt—
K2 followed by 15 Kt—Kt1, winning the imprisoned Queen!

**14 Kt—Q2　　　Kt—B6 !**

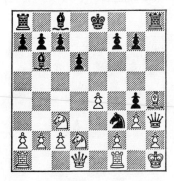

**8.**　**15 Kt×Kt　　　P×Kt**
　　　**16 R—KKt1　　　. . . .**

16 Q×BP instead would lose a
piece by 16 . . . R×B.

**9.**　**16 . . . .　　　P—Kt4**

Stronger than winning the exchange by 16 . . . B×P.

**17 Kt—Q5　　　Q—K3**

A prettier way to win a piece
than by 17 . . . P—QB3; 18
Kt×B, P×B, and the Knight must
not move away on account of the
deadly reply 19 . . . P×P.

**18 Q×P　　　. . . .**

18 B×P is impossible, as Black
would mate in two by 18 . . .
R×P*ch;* 19 K×R, Q—R6 mate.

**18 . . . .　　　P×B**

Black has won a piece, but there
are still some delightful finesses.

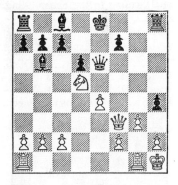

**10.**　**19 P×P　　　B—Q2**

If Black is permitted to castle,
White's present slim chances will
disappear completely.

**20 Kt—B6***ch*　**K—Q1**
**21 P—B3　　　. . . .**

To prevent Black from hitting at
the well-posted Knight by 21
. . . B—Q5.

## 11.

21 ....        B—B3

Black bears down on the diagonal leading to the enemy King.

22 R—Kt7        ....

Hoping for something like this: 22 ... K—K2; 23 Kt—Q5*ch*, B×Kt; 24 P×B, Q—B3 (otherwise 25 Q×P*ch* follows); 25 R—K1*ch,* and White wins the Queen.

## 12.

22 ....        R×P!

Black intends 23 ... R×P!

23 R—Kt8*ch*        K—K2
24 R×R        ....

All that is left. On 24 Kt—Q5*ch*, B×Kt; 25 P×B, Q—K4 (again threatening 26 ... Q×P mate!) is decisive.

## 13.

24 ....        Q×Kt

Forcing White to exchange Queens. If White refuses, say by 25 Q—Kt3, then comes 25 ... B×P*ch*; 26 K—Kt1 (if 26 P—B3, Q×P*ch*; 27 Q×Q, B×Q mate), R—Kt5! 27 Q×R, Q×P mate.

25 Q×Q*ch*        K×Q
26 P—B3        ....

Protects the King Pawn—he thinks!

26 ....        R×P!

Clearly if 27 P×R in reply, 27 ... B×P mates artistically.

27 K—Kt2        R—K7*ch*
28 Resigns

### 49. MOSCOW 1945

#### Queen's Pawn Game

*Black's attack begins on the Queen side, moves to the center, and suddenly shifts to the King side. With lightning speed Boleslavsky's pieces penetrate the enemy lines, and with their entrance the opponent's position disintegrates.*

| WHITE | BLACK |
|-------|-------|
| A. Kotov | I. Boleslavsky |
| 1 P—Q4 | Kt—KB3 |
| 2 B—Kt5 | Kt—K5 |
| 3 B—B4 | P—Q3 |
| 4 P—KB3 | Kt—KB3 |
| 5 P—K4 | .... |

and the position is shown on the diagram below:

**1.** Only a few moves have been made, but the players have already reached a position which is completely original.

| 5 .... | P—KKt3 |
|--------|--------|
| 6 Q—Q2 | QKt—Q2 |
| 7 B—KR6 | .... |

**2.** White wastes time in forcing the exchange of Bishops, when he should be putting his other pieces to work.

| 7 .... | B×B |
|--------|-----|
| 8 Q×B | P—B4 ! |

**3.**

| 9 P—B3 | Q—Kt3 |
|--------|-------|

Threatening to win a Pawn by 10 . . . Q×P, or 10 . . . P×P; 11 P×P, Q×QP.

**10 Q—Q2 . . . .**

This, and White's previous move have taken away the best squares for the development of his Queen Knight.

**10 . . . . P×P**
**11 P×P P—K4 !**

Black insists on breaking up the center!

**12 Kt—QR3 P—Q4 !**

A vigorous thrust which is much stronger than trying to win the Queen Pawn. If, for example, 12 . . . Q×QP; 13 Q×Q, P×Q; 14 Kt—Kt5 regains the Pawn, with the better game.

**4.** **13 QP×P Kt(Q2)×P**
**14 B—Kt5ch K—B1 !**

Better than 14 . . . B—Q2, as Black wants to keep his Bishop for the attack.

**15 P×P K—Kt2**

**16 Kt—K2 . . . .**

White does not risk castling as the reply would be 16 . . . B—B4, and 17 . . . QR—B1ch.

**5.** **16 . . . . P—QR3 !**
**17 B—B4 . . . .**

On 17 B—R4, Black plays 17 . . . B—B4 (threatening 18 . . . Kt—Q6ch) and . . . QR—Q1.

**17 . . . . R—K1**

**6.** **18 R—Q1 B—R6 !!**

Not merely a surface brilliancy (19 P×B, Kt×P*ch*) but the first move of a charming combination. On 19 R—KKt1 Black wins nicely by 19 . . . Kt×P*ch;* 20 K—B1, Kt×P*ch;* 21 K—K1, Q× R mate.

> *19 K—B1* . . . .

19 P—B4 loses by 19 . . . B×P; 20 P×Kt, Kt—K5; 21 Q—Q4, Q×Q; 22 Kt×Q, B×R.

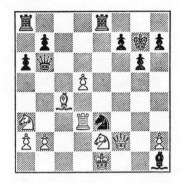

**8.**
> 24 . . . . **Q—Kt5***ch*
> 25 R—Q2 . . . .

Forced, as 25 R—B3 loses by 25 . . . Kt×P, and 25 Kt—B3 costs the Queen by the discovered check.

> 25 . . . . **QR—B1**

Threatens to win a piece by 26 . . . Kt×B; 27 Kt×Kt, R×Kt.

**7.**
> 19 . . . . **Kt×BP !**
> 20 Q—B4 . . . .

On 20 Q—B3, Black plays 20 . . . R—K6. Then if 21 R—Q3 (21 B—Q3, R—QB1 also loses), B×P*ch;* 22 K×B, R×Kt*ch;* 23 K×Kt, Q—B7 is mate.

> 20 . . . . **Kt—Kt5 !**
> 21 Q×Kt(B3) **Kt—K6***ch*
> 22 K—K1 **B×P**
> 23 Q—B2 **B×R**
> 24 R—Q3 . . . .

White is the exchange down, but he is not yet convinced.

**9.**
> 26 B—Kt3 **B×P**
> 27 B×B **Kt×B**

With the pretty idea of mate in one by 28 . . . R—B8.

| 28 Q—Q4*ch* | Q×Q |
| 29 R×Q | Kt—B3 |
| 30 Resigns | |

## 50. MOSCOW 1945

### Sicilian Defense

*Flawless mid-game play by Ragozin leads to a superb sacrificial combination.*

| WHITE | BLACK |
| --- | --- |
| V. Ragozin | G. Veresov |

| 1 P—K4 | P—QB4 |
| 2 Kt—KB3 | Kt—QB3 |
| 3 P—Q4 | P×P |
| 4 Kt×P | Kt—B3 |
| 5 Kt—QB3 | P—Q3 |
| 6 B—K2 | P—KKt3 |

and the position is shown on the diagram below:

**1.** Black intends to develop his King Bishop at Kt2,

where it will exert a great deal of pressure on the long diagonal.

| 7 O—O | B—Kt2 |
| 8 B—K3 | O—O |
| 9 Kt—Kt3 | .... |

To prevent Black from simplifying by 9 ... P—Q4; 10 P×P, Kt—QKt5.

9 ....     B—K3

**2.** Black hopes to force an early ... P—Q4.

10 P—B4     ....

Ready to reply to 10 ... P—Q4 with 11 P—K5.

10 ....     Q—B1

Better 10 ... Kt—QR4, and if 11 P—B5, B—B5 !

11 Q—K1     ....

Permits the exchange of one of his Bishops. White could have prevented it with 11 P—KR3, but he is eager to attack, and does not want to lose time by making defensive moves.

| 11 .... | Kt—KKt5 |
|---|---|
| 12 B×Kt | B×B |

**3.** Black has attained his objective—the advantage of the two Bishops. But now Ragozin, by a clever maneuver, opens up lines for his pieces, and they spring into action.

| 13 P—B5 ! | .... |
|---|---|

Intending to win the Bishop by 14 P—KR3, B—R4; 15 P—Kt4.

| **4.** | 13 .... | P×P |
|---|---|---|
| | 14 P—KR3 | P—B5 |

Not at once 14 . . . B—R4, as after 15 P×P the Bishop cannot get to Kt3.

| 15 R×P | B—R4 |
|---|---|
| 16 Kt—Q5 | .... |

An excellent outpost for the Knight.

White's threat is 17 Kt—Q4, P—K3 (or 17 . . . P—K4); 18 Kt×Kt winning.

| 16 .... | Q—Q2 |
|---|---|

If 16 . . . B×P; 17 B—Q4 !, B×R; 18 B×B, and White has a powerful attack for the sacrificed exchange.

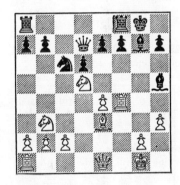

| **5.** | 17 Q—R4 | B—Kt3 |
|---|---|---|
| | 18 QR—KB1 | QR—B1 |

If 18 . . . B×KtP; 19 P—B3 keeps Black's Bishop from getting back into the game.

| 19 P—B3 | KR—K1 |
|---|---|
| 20 R—Kt4 | .... |

Beginning the final phase—direct attack on the adverse King.

**6.** 20 ....      P—Kt4
     21 Kt—Q4      ....

Aiming for B5, to force the exchange of one of Black's Bishops.

     21 ....      Kt×Kt
     22 B×Kt      R—B5

22 . . . P—B3 might have held out longer.

**8.** 25 R—B7*ch* !      K×R
     26 Q×RP*ch*      K—K3

Or 26 . . . K—B1; 27 Kt—B4 !, KR—B1; 28 Kt×P*ch*, K—K1; 29 Q—Kt8 mate.

     27 Q×KtP*ch*      K—K4

**7.** 23 B×B      K×B
     24 R×B*ch* !!      BP×R

If 24 . . . K×R; 25 Q—Kt3*ch*, K—R3; 26 R—B4 followed by 27 R—R4 mate.

**9.** 28 Q—Kt7*ch*      K×P

If 28 . . . K—K3; 29 Kt—B4 mate!

     29 Kt—B6*ch* !      P×Kt
     30 Q×Q      Resigns

An elegant ending.

## 51. MOSCOW 1951
### Nimzovich Defense

*Smyslov's way of pouncing on a weakness is quite original. In order to dominate the square QB5 he moves pieces twice in the opening, and develops them to the side of the board instead of towards the center. This strategy (which would horrify Tarrasch) proves so fruitful that he is able to effect checkmate while his opponent is still organizing a King-side attack.*

| WHITE | BLACK |
|-------|-------|
| **I. Lipnitsky** | **V. Smyslov** |
| *1* P—Q4 | Kt—KB3 |
| *2* P—QB4 | P—K3 |
| *3* Kt—QB3 | B—Kt5 |
| *4* Q—B2 | Kt—B3 |
| *5* Kt—B3 | P—Q4 |
| *6* P—QR3 | B×Kt*ch* |
| *7* P×B | .... |

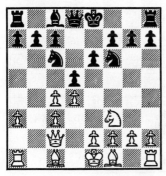

**1.** For the moment White seems to have the better of

it. He has the two Bishops, and an open file for his Queen Rook.

| *7* .... | Kt—QR4! |

Attacks the Pawn at White's QB4, and as we shall see, the square on which it stands.

| *8* Kt—K5 | Kt—Q2 |

The purpose of this is to rid the board of White's Knight, protector of the Bishop Pawn.

| *9* Kt×Kt | B×Kt |
| *10* P×P | P×P |
| *11* B—B4 | .... |

Anticipating no danger in a position that looks placid, White makes a routine developing move. A more suitable course was 11 P—K3 followed by 12 B—Q3 and 13 O—O.

| *11* .... | B—Kt4! |

**2.** This gives Black a firm grip on the square B5, a fine

outpost for his Knight. White
meanwhile can never advance the
Queen Bishop Pawn, a move
which would free his game.

|      |        |      |
|------|--------|------|
| 12   | P—KR4  | O—O  |
| 13   | R—QKt1 | Q—Q2 |
| 14   | R—R3   | .... |

White is playing for a King-side
attack. The tempting 14 B × P
(hoping for 14 . . . Q × B; 15 R × B)
would lose by 14 . . . B—R5 followed by 15 . . . Q × B.

|      |        |        |
|------|--------|--------|
| 14   | ....   | KR—K1  |
| 15   | R—KKt3 | Kt—B5  |

**3.** Threatens 16 . . . Kt × P
winning the exchange,
which White meets with a coun-
ter-threat.

|      |       |        |
|------|-------|--------|
| 16   | B—R6  | P—KKt3 |
| 17   | Q—B1  | Kt—Q3! |
| 18   | Q—B4  | ....   |

Threatens 19 Q—B6 and quick
mate.

**4.** 18 . . . .               B—R3

Black avoids the plausible 18 . . .
Kt—B4, which could lead to 19
R × B, Kt × R; 20 P × Kt, Q × R; 21
Q—B6 and mate at Kt7.

|      |       |        |
|------|-------|--------|
| 19   | P—K3  | Kt—B4  |
| 20   | B × B | P × B  |
| 21   | R—Kt7 | QR—Kt1! |
| 22   | R × BP | ....  |

**5.** White's position certainly
looks formidable but two

smart moves by Smyslov change the whole picture.

| 22 . . . . | R—Kt8*ch* |
| 23 K—K2 | Q—R5! |

Suddenly there is a threat of mate, which White can delay for only a move or two.

*24* **Resigns**

## 52. STOCKHOLM 1952

### Queen's Gambit Declined

*One of the marks of a great player is the flexibility with which he adapts himself to changing circumstances. In this game, Petrosian prepares to embark on the minority attack—standard procedure in this form of the Queen's Gambit. Our hearts sink as we envision a long positional struggle, with Petrosian squeezing out a win on the 89th move. But Petrosian can be as alert as Alekhine, given a glimmer of opportunity. Here he gets the chance, and in a flash shifts his attack to the King-side and wins the game in brilliant style.*

| WHITE | BLACK |
| T. Petrosian | P. Vaitonis |
| *1* P—Q4 | Kt—KB3 |
| *2* P—QB4 | P—K3 |
| *3* Kt—KB3 | P—Q4 |
| *4* Kt—B3 | B—K2 |
| *5* P×P | . . . . |

The Exchange Variation—favored by such disparate personalities as Marshall, Reshevsky and Petrosian.

| *5* . . . . | P×P |
| *6* Q—B2 | O—O |
| *7* B—Kt5 | QKt—Q2 |
| *8* P—K3 | P—B3 |
| *9* B—Q3 | R—K1 |
| *10* O—O | . . . . |

**1.** Black's game is cramped, and it is not easy to equalize. If he tries to simplify by 10 . . . Kt—K5, then 11 B×Kt, B×B; 12 B×P*ch* costs him a Pawn. Or if 11 . . . P—KR3; 12 B—KB4, Kt—R4; 13 Kt×P!, and Black is in the famous trap that caught Rubinstein.

|    |    |    |    |
|----|----|----|----|
| 10 . . . . | | Kt—B1 |
| 11 R—QKt1 | | . . . . |

The key move for the famous minority attack, the idea of which is to disrupt Black's Queen-side by P—QKt4 and P—QKt5.

|    |    |    |    |
|----|----|----|----|
| 11 . . . . | | Kt—K5 |
| 12 B—KB4 | | P—KB4 |
| 13 Kt—K5 | | . . . . |

White immediately seizes this fine square as an outpost for his Knight. One reason this spot is so desirable is that there are no Pawns to drive the Knight away.

|    |    |    |    |
|----|----|----|----|
| 13 . . . . | | B—B3 |
| 14 P—B3 | | . . . . |

But Black's Knight can be driven off by a Pawn!

|    |    |    |    |
|----|----|----|----|
| 14 . . . . | | Kt—Q3 |

**2.**    15 QR—K1!    . . . .

Petrosian is not stubborn. The Rook can be more useful on the King-side, since the position is ripe for a King-side attack.

|    |    |    |    |
|----|----|----|----|
| 15 . . . . | | P—KKt3 |
| 16 P—KR3 | | . . . . |

Indicating that he intends to follow with 17 P—KKt4, breaking up the adverse position, whether Black exchanges Pawns or not.

|    |    |    |    |
|----|----|----|----|
| 16 . . . . | | B—K3 |
| 17 P—KKt4 | | R—B1 |
| 18 Q—R2 | | . . . . |

**3.**    The Queen swings over to the King-side, gaining a tempo because of the threat 19 Kt×KtP, P×Kt; 20 B×Kt, winning a Pawn.

|    |    |    |    |
|----|----|----|----|
| 18 . . . . | | B—K2 |
| 19 K—R1 | | . . . . |

Clears a square for use by the Rook.

|    |    |    |    |
|----|----|----|----|
| 19 . . . . | | P×P |
| 20 RP×P | | Kt—B2 |
| 21 Kt×Kt | | B×Kt |
| 22 B—K5 | | . . . . |

The Knight has disappeared, but another piece occupies the outpost.

| 22 .... | B—B3 |
| 23 P—B4 | B × B |
| 24 QP × B | .... |

The Bishop has been disposed of, but now White has a passed Pawn, and threats in the offing—such as 25 P—B5 followed by 26 P—K6, for example.

| 24 .... | Q—K2 |

Ready to meet 25 P—B5 with 25 ...Q × P.

| 25 Kt—K2 | .... |

The idea of this is to maneuver the Knight over to B3 by way of Kt1 or Q4. At B3, the Knight would be an additional protector of the King Pawn, enabling White to carry out his plan to advance the Bishop Pawn.

| 25 .... | P—QR3 |
| 26 Kt—Q4 | Kt—K3 |

**4.**   27 Kt—B5!   ....

Petrosian, as I mentioned before, is alert and rises to the occasion.

| 27 .... | P × Kt |

Forced, as otherwise 28 Kt—Q6 wins the exchange.

| 28 P × P | Kt—B1 |

Protects the Rook Pawn. If instead 28 ... Kt—B4; 29 P—B6 attacks the Queen and also threatens 30 Q × P*ch* and mate next move.

| 29 R—Kt1*ch* | K—R1 |
| 30 Q—R6 | Kt—Kt3 |

If 30 ... B—Kt1 instead (to meet the threat of 31 Q—Kt7 mate) White wins neatly by 31 P—B6, Q—Q2; 32 Q—Kt7*ch*, Q × Q; 33 P × Q mate.

| 31 P × Kt | B × P |

Here if 31 ... B—K3, White mates in three, beginning with 32 P—Kt7*ch*.

| 32 R × B | **Resigns** |

## 53. MOSCOW 1956

### Two Knights' Defense

*There are so many marvellous players around! There is Bronstein, for instance, whose brave combinations and fierce attacking play put him on a level with the old-time giants of aggression.*

*Here, with no definite attack in sight, Bronstein gives up a Bishop cheerfully for two Pawns. No attack in sight? N'importe. Bronstein gets an army of Pawns moving. So* formidable is the effect of eight Pawns marching up the board that Rojahn is overwhelmed, and runs out of time trying to meet their threats.

| WHITE | BLACK |
|---|---|
| D. Bronstein | E. Rojahn |
| 1 P—K4 | P—K4 |
| 2 Kt—KB3 | Kt—QB3 |
| 3 B—B4 | Kt—B3 |
| 4 Kt—Kt5 | P—Q4 |
| 5 P×P | Kt—QR4 |
| 6 P—Q3 | P—KR3 |
| 7 Kt—KB3 | P—K5 |

***1.*** The usual play at this point is 8 Q—K2, but Bronstein springs an innovation.

| 8 P×P! | Kt×B |
| 9 Q—Q4 | Kt—Kt3 |
| 10 P—B4 | P—B4 |

To prevent 11 P—B5, but 10 ... P—B3 might have been better, with the idea of returning the piece for two Pawns.

| 11 Q—Q3 | B—Kt5 |
| 12 QKt—Q2 | B—K2 |
| 13 0—0 | 0—0 |
| 14 Kt—K5 | B—R4 |

Not a happy spot for the Bishop, but White was threatening 15 Kt×B, Kt×Kt; 16 P—B4.

| 15 P—QKt3 | QKt—Q2 |
| 16 B—Kt2 | Kt×Kt |
| 17 B×Kt | Kt—Q2 |
| 18 B—B3 | B—B3 |

***2.*** Black is intent on exchanging, and bringing it to an ending where his extra material will give him the advantage.

| 19 QR—K1 | .... |

Preparing for the Pawn advance 20 P—B4 followed by 21 P—K5.

| 19 .... | B×B |
| 20 Q×B | Q—B3 |

Still bent on exchanging as many pieces as possible. More to the point though was 20 ... P—B3 instead, to restrain the opposing Pawns.

*21* **P—K5** . . . .

Stronger than the plausible 21 Q—R3 (attacking two loose pieces) which might allow Black sufficient counter-play to change the aspect of things: 21 . . . Q—Kt7; 22 Kt—Kt1, B—K7; 23 Q× Kt, B×R; 24 R×B, Q×RP, and Black has good chances.

*21* . . . .      **Q—B4**
*22* **P—B4**      **B—Kt3**
*23* **Kt—K4**      . . . .

To prevent Black from coming in by 23 . . . Q—Q6.

*23* . . . .      **QR—Kt1**
*24* **Q—B3**      . . . .

With two dire threats : 25 P—KKt4, and 25 Kt—Kt3, Q—B7; 26 R—K2, with a decisive gain of material in either case.

**3.** *24* . . . .      **B—R2**

Clears a spot for the Queen.

*25* **P—KKt4**      **Q—Kt3**
*26* **P—B5**      **Q—Kt3**

If instead 26 . . . Kt×P; 27 P×Q, Kt×Q*ch*; 28 R×Kt, B×P; 29 Kt×P, and White wins.

*27* **Q—Kt3**      . . . .

Intending either 28 Kt—Q6 followed by 29 P—K6, or 28 P—KR4 and 29 P—Kt5, breaking through on the King-side.

*27* . . . .      **P—B3**
*28* **P—K6**      **Kt—K4**
*29* **P—KR4**      **K—R1**
*30* **P—Kt5**      **QR—B1**
*31* **K—R1**      **Q—Q1**
*32* **P—Kt6**      . . . .

Bronstein notes that he also had choice of winning by 32 Kt×KBP, P×Kt; 33 R×Kt, P×R; 34 Q×P*ch*, K—Kt1; 35 P—K7.

*32* . . . .      **B×P**

Or 32 . . . B—Kt1; 33 P—Q6, and Black is helpless.

*33* **P×B**      **P—Kt4**
*34* **P—Q6**      **Q—Kt3**
*35* **P—Q7**      **Kt×QP**
*36* **P×Kt**      **QR—Q1**
*37* **Kt×KBP!**      **Q—B3***ch*

The alternatives are: 37 . . . P×Kt; 38 P—Kt7*ch*, winning a Rook, and 37 . . . R×Kt; 38 R—K8*ch* and mate in two.

*38* **Q—Kt2**      . . . .

*face) that bears the stamp of genius.*

| WHITE | BLACK |
|-------|-------|
| **M. Tal** | **K. Klaman** |
| *1* P—K4 | P—QB4 |
| *2* Kt—KB3 | Kt—QB3 |
| *3* P—Q4 | P×P |
| *4* Kt×P | Kt—B3 |
| *5* Kt—QB3 | P—Q3 |
| *6* B—KKt5 | B—Q2 |
| *7* Q—Q2 | Kt×Kt |
| *8* Q×Kt | Q—R4 |
| *9* B×Kt | KtP×B |

**4.** At this point Black overstepped the time limit and lost. Had play continued, it might have gone something like this: 38 ...Q×Qch; 39 K×Q, P×Kt; 40 R—K7 (threatening 41 P—Kt7*ch*), R—KKt1; 41 R—R7 mate! Too bad Bronstein was deprived of this neat finish, but he has the gratification of achieving it in the notes.

## 54. MOSCOW 1957

### Sicilian Defense

*The fiery Tal is in his element in this game. Confronted by a position that looks impenetrable, he finds a way to rip it open by sacrificing two pieces. The attack on the King which follows is easy enough (for Tal) but it is the Knight fork at the end (which Klaman refuses to*

**1.** This weakens Black's Pawn position, but in compensation he does have the two Bishops. An interesting possibility (instead of the actual exchange) was 9 B—R4, R—B1; 10 B—K2, P—K4; 11 Q—Q3, Kt×P; 12 Q×Kt, R×Kt!, with winning chances for Black.

| | | |
|---|---|---|
| *10* O—O—O | R—B1 |
| *11* P—B4 | R—KKt1 |
| *12* P—KKt3 | P—K3 |
| *13* B—R3 | .... |

Tal is clearly not interested in 13 Q × BP, B—Kt2, and the initiative changes hands.

| 13 . . . . | Q—QB4 |
| 14 Q—Q2 | P—Kt4 |
| 15 KR—K1 | P—Kt5 |

Instead of this, if 15 . . . Q—R4, White has a powerful reply in 16 Kt—Q5, threatening 17 Kt × P*ch*. Then if 16 . . . B—Kt2; 17 Kt—K7 is a startling winning move.

| 16 Kt—K2 | Q—B5 |
| 17 K—Kt1 | Q × KP |

**2.** This is probably the losing move. Considerably safer was 17 . . . B—K2 to complete his development.

| 18 Kt—Q4 | Q—Kt2 |
| 19 Q—Q3 | . . . . |

Attacks the Rook Pawn, which can be defended only by the miserable 19 . . . R—KR1 or by 19 . . . R—Kt2, allowing 20 Kt—B5, which strikes at the Rook and the Queen Pawn.

| 19 . . . . | B—K2 |
| 20 Q × P | R—B1 |
| 21 B—Kt4 | . . . . |

Intending to continue with 22 B—R5, adding pressure on the Pawns at Black's B2 and K3. A possibility (pointed out by several annotators) is this pretty line of play: 21 . . . K—Q1; 22 B—R5, B—K1; 23 R × P!, P × R; 24 Kt × P*ch*, K—Q2; 25 Kt × R*ch*, K—Q1; 26 R × P*ch*!, B × R; 27 Kt—K6 mate!

| 21 . . . . | Q—B2 |
| 22 K—R1 | . . . . |

To prevent the Pawn being captured with check when the Queen and Knight move away from its protection.

| 22 . . . . | P—B4 |

This gives Tal his chance, but passive resistance was no better. Tal would either find a combination, or start pushing his passed Pawn.

**3.** 23 B × P!     . . . .

Begins an attractive combination.

| 23 .... | P×B |
| 24 R×B*ch*! | K×R |
| 25 R—K1*ch* | K—Q1 |

If 25 ... B—K3 instead, 26 Kt×B wins. Note that if White's King were still at Kt1, Black could allow this and turn the tables by continuing 26 ... Q×P*ch* and mate in two.

| 26 Q—R4*ch* | P—B3 |
| 27 Q—R6 | .... |

Attacks the helpless Rook. Black cannot defend the Rook, and moving it allows a quick mate.

| 27 .... | Q—R4 |

Gives the King a flight-square, and puts temptation in Tal's path. If Tal captures hurriedly ("Take first and think it over later") this might happen: 28 Q×R*ch*, K—B2; 29 Q×BP, P—Kt6, and Black threatens two instant mates.

| 28 Kt—Kt3 | Q—Q4 |
| 29 Q×R*ch* | K—B2 |
| 30 Q×BP | R—K1 |
| 31 R—QB1 | .... |

Intending 32 P—B3 next, opening the Bishop file for the Rook.

| 31 .... | B—R5 |
| 32 Q—Q4 | Q—Kt2 |
| 33 R—Q1 | R—K3 |

Protecting the Pawn by 33 ... R—Q1 allows 34 Kt—B5 in reply. The Knight would then attack Queen and Bishop, and also threaten the Rook by 35 Kt—K6*ch*.

| 34 Q—B4*ch* | Resigns |

**4.** This is the final position, but why didn't Black play one more move, and give us the pleasure of seeing the following continuation?

| 34 .... | K—Q2 |

To protect the Rook.

| 35 Kt—B5*ch*! |

And the Knight (which cannot be taken) attacks King, Queen, Rook and Bishop!

**5.**

## 55. PORTOROZ 1958

### Caro-Kann Defense

*Tal wins this from a strong opponent as effortlessly as though this were another game in the series Morphy vs. Amateur.*

*A slashing stroke rips the position wide open, and the combinations come tumbling down.*

| WHITE | BLACK |
|-------|-------|
| **M. Tal** | **G. Füster** |
| *1* P—K4 | P—QB3 |
| *2* P—Q4 | P—Q4 |
| *3* Kt—QB3 | P×P |
| *4* Kt×P | Kt—Q2 |

The order of moves is important; if at once 4 ... Kt—KB3; 5 Kt× Kt*ch* disrupts Black's Pawn position.

**5 Kt—KB3 . . . .**

A trappy alternative is 5 B—QB4, after which there could follow 5 ... KKt—B3; 6 Kt—Kt5, P—K3; 7 Q—K2, Kt—Kt3 (definitely not 7 ... P—KR3, as 8 Kt×BP, K×Kt; 9 Q×P*ch*, K—Kt3; 10 B—Q3*ch*, K—R4; 11 Q—R3 mate would be the punishment); 8 B—Kt3, Q×P; 9KKt—B3, followed by 10 Kt—K5.

| 5 . . . . | KKt—B3 |
|-----------|--------|
| 6 Kt× Kt*ch* | Kt× Kt |
| 7 B—QB4 | B—B4 |

Carefully avoiding 7 ... B—Kt5, which loses a Pawn by 8 B×P*ch*, K×B; 9 Kt—K5*ch*.

| *8* Q—K2 | P—K3 |
|----------|------|
| *9* B—KKt5 | B—K2 |
| *10* 0—0—0 | P—KR3 |

***1.*** An instinctive attempt to brush the Bishop away, but it weakens the Pawn position. It seems dangerous to Castle since White can initiate an attack by 11 Kt—K5, followed by P—KKt4 and P—KR4. Safest is probably 10 ... Kt—Q4, to free the position by exchanges.

| *11* B—R4 | Kt—K5 |
|-----------|-------|

Hoping for 12 B—Kt3, Kt×B and the simple life, but Tal throws a monkey-wrench into the machinery.

| *12* P—KKt4! | B—R2 |
|--------------|------|

Prudently retreating, since other lines of play lead to trouble:

(*a*) If ... 12 B×P; 13 B×B, B×Kt (or Q×B; 14 Q×Kt

winning a piece); 14 Q × B, Q × B;
15 Q × Kt, and White has won a
piece.

   (*b*) If 12 ... B × B; 13 P × B,
Kt × P; 14 P × P, Kt × QR; 15
P × P*ch*, K—Q2 (or K—B1; 16
Kt—K5); 16 B—K6*ch*, K—B2;
17 Kt × B, Q × Kt; 18 Q—K5*ch*,
K—Kt3; 19 R × Kt, Q—Kt4*ch*;
20 K—Kt1, and White should
win.

|     |       |        |
| --- | ----- | ------ |
| *13* | B—KKt3 | Kt × B |
| *14* | BP × Kt! | . . . . |

The books say, "Pawn captures
must be made towards the center,"
But Tal sees that the open Bishop
file can be more useful than the
Rook file.

|     |       |        |
| --- | ----- | ------ |
| *14* | . . . . | Q—B2 |

Develops the Queen, and prepares
for Castling Queen-side (if Tal
permits it).

|     |       |        |
| --- | ----- | ------ |
| *15* | Kt—K5 | B—Q3 |
| *16* | P—KR4 | P—B3 |

Black wants to evict the Knight by
force, since he dares not Castle
King-side on account of the reply
17 P—Kt5, breaking into his position, and if 16 ... O—O—O; 17
Kt × KBP, Q × Kt; 18 B × P*ch*, and
White wins the Queen. The move
Black does make gives Tal the
opportunity he wants—a sacrifice
which tears away the King's Pawn
protection.

**2.** *17* B × P!          . . . .

This confines Black's King to the
center.

|     |       |        |
| --- | ----- | ------ |
| *17* | . . . . | P × Kt |
| *18* | P × P | B—K2 |

Black loses quickly after 18 ...
B × P; 19 KR—K1. The combinations are easy, but pretty:

   (*a*) 19 ... B × KtP; 20 B—Q7*ch*,
K—B2; 21 Q—K7*ch*, K—Kt3; 22
P—R5 mate.

   (*b*) 19 ... B—B3; 20 B—B8*ch*,
K—B2 (if B—K2; 21 B—Q7*ch*,
and Black must give up his Queen
—as a start); 21 Q—K6*ch*, K—
Kt3; 22 P—R5*ch*, K—Kt4; 23 Q—
K3*ch* and mate next.

   (*c*) 19 ... B—B3; 20 B—B8*ch*,
Q—K2; 21 Q—Q2, R × B; 22 Q—
Q7*ch*, K—B2; 23 R × Q*ch*, B × R;
24 R—B1*ch*, K—Kt3; 25 Q—B5
mate.

|     |       |        |
| --- | ----- | ------ |
| *19* | KR—B1 | . . . . |

With mating threats: 20 B—B7*ch*, K—B1; 21 B—Kt6*ch*, K—Kt1; 22 Q—B4 mate.

| 19 . . . . | KR—B1 |
| 20 R×R*ch* | B×R |
| 21 Q—B3! | . . . . |

**3.** To which the natural reply is fatal: 21 . . . R—Q1; 22 R×R*ch*, K×R (or Q×R; 23 Q—B7 mate); 23 Q×B mate.

| 21 . . . . | Q—K2 |
| 22 Q—Kt3! | . . . . |

Institutes a new threat: 23 B—Q7*ch*, Q×B; 24 R×Q, K×R; 25 Q×P*ch*, winning an innocent Rook that wasn't even in the fight.

| 22 . . . . | R—Kt1 |

This move loses, but so does everything else. White can always win the Queen for Rook and Bishop by B—Q7*ch* and retain a winning attack.

| 23 B—Q7*ch* | Q×B |

Or 23 . . . K—Q1; 24 B—B5*ch*, followed by 25 B×B.

| 24 R×Q | K×R |
| 25 Q—B7*ch* | B—K2 |
| 26 P—K6*ch* | K—Q1 |

Or 26 . . . K—Q3; 27 Q—B4*ch*, and wins the Rook.

| 27 Q×P | Resigns |

The Bishop is lost. After 27 . . . B—K5; 28 Q—K5 attacks two unprotected pieces. The game is a good illustration of the power of the Queen in attack (or is it the power of Tal?).

**4.**

## 56. COPENHAGEN 1960
### Dutch Defense

*Petrosian's Knight accomplishes so much while appearing to do so little! Early in the game the Queen Knight zig-zags over to QB5, and simply stays on that spot. Never another move does that piece make, but its threats of leaping over to K6 with a deadly check are enough to terrify the opponent into submission.*

| WHITE | BLACK |
|-------|-------|
| **T. Petrosian** | **Nielsen** |
| *1* P—Q4 | P—KB4 |
| *2* B—Kt5 | P—KKt3 |
| *3* Kt—Q2 | B—Kt2 |
| *4* P—QB3 | Kt—KB3 |
| *5* P—K3 | P—Q3 |

Petrosian plays the opening in original style, having left the books as early as the second move.

| *6* KKt—B3 | Kt—B3 |
|-----------|-------|
| *7* Q—Kt3 | P—KR3 |
| *8* B×Kt  | . . . . |

Here too Petrosian is not bound by tradition, but cheerfully lets his opponent have the two Bishops.

| *8* . . . . | B×B |
|------------|-----|
| *9* P—K4   | P—K4 |
| *10* B—Kt5 | . . . . |

**1.** A critical stage. Black must guard against the threat 11

P—Q5, P—R3; 12 P×Kt, P×B; 13 P×KtP, B×P; 14 Q×Pch, and White wins a piece.

| *10* . . . . | K—B1 |
|-------------|------|

Instead of this, if 10 . . . B—Q2; 11 P×BP, KtP×P; 12 B×Kt, B×B; 13 Q—K6ch, and the Bishop Pawn falls.

| *11* B×Kt  | P×B   |
|-----------|-------|
| *12* P×KP | QP×P  |
| *13* Q—R4 | Q—Q3  |

The hasty 13 . . . P×P instead would be bad, as after 14 Q×KP in reply, three Black Pawns would be attacked.

| *14* Kt—Kt3 | B—Q2 |
|------------|------|
| *15* R—Q1  | Q—K2 |
| *16* Kt—B5! | . . . . |

**2.** A beautiful move! The gallant Knight, unprotected, seizes an outpost station. From this vital square the Knight exerts pressure on the center and blockades the Queen-side Pawns as well.

| *16* . . . . | B—K1 |
|-------------|------|

The alternative of removing the Knight leads to trouble for Black: 16 . . . Q × Kt; 17 R × B, Q—Kt3; 18 Q—B4 (threatens mate), B—K2; 19 Q—K6, R—R2; 20 Kt × P, Q—B4 (if 20 . . . R—Kt2 to guard the KtP, 21 R × B, R × R; 22 Kt × P*ch* wins); 21 Kt×P*ch*, K—K1; 22 R × P, R—Kt2; 23 Kt × B, R × Kt; 24 Q—Kt8 mate.

| 17 P—QKt4 | . . . . |

Now the Knight stands like a rock!

| 17 . . . . | K—Kt2 |
| 18 O—O | R—KB1 |
| 19 Q—R6! | . . . . |

The strength of this move becomes apparent half-a-dozen moves later.

| 19 . . . . | P × P |

**3.** Black tries to get some counter-play, but the clever reply brings White's other Knight into the game.

| 20 Kt—Q2 | P—K6 |
| 21 Kt(Q2)—K4 | P × P*ch* |
| 22 R × P | B—Kt4 |

Exchanging some pieces would free his game. Or would it?

| 23 R × R | K × R |

Obviously, if 23 . . . Q × R; 24 Kt—K6*ch* wins the Queen.

| 24 Kt × B | P × Kt |

Here, too, if 24 . . . Q × Kt; 25 Kt—K6*ch* wins the Queen.

| 25 Q—Kt7! | . . . . |

**4.** This move, which traps the Rook (and was foreseen much earlier by Petrosian) certainly deserves a diagram.

| 25 . . . . | **Resigns** |

There was no escape for the unfortunate Rook, since 25 . . . R—Q1; 26 R × R, Q × R; 27 Kt—K6*ch* (again that terrible Knight check) loses the Queen.

# CATALOG OF DOVER BOOKS

# Books Explaining Science and Mathematics

**WHAT IS SCIENCE?, N. Campbell.** The role of experiment and measurement, the function of mathematics, the nature of scientific laws, the difference between laws and theories, the limitations of science, and many similarly provocative topics are treated clearly and without technicalities by an eminent scientist. "Still an excellent introduction to scientific philosophy," H. Margenau in PHYSICS TODAY. "A first-rate primer . . . deserves a wide audience," SCIENTIFIC AMERICAN. 192pp. 5⅜ x 8.          S43 Paperbound **$1.25**

**THE NATURE OF PHYSICAL THEORY, P. W. Bridgman.** A Nobel Laureate's clear, non-technical lectures on difficulties and paradoxes connected with frontier research on the physical sciences. Concerned with such central concepts as thought, logic, mathematics, relativity, probability, wave mechanics, etc. he analyzes the contributions of such men as Newton, Einstein, Bohr, Heisenberg, and many others. "Lucid and entertaining . . . recommended to anyone who wants to get some insight into current philosophies of science," THE NEW PHILOSOPHY. Index. xi + 138pp. 5⅜ x 8.          S33 Paperbound **$1.25**

**EXPERIMENT AND THEORY IN PHYSICS, Max Born.** A Nobel Laureate examines the nature of experiment and theory in theoretical physics and analyzes the advances made by the great physicists of our day: Heisenberg, Einstein, Bohr, Planck, Dirac, and others. The actual process of creation is detailed step-by-step by one who participated. A fine examination of the scientific method at work. 44pp. 5⅜ x 8.          S308 Paperbound **75¢**

**THE PSYCHOLOGY OF INVENTION IN THE MATHEMATICAL FIELD, J. Hadamard.** The reports of such men as Descartes, Pascal, Einstein, Poincaré, and others are considered in this investigation of the method of idea-creation in mathematics and other sciences and the thinking process in general. How do ideas originate? What is the role of the unconscious? What is Poincaré's forgetting hypothesis? are some of the fascinating questions treated. A penetrating analysis of Einstein's thought processes concludes the book. xiii + 145pp. 5⅜ x 8.          T107 Paperbound **$1.25**

**THE NATURE OF LIGHT AND COLOUR IN THE OPEN AIR, M. Minnaert.** Why are shadows sometimes blue, sometimes green, or other colors depending on the light and surroundings? What causes mirages? Why do multiple suns and moons appear in the sky? Professor Minnaert explains these unusual phenomena and hundreds of others in simple, easy-to-understand terms based on optical laws and the properties of light and color. No mathematics is required but artists, scientists, students, and everyone fascinated by these "tricks" of nature will find thousands of useful and amazing pieces of information. Hundreds of observational experiments are suggested which require no special equipment. 200 illustrations; 42 photos. xvi + 362pp. 5⅜ x 8.          T196 Paperbound **$1.95**

**THE UNIVERSE OF LIGHT, W. Bragg.** Sir William Bragg, Nobel Laureate and great modern physicist, is also well known for his powers of clear exposition. Here he analyzes all aspects of light for the layman: lenses, reflection, refraction, the optics of vision, x-rays, the photoelectric effect, etc. He tells you what causes the color of spectra, rainbows, and soap bubbles, how magic mirrors work, and much more. Dozens of simple experiments are described. Preface. Index. 199 line drawings and photographs, including 2 full-page color plates. x + 283pp. 5⅜ x 8.          T538 Paperbound **$1.85**

**SOAP-BUBBLES: THEIR COLOURS AND THE FORCES THAT MOULD THEM, C. V. Boys.** For continuing popularity and validity as scientific primer, few books can match this volume of easily-followed experiments, explanations. Lucid exposition of complexities of liquid films, surface tension and related phenomena, bubbles' reaction to heat, motion, music, magnetic fields. Experiments with capillary attraction, soap bubbles on frames, composite bubbles, liquid cylinders and jets, bubbles other than soap, etc. Wonderful introduction to scientific method, natural laws that have many ramifications in areas of modern physics. Only complete edition in print. New Introduction by S. Z. Lewin, New York University. 83 illustrations; 1 full-page color plate. xii + 190pp. 5⅜ x 8½.          T542 Paperbound **95¢**

# CATALOGUE OF DOVER BOOKS

**THE STORY OF X-RAYS FROM RONTGEN TO ISOTOPES, A. R. Bleich, M.D.** This book, by a member of the American College of Radiology, gives the scientific explanation of x-rays, their applications in medicine, industry and art, and their danger (and that of atmospheric radiation) to the individual and the species. You learn how radiation therapy is applied against cancer, how x-rays diagnose heart disease and other ailments, how they are used to examine mummies for information on diseases of early societies, and industrial materials for hidden weaknesses. 54 illustrations show x-rays of flowers, bones, stomach, gears with flaws, etc. 1st publication. Index. xix + 186pp. 5⅜ x 8. **T622 Paperbound $1.35**

**SPINNING TOPS AND GYROSCOPIC MOTION, John Perry.** A classic elementary text of the dynamics of rotation — the behavior and use of rotating bodies such as gyroscopes and tops. In simple, everyday English you are shown how quasi-rigidity is induced in discs of paper, smoke rings, chains, etc., by rapid motions; why a gyrostat falls and why a top rises; precession; how the earth's motion affects climate; and many other phenomena. Appendix on practical use of gyroscopes. 62 figures. 128pp. 5⅜ x 8. **T416 Paperbound $1.00**

**SNOW CRYSTALS, W. A. Bentley, M. J. Humphreys.** For almost 50 years W. A. Bentley photographed snow flakes in his laboratory in Jericho, Vermont; in 1931 the American Meteorological Society gathered together the best of his work, some 2400 photographs of snow flakes, plus a few ice flowers, windowpane frosts, dew, frozen rain, and other ice formations. Pictures were selected for beauty and scientific value. A very valuable work to anyone in meteorology, cryology; most interesting to layman; extremely useful for artist who wants beautiful, crystalline designs. All copyright free. Unabridged reprint of 1931 edition. 2453 illustrations. 227pp. 8 x 10½. **T287 Paperbound $2.95**

**A DOVER SCIENCE SAMPLER, edited by George Barkin.** A collection of brief, non-technical passages from 44 Dover Books Explaining Science for the enjoyment of the science-minded browser. Includes work of Bertrand Russell, Poincaré, Laplace, Max Born, Galileo, Newton; material on physics, mathematics, metallurgy, anatomy, astronomy, chemistry, etc. You will be fascinated by Martin Gardner's analysis of the sincere pseudo-scientist, Moritz's account of Newton's absentmindedness, Bernard's examples of human vivisection, etc. Illustrations from the Diderot Pictorial Encyclopedia and De Re Metallica. 64 pages. **FREE**

**THE STORY OF ATOMIC THEORY AND ATOMIC ENERGY, J. G. Feinberg.** A broader approach to subject of nuclear energy and its cultural implications than any other similar source. Very readable, informal, completely non-technical text. Begins with first atomic theory, 600 B.C. and carries you through the work of Mendelejeff, Röntgen, Madame Curie, to Einstein's equation and the A-bomb. New chapter goes through thermonuclear fission, binding energy, other events up to 1959. Radioactive decay and radiation hazards, future benefits, work of Bohr, moderns, hundreds more topics. "Deserves special mention . . . not only authoritative but thoroughly popular in the best sense of the word," Saturday Review. Formerly, "The Atom Story." Expanded with new chapter. Three appendixes. Index. 34 illustrations. vii + 243pp. 5⅜ x 8. **T625 Paperbound $1.45**

**THE STRANGE STORY OF THE QUANTUM, AN ACCOUNT FOR THE GENERAL READER OF THE GROWTH OF IDEAS UNDERLYING OUR PRESENT ATOMIC KNOWLEDGE, B. Hoffmann.** Presents lucidly and expertly, with barest amount of mathematics, the problems and theories which led to modern quantum physics. Dr. Hoffmann begins with the closing years of the 19th century, when certain trifling discrepancies were noticed, and with illuminating analogies and examples takes you through the brilliant concepts of Planck, Einstein, Pauli, Broglie, Bohr, Schroedinger, Heisenberg, Dirac, Sommerfeld, Feynman, etc. This edition includes a new, long postscript carrying the story through 1958. "Of the books attempting an account of the history and contents of our modern atomic physics which have come to my attention, this is the best," H. Margenau, Yale University, in "American Journal of Physics." 32 tables and line illustrations. Index. 275pp. 5⅜ x 8. **T518 Paperbound $1.45**

**SPACE AND TIME, E. Borel.** Written by a versatile mathematician of world renown with his customary lucidity and precision, this introduction to relativity for the layman presents scores of examples, analogies, and illustrations that open up new ways of thinking about space and time. It covers abstract geometry and geographical maps, continuity and topology, the propagation of light, the special theory of relativity, the general theory of relativity, theoretical researches, and much more. Mathematical notes. 2 Indexes. 4 Appendices. 15 figures. xvi + 243pp. 5⅜ x 8. **T592 Paperbound $1.45**

**FROM EUCLID TO EDDINGTON: A STUDY OF THE CONCEPTIONS OF THE EXTERNAL WORLD, Sir Edmund Whittaker.** A foremost British scientist traces the development of theories of natural philosophy from the western rediscovery of Euclid to Eddington, Einstein, Dirac, etc. The inadequacy of classical physics is contrasted with present day attempts to understand the physical world through relativity, non-Euclidean geometry, space curvature, wave mechanics, etc. 5 major divisions of examination: Space; Time and Movement; the Concepts of Classical Physics; the Concepts of Quantum Mechanics; the Eddington Universe. 212pp. 5⅜ x 8. **T491 Paperbound $1.35**

# Nature, Biology

**NATURE RECREATION: Group Guidance for the Out-of-doors, William Gould Vinal.** Intended for both the uninitiated nature instructor and the education student on the college level, this complete "how-to" program surveys the entire area of nature education for the young. Philosophy of nature recreation; requirements, responsibilities, important information for group leaders; nature games; suggested group projects; conducting meetings and getting discussions started; etc. Scores of immediately applicable teaching aids, plus completely updated sources of information, pamphlets, field guides, recordings, etc. Bibliography. 74 photographs. + 310pp. 5⅜ x 8½. **T1015 Paperbound $1.75**

**HOW TO KNOW THE WILD FLOWERS, Mrs. William Starr Dana.** Classic nature book that has introduced thousands to wonders of American wild flowers. Color-season principle of organization is easy to use, even by those with no botanical training, and the genial, refreshing discussions of history, folklore, uses of over 1,000 native and escape flowers, foliage plants are informative as well as fun to read. Over 170 full-page plates, collected from several editions, may be colored in to make permanent records of finds. Revised to conform with 1950 edition of Gray's Manual of Botany. xlii + 438pp. 5⅜ x 8½. **T332 Paperbound $1.85**

**HOW TO KNOW THE FERNS, F. T. Parsons.** Ferns, among our most lovely native plants, are all too little known. This classic of nature lore will enable the layman to identify almost any American fern he may come across. After an introduction on the structure and life of ferns, the 57 most important ferns are fully pictured and described (arranged upon a simple identification key). Index of Latin and English names. 61 illustrations and 42 full-page plates. xiv + 215pp. 5⅜ x 8. **T740 Paperbound $1.25**

**MANUAL OF THE TREES OF NORTH AMERICA, Charles Sprague Sargent.** Still unsurpassed as most comprehensive, reliable study of North American tree characteristics, precise locations and distribution. By dean of American dendrologists. Every tree native to U.S., Canada, Alaska, 185 genera, 717 species, described in detail—leaves, flowers, fruit, winterbuds, bark, wood, growth habits etc. plus discussion of varieties and local variants, immaturity variations. Over 100 keys, including unusual 11-page analytical key to genera, aid in identification. 783 clear illustrations of flowers, fruit, leaves. An unmatched permanent reference work for all nature lovers. Second enlarged (1926) edition. Synopsis of families. Analytical key to genera. Glossary of technical terms. Index. 783 illustrations, 1 map. Two volumes. Total of 982pp. 5⅜ x 8. **T277 Vol. I Paperbound $2.00**
**T278 Vol. II Paperbound $2.00**
**The set $4.00**

**TREES OF THE EASTERN AND CENTRAL UNITED STATES AND CANADA, W. M. Harlow.** A revised edition of a standard middle-level guide to native trees and important escapes. More than 140 trees are described in detail, and illustrated with more than 600 drawings and photographs. Supplementary keys will enable the careful reader to identify almost any tree he might encounter. xiii + 288pp. 5⅜ x 8. **T395 Paperbound $1.35**

**GUIDE TO SOUTHERN TREES, Ellwood S. Harrar and J. George Harrar.** All the essential information about trees indigenous to the South, in an extremely handy format. Introductory essay on methods of tree classification and study, nomenclature, chief divisions of Southern trees, etc. Approximately 100 keys and synopses allow for swift, accurate identification of trees. Numerous excellent illustrations, non-technical text make this a useful book for teachers of biology or natural science, nature lovers, amateur naturalists. Revised 1962 edition. Index. Bibliography. Glossary of technical terms. 920 illustrations; 201 full-page plates. ix + 709pp. 4⅝ x 6⅜. **T945 Paperbound $2.25**

**FRUIT KEY AND TWIG KEY TO TREES AND SHRUBS, W. M. Harlow.** Bound together in one volume for the first time, these handy and accurate keys to fruit and twig identification are the only guides of their sort with photographs (up to 3 times natural size). "Fruit Key": Key to over 120 different deciduous and evergreen fruits. 139 photographs and 11 line drawings. Synoptic summary of fruit types. Bibliography. 2 Indexes (common and scientific names). "Twig Key": Key to over 160 different twigs and buds. 173 photographs. Glossary of technical terms. Bibliography. 2 Indexes (common and scientific names). Two volumes bound as one. Total of xvii + 126pp. 5⅝ x 8⅜. **T511 Paperbound $1.25**

**INSECT LIFE AND INSECT NATURAL HISTORY, S. W. Frost.** A work emphasizing habits, social life, and ecological relations of insects, rather than more academic aspects of classification and morphology. Prof. Frost's enthusiasm and knowledge are everywhere evident as he discusses insect associations and specialized habits like leaf-rolling, leaf-mining, and case-making, the gall insects, the boring insects, aquatic insects, etc. He examines all sorts of matters not usually covered in general works, such as: insects as human food, insect music and musicians, insect response to electric and radio waves, use of insects in art and literature. The admirably executed purpose of this book, which covers the middle ground between elementary treatment and scholarly monographs, is to excite the reader to observe for himself. Over 700 illustrations. Extensive bibliography. x + 524pp. 5⅜ x 8. **T517 Paperbound $2.45**

# CATALOGUE OF DOVER BOOKS

**COMMON SPIDERS OF THE UNITED STATES, J. H. Emerton.** Here is a nature hobby you can pursue right in your own cellar! Only non-technical, but thorough, reliable guide to spiders for the layman. Over 200 spiders from all parts of the country, arranged by scientific classification, are identified by shape and color, number of eyes, habitat and range, habits, etc. Full text, 501 line drawings and photographs, and valuable introduction explain webs, poisons, threads, capturing and preserving spiders, etc. Index. New synoptic key by S. W. Frost. xxiv + 225pp. 5⅜ x 8.
T223 Paperbound **$1.35**

**THE LIFE STORY OF THE FISH: HIS MANNERS AND MORALS, Brian Curtis.** A comprehensive, non-technical survey of just about everything worth knowing about fish. Written for the aquarist, the angler, and the layman with an inquisitive mind, the text covers such topics as evolution, external covering and protective coloration, physics and physiology of vision, maintenance of equilibrium, function of the lateral line canal for auditory and temperature senses, nervous system, function of the air bladder, reproductive system and methods—courtship, mating, spawning, care of young—and many more. Also sections on game fish, the problems of conservation and a fascinating chapter on fish curiosities. "Clear, simple language . . . excellent judgment in choice of subjects . . . delightful sense of humor," New York Times. Revised (1949) edition. Index. Bibliography of 72 items. 6 full-page photographic plates. xii + 284pp. 5⅜ x 8.
T929 Paperbound **$1.50**

**BATS, Glover Morrill Allen.** The most comprehensive study of bats as a life-form by the world's foremost authority. A thorough summary of just about everything known about this fascinating and mysterious flying mammal, including its unique location sense, hibernation and cycles, its habitats and distribution, its wing structure and flying habits, and its relationship to man in the long history of folklore and superstition. Written on a middle-level, the book can be profitably studied by a trained zoologist and thoroughly enjoyed by the layman. "An absorbing text with excellent illustrations. Bats should have more friends and fewer thoughtless detractors as a result of the publication of this volume," William Beebe, Books. Extensive bibliography. 57 photographs and illustrations. x + 368pp. 5⅜ x 8½.
T984 Paperbound **$2.00**

**BIRDS AND THEIR ATTRIBUTES, Glover Morrill Allen.** A fine general introduction to birds as living organisms, especially valuable because of emphasis on structure, physiology, habits, behavior. Discusses relationship of bird to man, early attempts at scientific ornithology, feathers and coloration, skeletal structure including bills, legs and feet, wings. Also food habits, evolution and present distribution, feeding and nest-building, still unsolved questions of migrations and location sense, many more similar topics. Final chapter on classification, nomenclature. A good popular-level summary for the biologist; a first-rate introduction for the layman. Reprint of 1925 edition. References and index. 51 illustrations. viii + 338pp. 5⅜ x 8½.
T957 Paperbound **$1.85**

**LIFE HISTORIES OF NORTH AMERICAN BIRDS, Arthur Cleveland Bent.** Bent's monumental series of books on North American birds, prepared and published under auspices of Smithsonian Institute, is the definitive coverage of the subject, the most-used single source of information. Now the entire set is to be made available by Dover in inexpensive editions. This encyclopedic collection of detailed, specific observations utilizes reports of hundreds of contemporary observers, writings of such naturalists as Audubon, Burroughs, William Brewster, as well as author's own extensive investigations. Contains literally everything known about life history of each bird considered: nesting, eggs, plumage, distribution and migration, voice, enemies, courtship, etc. These not over-technical works are musts for ornithologists, conservationists, amateur naturalists, anyone seriously interested in American birds.

**BIRDS OF PREY.** More than 100 subspecies of hawks, falcons, eagles, buzzards, condors and owls, from the common barn owl to the extinct caracara of Guadaloupe Island. 400 photographs. Two volume set. Index for each volume. Bibliographies of 403, 520 items. 197 full-page plates. Total of 907pp. 5⅜ x 8½.
Vol. I T931 Paperbound **$2.35**
Vol. II T932 Paperbound **$2.35**

**WILD FOWL.** Ducks, geese, swans, and tree ducks—73 different subspecies. Two volume set. Index for each volume. Bibliographies of 124, 144 items. 106 full-page plates. Total of 685pp. 5⅜ x 8½.
Vol. I T285 Paperbound **$2.35**
Vol. II T286 Paperbound **$2.35**

**SHORE BIRDS.** 81 varieties (sandpipers, woodcocks, plovers, snipes, phalaropes, curlews, oyster catchers, etc.). More than 200 photographs of eggs, nesting sites, adult and young of important species. Two volume set. Index for each volume. Bibliographies of 261, 188 items. 121 full-page plates. Total of 860pp. 5⅜ x 8½.
Vol. I T933 Paperbound **$2.35**
Vol. II T934 Paperbound **$2.35**

**THE LIFE OF PASTEUR, R. Vallery-Radot.** 13th edition of this definitive biography, cited in Encyclopaedia Britannica. Authoritative, scholarly, well-documented with contemporary quotes, observations; gives complete picture of Pasteur's personal life; especially thorough presentation of scientific activities with silkworms, fermentation, hydrophobia, inoculation, etc. Introduction by Sir William Osler. Index. 505pp. 5⅜ x 8.
T632 Paperbound **$2.00**

# Puzzles, Mathematical Recreations

**SYMBOLIC LOGIC and THE GAME OF LOGIC, Lewis Carroll.** "Symbolic Logic" is not concerned with modern symbolic logic, but is instead a collection of over 380 problems posed with charm and imagination, using the syllogism, and a fascinating diagrammatic method of drawing conclusions. In "The Game of Logic" Carroll's whimsical imagination devises a logical game played with 2 diagrams and counters (included) to manipulate hundreds of tricky syllogisms. The final section, "Hit or Miss" is a lagniappe of 101 additional puzzles in the delightful Carroll manner. Until this reprint edition, both of these books were rarities costing up to $15 each. Symbolic Logic: Index. xxxi + 199pp. The Game of Logic: 96pp. 2 vols. bound as one. 5⅜ x 8.                                             T492 Paperbound **$1.50**

**PILLOW PROBLEMS and A TANGLED TALE, Lewis Carroll.** One of the rarest of all Carroll's works, "Pillow Problems" contains 72 original math puzzles, all typically ingenious. Particularly fascinating are Carroll's answers which remain exactly as he thought them out, reflecting his actual mental process. The problems in "A Tangled Tale" are in story form, originally appearing as a monthly magazine serial. Carroll not only gives the solutions, but uses answers sent in by readers to discuss wrong approaches and misleading paths, and grades them for insight. Both of these books were rarities until this edition, "Pillow Problems" costing up to $25, and "A Tangled Tale" $15. Pillow Problems: Preface and Introduction by Lewis Carroll. xx + 109pp. A Tangled Tale: 6 illustrations. 152pp. Two vols. bound as one. 5⅜ x 8.                                             T493 Paperbound **$1.50**

**AMUSEMENTS IN MATHEMATICS, Henry Ernest Dudeney.** The foremost British originator of mathematical puzzles is always intriguing, witty, and paradoxical in this classic, one of the largest collections of mathematical amusements. More than 430 puzzles, problems, and paradoxes. Mazes and games, problems on number manipulation, unicursal and other route problems, puzzles on measuring, weighing, packing, age, kinship, chessboards, joiners', crossing river, plane figure dissection, and many others. Solutions. More than 450 illustrations. vii + 258pp. 5⅜ x 8.                                             T473 Paperbound **$1.25**

**THE CANTERBURY PUZZLES, Henry Dudeney.** Chaucer's pilgrims set one another problems in story form. Also Adventures of the Puzzle Club, the Strange Escape of the King's Jester, the Monks of Riddlewell, the Squire's Christmas Puzzle Party, and others. All puzzles are original, based on dissecting plane figures, arithmetic, algebra, elementary calculus and other branches of mathematics, and purely logical ingenuity. "The limit of ingenuity and intricacy," The Observer. Over 110 puzzles. Full Solutions. 150 illustrations. vii + 225pp. 5⅜ x 8.
T474 Paperbound **$1.25**

**MATHEMATICAL EXCURSIONS, H. A. Merrill.** Even if you hardly remember your high school math, you'll enjoy the 90 stimulating problems contained in this book and you will come to understand a great many mathematical principles with surprisingly little effort. Many useful shortcuts and diversions not generally known are included: division by inspection, Russian peasant multiplication, memory systems for pi, building odd and even magic squares, square roots by geometry, dyadic systems, and many more. Solutions to difficult problems. 50 illustrations. 145pp. 5⅜ x 8.                                             T350 Paperbound **$1.00**

**MAGIC SQUARES AND CUBES, W. S. Andrews.** Only book-length treatment in English, a thorough non-technical description and analysis. Here are nasik, overlapping, pandiagonal, serrated squares; magic circles, cubes, spheres, rhombuses. Try your hand at 4-dimensional magical figures! Much unusual folklore and tradition included. High school algebra is sufficient. 754 diagrams and illustrations. viii + 419pp. 5⅜ x 8.                                             T658 Paperbound **$1.85**

**CALIBAN'S PROBLEM BOOK: MATHEMATICAL, INFERENTIAL AND CRYPTOGRAPHIC PUZZLES, H. Phillips (Caliban), S. T. Shovelton, G. S. Marshall.** 105 ingenious problems by the greatest living creator of puzzles based on logic and inference. Rigorous, modern, piquant; reflecting their author's unusual personality, these intermediate and advanced puzzles all involve the ability to reason clearly through complex situations; some call for mathematical knowledge, ranging from algebra to number theory. Solutions. xi + 180pp. 5⅜ x 8.
T736 Paperbound **$1.25**

**MATHEMATICAL PUZZLES FOR BEGINNERS AND ENTHUSIASTS, G. Mott-Smith.** 188 mathematical puzzles based on algebra, dissection of plane figures, permutations, and probability, that will test and improve your powers of inference and interpretation. The Odic Force, The Spider's Cousin, Ellipse Drawing, theory and strategy of card and board games like tit-tat-toe, go moku, salvo, and many others. 100 pages of detailed mathematical explanations. Appendix of primes, square roots, etc. 135 illustrations. 2nd revised edition. 248pp. 5⅜ x 8.
T198 Paperbound **$1.00**

**MATHEMAGIC, MAGIC PUZZLES, AND GAMES WITH NUMBERS, R. V. Heath.** More than 60 new puzzles and stunts based on the properties of numbers. Easy techniques for multiplying large numbers mentally, revealing hidden numbers magically, finding the date of any day in any year, and dozens more. Over 30 pages devoted to magic squares, triangles, cubes, circles, etc. Edited by J. S. Meyer. 76 illustrations. 128pp. 5⅜ x 8.                                             T110 Paperbound **$1.00**

# CATALOGUE OF DOVER BOOKS

**THE BOOK OF MODERN PUZZLES, G. L. Kaufman.** A completely new series of puzzles as fascinating as crossword and deduction puzzles but based upon different principles and techniques. Simple 2-minute teasers, word labyrinths, design and pattern puzzles, logic and observation puzzles — over 150 braincrackers. Answers to all problems. 116 illustrations. 192pp. 5⅜ x 8.
T143 Paperbound **$1.00**

**NEW WORD PUZZLES, G. L. Kaufman.** 100 ENTIRELY NEW puzzles based on words and their combinations that will delight crossword puzzle, Scrabble and Jotto fans. Chess words, based on the moves of the chess king; design-onyms, symmetrical designs made of synonyms; rhymed double-crostics; syllable sentences; addle letter anagrams; alphagrams; linkograms; and many others all brand new. Full solutions. Space to work problems. 196 figures. vi + 122pp. 5⅜ x 8.
T344 Paperbound **$1.00**

**MAZES AND LABYRINTHS: A BOOK OF PUZZLES, W. Shepherd.** Mazes, formerly associated with mystery and ritual, are still among the most intriguing of intellectual puzzles. This is a novel and different collection of 50 amusements that embody the principle of the maze: mazes in the classical tradition; 3-dimensional, ribbon, and Möbius-strip mazes; hidden messages; spatial arrangements; etc.—almost all built on amusing story situations. 84 illustrations. Essay on maze psychology. Solutions. xv + 122pp. 5⅜ x 8.
T731 Paperbound **$1.00**

**MAGIC TRICKS & CARD TRICKS, W. Jonson.** Two books bound as one. 52 tricks with cards, 37 tricks with coins, bills, eggs, smoke, ribbons, slates, etc. Details on presentation, misdirection, and routining will help you master such famous tricks as the Changing Card, Card in the Pocket, Four Aces, Coin Through the Hand, Bill in the Egg, Afghan Bands, and over 75 others. If you follow the lucid exposition and key diagrams carefully, you will finish these two books with an astonishing mastery of magic. 106 figures. 224pp. 5⅜ x 8. T909 Paperbound **$1.00**

**PANORAMA OF MAGIC, Milbourne Christopher.** A profusely illustrated history of stage magic, a unique selection of prints and engravings from the author's private collection of magic memorabilia, the largest of its kind. Apparatus, stage settings and costumes; ingenious ads distributed by the performers and satiric broadsides passed around in the streets ridiculing pompous showmen; programs; decorative souvenirs. The lively text, by one of America's foremost professional magicians, is full of anecdotes about almost legendary wizards: Dede, the Egyptian; Philadelphia, the wonder-worker; Robert-Houdin, "the father of modern magic;" Harry Houdini; scores more. Altogether a pleasure package for anyone interested in magic, stage setting and design, ethnology, psychology, or simply in unusual people. A Dover original. 295 illustrations; 8 in full color. Index. viii + 216pp. 8⅜ x 11¼.
T774 Paperbound **$2.25**

**HOUDINI ON MAGIC, Harry Houdini.** One of the greatest magicians of modern times explains his most prized secrets. How locks are picked, with illustrated picks and skeleton keys; how a girl is sawed into twins; how to walk through a brick wall — Houdini's explanations of 44 stage tricks with many diagrams. Also included is a fascinating discussion of great magicians of the past and the story of his fight against fraudulent mediums and spiritualists. Edited by W.B. Gibson and M.N. Young. Bibliography. 155 figures, photos. xv + 280pp. 5⅜ x 8.
T384 Paperbound **$1.25**

**MATHEMATICS, MAGIC AND MYSTERY, Martin Gardner.** Why do card tricks work? How do magicians perform astonishing mathematical feats? How is stage mind-reading possible? This is the first book length study explaining the application of probability, set theory, theory of numbers, topology, etc., to achieve many startling tricks. Non-technical, accurate, detailed! 115 sections discuss tricks with cards, dice, coins, knots, geometrical vanishing illusions, how a Curry square "demonstrates" that the sum of the parts may be greater than the whole, and dozens of others. No sleight of hand necessary! 135 illustrations. xii + 174pp. 5⅜ x 8.
T335 Paperbound **$1.00**

**EASY-TO-DO ENTERTAINMENTS AND DIVERSIONS WITH COINS, CARDS, STRING, PAPER AND MATCHES, R. M. Abraham.** Over 300 tricks, games and puzzles will provide young readers with absorbing fun. Sections on card games; paper-folding; tricks with coins, matches and pieces of string; games for the agile; toy-making from common household objects; mathematical recreations; and 50 miscellaneous pastimes. Anyone in charge of groups of youngsters, including hard-pressed parents, and in need of suggestions on how to keep children sensibly amused and quietly content will find this book indispensable. Clear, simple text, copious number of delightful line drawings and illustrative diagrams. Originally titled "Winter Nights Entertainments." Introduction by Lord Baden Powell. 329 illustrations. v + 186pp. 5⅜ x 8½.
T921 Paperbound **$1.00**

**STRING FIGURES AND HOW TO MAKE THEM, Caroline Furness Jayne.** 107 string figures plus variations selected from the best primitive and modern examples developed by Navajo, Apache, pygmies of Africa, Eskimo, in Europe, Australia, China, etc. The most readily understandable, easy-to-follow book in English on perennially popular recreation. Crystal-clear exposition; step-by-step diagrams. Everyone from kindergarten children to adults looking for unusual diversion will be endlessly amused. Index. Bibliography. Introduction by A. C. Haddon. 17 full-page plates. 960 illustrations. xxiii + 401pp. 5⅜ x 8½.
T152 Paperbound **$2.00**

# Entertainments, Humor

**ODDITIES AND CURIOSITIES OF WORDS AND LITERATURE, C. Bombaugh, edited by M. Gardner.** The largest collection of idiosyncratic prose and poetry techniques in English, a legendary work in the curious and amusing bypaths of literary recreations and the play technique in literature—so important in modern works. Contains alphabetic poetry, acrostics, palindromes, scissors verse, centos, emblematic poetry, famous literary puns, hoaxes, notorious slips of the press, hilarious mistranslations, and much more. Revised and enlarged with modern material by Martin Gardner. 368pp. 5⅜ x 8. **T759 Paperbound $1.50**

**A NONSENSE ANTHOLOGY, collected by Carolyn Wells.** 245 of the best nonsense verses ever written, including nonsense puns, absurd arguments, mock epics and sagas, nonsense ballads, odes, "sick" verses, dog-Latin verses, French nonsense verses, songs. By Edward Lear, Lewis Carroll, Gelett Burgess, W. S. Gilbert, Hilaire Belloc, Peter Newell, Oliver Herford, etc., 83 writers in all plus over four score anonymous nonsense verses. A special section of limericks, plus famous nonsense such as Carroll's "Jabberwocky" and Lear's "The Jumblies" and much excellent verse virtually impossible to locate elsewhere. For 50 years considered the best anthology available. Index of first lines specially prepared for this edition. Introduction by Carolyn Wells. 3 indexes: Title, Author, First lines. xxxiii + 279pp. **T499 Paperbound $1.25**

**THE BAD CHILD'S BOOK OF BEASTS, MORE BEASTS FOR WORSE CHILDREN, and A MORAL ALPHABET, H. Belloc.** Hardly an anthology of humorous verse has appeared in the last 50 years without at least a couple of these famous nonsense verses. But one must see the entire volumes—with all the delightful original illustrations by Sir Basil Blackwood—to appreciate fully Belloc's charming and witty verses that play so subacidly on the platitudes of life and morals that beset his day—and ours. A great humor classic. Three books in one. Total of 157pp. 5⅜ x 8. **T749 Paperbound $1.00**

**THE DEVIL'S DICTIONARY, Ambrose Bierce.** Sardonic and irreverent barbs puncturing the pomposities and absurdities of American politics, business, religion, literature, and arts, by the country's greatest satirist in the classic tradition. Epigrammatic as Shaw, piercing as Swift, American as Mark Twain, Will Rogers, and Fred Allen, Bierce will always remain the favorite of a small coterie of enthusiasts, and of writers and speakers whom he supplies with "some of the most gorgeous witticisms of the English language" (H. L. Mencken). Over 1000 entries in alphabetical order. 144pp. 5⅜ x 8. **T487 Paperbound $1.00**

**THE PURPLE COW AND OTHER NONSENSE, Gelett Burgess.** The best of Burgess's early nonsense, selected from the first edition of the "Burgess Nonsense Book." Contains many of his most unusual and truly awe-inspiring pieces: 36 nonsense quatrains, the Poems of Patagonia, Alphabet of Famous Goops, and the other hilarious (and rare) adult nonsense that place him in the forefront of American humorists. All pieces are accompanied by the original Burgess illustrations. 123 illustrations. xiii + 113pp. 5⅜ x 8. **T772 Paperbound $1.00**

**MY PIOUS FRIENDS AND DRUNKEN COMPANIONS and MORE PIOUS FRIENDS AND DRUNKEN COMPANIONS, Frank Shay.** Folksingers, amateur and professional, and everyone who loves singing: here, available for the first time in 30 years, is this valued collection of 132 ballads, blues, vaudeville numbers, drinking songs, sea chanties, comedy songs. Songs of pre-Beatnik Bohemia; songs from all over America, England, France, Australia; the great songs of the Naughty Nineties and early twentieth-century America. Over a third with music. Woodcuts by John Held, Jr. convey perfectly the brash insouciance of an era of rollicking unabashed song. 12 illustrations by John Held, Jr. Two indexes (Titles and First lines and Choruses). Introductions by the author. Two volumes bound as one. Total of xvi + 235pp. 5⅜ x 8½. **T946 Paperbound $1.00**

**HOW TO TELL THE BIRDS FROM THE FLOWERS, R. W. Wood.** How not to confuse a carrot with a parrot, a grape with an ape, a puffin with nuffin. Delightful drawings, clever puns, absurd little poems point out far-fetched resemblances in nature. The author was a leading physicist. Introduction by Margaret Wood White. 106 illus. 60pp. 5⅜ x 8. **T523 Paperbound 75¢**

**PECK'S BAD BOY AND HIS PA, George W. Peck.** The complete edition, containing both volumes, of one of the most widely read American humor books. The endless ingenious pranks played by bad boy "Hennery" on his pa and the grocery man, the outraged pomposity of Pa, the perpetual ridiculing of middle class institutions, are as entertaining today as they were in 1883. No pale sophistications or subtleties, but rather humor vigorous, raw, earthy, imaginative, and, as folk humor often is, sadistic. This peculiarly fascinating book is also valuable to historians and students of American culture as a portrait of an age. 100 original illustrations by True Williams. Introduction by E. F. Bleiler. 347pp. 5⅜ x 8. **T497 Paperbound $1.35**

# CATALOGUE OF DOVER BOOKS

**THE HUMOROUS VERSE OF LEWIS CARROLL.** Almost every poem Carroll ever wrote, the largest collection ever published, including much never published elsewhere: 150 parodies, burlesques, riddles, ballads, acrostics, etc., with 130 original illustrations by Tenniel, Carroll, and others. "Addicts will be grateful . . . there is nothing for the faithful to do but sit down and fall to the banquet," N. Y. Times. Index to first lines. xiv + 446pp. 5⅜ x 8.
T654 Paperbound **$1.85**

**DIVERSIONS AND DIGRESSIONS OF LEWIS CARROLL.** A major new treasure for Carroll fans! Rare privately published humor, fantasy, puzzles, and games by Carroll at his whimsical best, with a new vein of frank satire. Includes many new mathematical amusements and recreations, among them the fragmentary Part III of "Curiosa Mathematica." Contains "The Rectory Umbrella," "The New Belfry," "The Vision of the Three T's," and much more. New 32-page supplement of rare photographs taken by Carroll. x + 375pp. 5⅜ x 8.
T732 Paperbound **$1.65**

**THE COMPLETE NONSENSE OF EDWARD LEAR.** This is the only complete edition of this master of gentle madness available at a popular price. A BOOK OF NONSENSE, NONSENSE SONGS, MORE NONSENSE SONGS AND STORIES in their entirety with all the old favorites that have delighted children and adults for years. The Dong With A Luminous Nose, The Jumblies, The Owl and the Pussycat, and hundreds of other bits of wonderful nonsense. 214 limericks, 3 sets of Nonsense Botany, 5 Nonsense Alphabets, 546 drawings by Lear himself, and much more. 320pp. 5⅜ x 8.
T167 Paperbound **$1.00**

**THE MELANCHOLY LUTE, The Humorous Verse of Franklin P. Adams ("FPA").** The author's own selection of light verse, drawn from thirty years of FPA's column, "The Conning Tower," syndicated all over the English-speaking world. Witty, perceptive, literate, these ninety-six poems range from parodies of other poets, Millay, Longfellow, Edgar Guest, Kipling, Masefield, etc., and free and hilarious translations of Horace and other Latin poets, to satiric comments on fabled American institutions—the New York Subways, preposterous ads, suburbanites, sensational journalism, etc. They reveal with vigor and clarity the humor, integrity and restraint of a wise and gentle American satirist. Introduction by Robert Hutchinson. vi + 122pp. 5⅜ x 8½.
T108 Paperbound **$1.00**

**SINGULAR TRAVELS, CAMPAIGNS, AND ADVENTURES OF BARON MUNCHAUSEN, R. E. Raspe,** with 90 illustrations by Gustave Doré. The first edition in over 150 years to reestablish the deeds of the Prince of Liars exactly as Raspe first recorded them in 1785—the genuine Baron Munchausen, one of the most popular personalities in English literature. Included also are the best of the many sequels, written by other hands. Introduction on Raspe by J. Carswell. Bibliography of early editions. xliv + 192pp. 5⅜ x 8.
T698 Paperbound **$1.00**

**THE WIT AND HUMOR OF OSCAR WILDE, ed. by Alvin Redman.** Wilde at his most brilliant, in 1000 epigrams exposing weaknesses and hypocrisies of "civilized" society. Divided into 49 categories—sin, wealth, women, America, etc.—to aid writers, speakers. Includes excerpts from his trials, books, plays, criticism. Formerly "The Epigrams of Oscar Wilde." Introduction by Vyvyan Holland, Wilde's only living son. Introductory essay by editor. 260pp. 5⅜ x 8.
T602 Paperbound **$1.00**

**MAX AND MORITZ, Wilhelm Busch.** Busch is one of the great humorists of all time, as well as the father of the modern comic strip. This volume, translated by H. A. Klein and other hands, contains the perennial favorite "Max and Moritz" (translated by C. T. Brooks), Plisch and Plum, Das Rabennest, Eispeter, and seven other whimsical, sardonic, jovial, diabolical cartoon and verse stories. Lively English translations parallel the original German. This work has delighted millions, since it first appeared in the 19th century, and is guaranteed to please almost anyone. Edited by H. A. Klein, with an afterword. x + 205pp. 5⅝ x 8½.
T181 Paperbound **$1.00**

**HYPOCRITICAL HELENA, Wilhelm Busch.** A companion volume to "Max and Moritz," with the title piece (Die Fromme Helena) and 10 other highly amusing cartoon and verse stories, all newly translated by H. A. Klein and M. C. Klein: Adventure on New Year's Eve (Abenteuer in der Neujahrsnacht), Hangover on the Morning after New Year's Eve (Der Katzenjammer am Neujahrsmorgen), etc. English and German in parallel columns. Hours of pleasure, also a fine language aid. x + 205pp. 5⅝ x 8½.
T184 Paperbound **$1.00**

**THE BEAR THAT WASN'T, Frank Tashlin.** What does it mean? Is it simply delightful wry humor, or a charming story of a bear who wakes up in the midst of a factory, or a satire on Big Business, or an existential cartoon-story of the human condition, or a symbolization of the struggle between conformity and the individual? New York Herald Tribune said of the first edition: ". . . a fable for grownups that will be fun for children. Sit down with the book and get your own bearings." Long an underground favorite with readers of all ages and opinions. v + 51pp. Illustrated. 5⅜ x 8½.
T939 Paperbound **75¢**

**RUTHLESS RHYMES FOR HEARTLESS HOMES and MORE RUTHLESS RHYMES FOR HEARTLESS HOMES, Harry Graham ("Col. D. Streamer").** Two volumes of Little Willy and 48 other poetic disasters. A bright, new reprint of oft-quoted, never forgotten, devastating humor by a precursor of today's "sick" joke school. For connoisseurs of wicked, wacky humor and all who delight in the comedy of manners. Original drawings are a perfect complement. 61 illustrations. Index. vi + 69pp. Two vols. bound as one. 5⅜ x 8½.
T930 Paperbound **75¢**

# CATALOGUE OF DOVER BOOKS

## Say It language phrase books

These handy phrase books (128 to 196 pages each) make grammatical drills unnecessary for an elementary knowledge of a spoken foreign language. Covering most matters of travel and everyday life each volume contains:

Over 1000 phrases and sentences in immediately useful forms — foreign language plus English.

Modern usage designed for Americans. Specific phrases like, "Give me small change," and "Please call a taxi."

Simplified phonetic transcription you will be able to read at sight.

The only completely indexed phrase books on the market.

Covers scores of important situations: — Greetings, restaurants, sightseeing, useful expressions, etc.

These books are prepared by native linguists who are professors at Columbia, N.Y.U., Fordham and other great universities. Use them independently or with any other book or record course. They provide a supplementary living element that most other courses lack. Individual volumes in:

| | | | |
|---|---|---|---|
| Russian 75¢ | Italian 75¢ | Spanish 75¢ | German 75¢ |
| Hebrew 75¢ | Danish 75¢ | Japanese 75¢ | Swedish 75¢ |
| Dutch 75¢ | Esperanto 75¢ | Modern Greek 75¢ | Portuguese 75¢ |
| Norwegian 75¢ | Polish 75¢ | French 75¢ | Yiddish 75¢ |
| Turkish 75¢ | | English for German-speaking people 75¢ | |
| English for Italian-speaking people 75¢ | | English for Spanish-speaking people 75¢ | |

Large clear type. 128-196 pages each. 3½ x 5¼. Sturdy paper binding.

## Listen and Learn language records

LISTEN & LEARN is the only language record course designed especially to meet your travel and everyday needs. It is available in separate sets for FRENCH, SPANISH, GERMAN, JAPANESE, RUSSIAN, MODERN GREEK, PORTUGUESE, ITALIAN and HEBREW, and each set contains three 33⅓ rpm long-playing records—1½ hours of recorded speech by eminent native speakers who are professors at Columbia, New York University, Queens College.

Check the following special features found only in LISTEN & LEARN:

- **Dual-language recording. 812 selected phrases and sentences, over 3200 words,** spoken first in English, then in their foreign language equivalents. A suitable pause follows each foreign phrase, allowing you time to repeat the expression. You learn by unconscious assimilation.

- **128 to 206-page manual** contains everything on the records, plus a simple phonetic pronunciation guide.

- **Indexed for convenience. The only set on the market** that is completely indexed. No more puzzling over where to find the phrase you need. Just look in the rear of the manual.

- **Practical.** No time wasted on material you can find in any grammar. LISTEN & LEARN covers central core material with phrase approach. Ideal for the person with limited learning time.

- **Living, modern expressions,** not found in other courses. Hygienic products, modern equipment, shopping—expressions used every day, like "nylon" and "air-conditioned."

- **Limited objective.** Everything you learn, no matter where you stop, is immediately useful. You have to finish other courses, wade through grammar and vocabulary drill, before they help you.

- **High-fidelity recording.** LISTEN & LEARN records equal in clarity and surface-silence any record on the market costing up to $6.

"Excellent . . . the spoken records . . . impress me as being among the very best on the market," **Prof. Mario Pei,** Dept. of Romance Languages, Columbia University. "Inexpensive and well-done . . . it would make an ideal present," CHICAGO SUNDAY TRIBUNE. "More genuinely helpful than anything of its kind which I have previously encountered," **Sidney Clark,** well-known author of "ALL THE BEST" travel books.

UNCONDITIONAL GUARANTEE. Try LISTEN & LEARN, then return it within 10 days for full refund if you are not satisfied.

Each set contains three twelve-inch 33⅓ records, manual, and album.

| | | | |
|---|---|---|---|
| SPANISH | the set $5.95 | GERMAN | the set $5.95 |
| FRENCH | the set $5.95 | ITALIAN | the set $5.95 |
| RUSSIAN | the set $5.95 | JAPANESE | the set $5.95 |
| PORTUGUESE | the set $5.95 | MODERN GREEK | the set $5.95 |
| MODERN HEBREW | the set $5.95 | | |

# Americana

**THE EYES OF DISCOVERY, J. Bakeless.** A vivid reconstruction of how unspoiled America appeared to the first white men. Authentic and enlightening accounts of Hudson's landing in New York, Coronado's trek through the Southwest; scores of explorers, settlers, trappers, soldiers. America's pristine flora, fauna, and Indians in every region and state in fresh and unusual new aspects. "A fascinating view of what the land was like before the first highway went through," Time. 68 contemporary illustrations, 39 newly added in this edition. Index. Bibliography. x + 500pp. 5⅜ x 8. **T761 Paperbound $2.00**

**AUDUBON AND HIS JOURNALS, J. J. Audubon.** A collection of fascinating accounts of Europe and America in the early 1800's through Audubon's own eyes. Includes the Missouri River Journals —an eventful trip through America's untouched heartland, the Labrador Journals, the European Journals, the famous "Episodes", and other rare Audubon material, including the descriptive chapters from the original letterpress edition of the "Ornithological Studies", omitted in all later editions. Indispensable for ornithologists, naturalists, and all lovers of Americana and adventure. 70-page biography by Audubon's granddaughter. 38 illustrations. Index. Total of 1106pp. 5⅜ x 8.
**T675 Vol I Paperbound $2.00**
**T676 Vol II Paperbound $2.00**
**The set $4.00**

**TRAVELS OF WILLIAM BARTRAM, edited by Mark Van Doren.** The first inexpensive illustrated edition of one of the 18th century's most delightful books is an excellent source of first-hand material on American geography, anthropology, and natural history. Many descriptions of early Indian tribes are our only source of information on them prior to the infiltration of the white man. "The mind of a scientist with the soul of a poet," John Livingston Lowes. 13 original illustrations and maps. Edited with an introduction by Mark Van Doren. 448pp. 5⅜ x 8.
**T13 Paperbound $2.00**

**GARRETS AND PRETENDERS: A HISTORY OF BOHEMIANISM IN AMERICA, A. Parry.** The colorful and fantastic history of American Bohemianism from Poe to Kerouac. This is the only complete record of hoboes, cranks, starving poets, and suicides. Here are Pfaff, Whitman, Crane, Bierce, Pound, and many others. New chapters by the author and by H. T. Moore bring this thorough and well-documented history down to the Beatniks. "An excellent account," N. Y. Times. Scores of cartoons, drawings, and caricatures. Bibliography. Index. xxviii + 421pp. 5⅝ x 8⅜. **T708 Paperbound $1.95**

**THE EXPLORATION OF THE COLORADO RIVER AND ITS CANYONS, J. W. Powell.** The thrilling first-hand account of the expedition that filled in the last white space on the map of the United States. Rapids, famine, hostile Indians, and mutiny are among the perils encountered as the unknown Colorado Valley reveals its secrets. This is the only uncut version of Major Powell's classic of exploration that has been printed in the last 60 years. Includes later reflections and subsequent expedition. 250 illustrations, new map. 400pp. 5⅝ x 8⅜.
**T94 Paperbound $2.00**

**THE JOURNAL OF HENRY D. THOREAU, Edited by Bradford Torrey and Francis H. Allen.** Henry Thoreau is not only one of the most important figures in American literature and social thought; his voluminous journals (from which his books emerged as selections and crystallizations) constitute both the longest, most sensitive record of personal internal development and a most penetrating description of a historical moment in American culture. This present set, which was first issued in fourteen volumes, contains Thoreau's entire journals from 1837 to 1862, with the exception of the lost years which were found only recently. We are reissuing it, complete and unabridged, with a new introduction by Walter Harding, Secretary of the Thoreau Society. Fourteen volumes reissued in two volumes. Foreword by Henry Seidel Canby. Total of 1888pp. 8⅜ x 12¼. **T312-3 Two volume set, Clothbound $20.00**

**GAMES AND SONGS OF AMERICAN CHILDREN, collected by William Wells Newell.** A remarkable collection of 190 games with songs that accompany many of them; cross references to show similarities, differences among them; variations; musical notation for 38 songs. Textual discussions show relations with folk-drama and other aspects of folk tradition. Grouped into categories for ready comparative study: Love-games, histories, playing at work, human life, bird and beast, mythology, guessing-games, etc. New introduction covers relations of songs and dances to timeless heritage of folklore, biographical sketch of Newell, other pertinent data. A good source of inspiration for those in charge of groups of children and a valuable reference for anthropologists, sociologists, psychiatrists. Introduction by Carl Withers. New indexes of first lines, games. 5⅜ x 8½. xii + 242pp. **T354 Paperbound $1.65**

# Art, History of Art, Antiques, Graphic Arts, Handcrafts

**ART STUDENTS' ANATOMY, E. J. Farris.** Outstanding art anatomy that uses chiefly living objects for its illustrations. 71 photos of undraped men, women, children are accompanied by carefully labeled matching sketches to illustrate the skeletal system, articulations and movements, bony landmarks, the muscular system, skin, fasciae, fat, etc. 9 x-ray photos show movement of joints. Undraped models are shown in such actions as serving in tennis, drawing a bow in archery, playing football, dancing, preparing to spring and to dive. Also discussed and illustrated are proportions, age and sex differences, the anatomy of the smile, etc. 8 plates by the great early 18th century anatomic illustrator Siegfried Albinus are also included. Glossary. 158 figures, 7 in color. x + 159pp. 5⅝ x 8⅜.				T744 Paperbound **$1.45**

**AN ATLAS OF ANATOMY FOR ARTISTS, F Schider.** A new 3rd edition of this standard text enlarged by 52 new illustrations of hands, anatomical studies by Cloquet, and expressive life studies of the body by Barcsay. 189 clear, detailed plates offer you precise information of impeccable accuracy. 29 plates show all aspects of the skeleton, with closeups of special areas, while 54 full-page plates, mostly in two colors, give human musculature as seen from four different points of view, with cutaways for important portions of the body. 14 full-page plates provide photographs of hand forms, eyelids, female breasts, and indicate the location of muscles upon models. 59 additional plates show how great artists of the past utilized human anatomy. They reproduce sketches and finished work by such artists as Michelangelo, Leonardo da Vinci, Goya, and 15 others. This is a lifetime reference work which will be one of the most important books in any artist's library. "The standard reference tool," AMERICAN LIBRARY ASSOCIATION. "Excellent," AMERICAN ARTIST. Third enlarged edition. 189 plates, 647 illustrations. xxvi + 192pp. 7⅞ x 10⅝.				T241 Clothbound **$6.00**

**AN ATLAS OF ANIMAL ANATOMY FOR ARTISTS, W. Ellenberger, H. Baum, H. Dittrich.** The largest, richest animal anatomy for artists available in English. 99 detailed anatomical plates of such animals as the horse, dog, cat, lion, deer, seal, kangaroo, flying squirrel, cow, bull, goat, monkey, hare, and bat. Surface features are clearly indicated, while progressive beneath-the-skin pictures show musculature, tendons, and bone structure. Rest and action are exhibited in terms of musculature and skeletal structure and detailed cross-sections are given for heads and important features. The animals chosen are representative of specific families so that a study of these anatomies will provide knowledge of hundreds of related species. "Highly recommended as one of the very few books on the subject worthy of being used as an authoritative guide," DESIGN. "Gives a fundamental knowledge," AMERICAN ARTIST. Second revised, enlarged edition with new plates from Cuvier, Stubbs, etc. 288 illustrations. 153pp. 11⅜ x 9.				T82 Clothbound **$6.00**

**THE HUMAN FIGURE IN MOTION, Eadweard Muybridge.** The largest selection in print of Muybridge's famous high-speed action photos of the human figure in motion. 4789 photographs illustrate 162 different actions: men, women, children—mostly undraped—are shown walking, running, carrying various objects, sitting, lying down, climbing, throwing, arising, and performing over 150 other actions. Some actions are shown in as many as 150 photographs each. All in all there are more than 500 action strips in this enormous volume, series shots taken at shutter speeds of as high as 1/6000th of a second! These are not posed shots, but true stopped motion. They show bone and muscle in situations that the human eye is not fast enough to capture. Earlier, smaller editions of these prints have brought $40 and more on the out-of-print market. "A must for artists," ART IN FOCUS. "An unparalleled dictionary of action for all artists," AMERICAN ARTIST. 390 full-page plates, with 4789 photographs. Printed on heavy glossy stock. Reinforced binding with headbands. xxi + 390pp. 7⅞ x 10⅝.				T204 Clothbound **$10.00**

**ANIMALS IN MOTION, Eadweard Muybridge.** This is the largest collection of animal action photos in print. 34 different animals (horses, mules, oxen, goats, camels, pigs, cats, guanacos, lions, gnus, deer, monkeys, eagles—and 21 others) in 132 characteristic actions. The horse alone is shown in more than 40 different actions. All 3919 photographs are taken in series at speeds up to 1/6000th of a second. The secrets of leg motion, spinal patterns, head movements, strains and contortions shown nowhere else are captured. You will see exactly how a lion sets his foot down; how an elephant's knees are like a human's—and how they differ; the position of a kangaroo's legs in mid-leap; how an ostrich's head bobs; details of the flight of birds—and thousands of facets of motion only the fastest cameras can catch. Photographed from domestic animals and animals in the Philadelphia zoo, it contains neither semiposed artificial shots nor distorted telephoto shots taken under adverse conditions. Artists, biologists, decorators, cartoonists, will find this book indispensable for understanding animals in motion. "A really marvelous series of plates," NATURE (London). "The dry plate's most spectacular early use was by Eadweard Muybridge," LIFE. 3919 photographs; 380 full pages of plates. 440pp. Printed on heavy glossy paper. Deluxe binding with headbands. 7⅞ x 10⅝.				T203 Clothbound **$10.00**

# CATALOGUE OF DOVER BOOKS

**THE AUTOBIOGRAPHY OF AN IDEA, Louis Sullivan.** The pioneer architect whom Frank Lloyd Wright called "the master" reveals an acute sensitivity to social forces and values in this passionately honest account. He records the crystallization of his opinions and theories, the growth of his organic theory of architecture that still influences American designers and architects, contemporary ideas, etc. This volume contains the first appearance of 34 full-page plates of his finest architecture. Unabridged reissue of 1924 edition. New introduction by R. M. Line. Index. xiv + 335pp. 5⅜ x 8.                                      T281 Paperbound **$2.00**

**THE DRAWINGS OF HEINRICH KLEY.** The first uncut republication of both of Kley's devastating sketchbooks, which first appeared in pre-World War I Germany. One of the greatest cartoonists and social satirists of modern times, his exuberant and iconoclastic fantasy and his extraordinary technique place him in the great tradition of Bosch, Breughel, and Goya, while his subject matter has all the immediacy and tension of our century. 200 drawings. viii + 128pp. 7¾ x 10¾.                                                                    T24 Paperbound **$1.85**

**MORE DRAWINGS BY HEINRICH KLEY.** All the sketches from Leut' Und Viecher (1912) and Sammel-Album (1923) not included in the previous Dover edition of Drawings. More of the bizarre, mercilessly iconoclastic sketches that shocked and amused on their original publication. Nothing was too sacred, no one too eminent for satirization by this imaginative, individual and accomplished master cartoonist. A total of 158 illustrations. Iv + 104pp. 7¾ x 10¾.                                                                    T41 Paperbound **$1.85**

**PINE FURNITURE OF EARLY NEW ENGLAND, R. H. Kettell.** A rich understanding of one of America's most original folk arts that collectors of antiques, interior decorators, craftsmen, woodworkers, and everyone interested in American history and art will find fascinating and immensely useful. 413 illustrations of more than 300 chairs, benches, racks, beds, cupboards, mirrors, shelves, tables, and other furniture will show all the simple beauty and character of early New England furniture. 55 detailed drawings carefully analyze outstanding pieces. "With its rich store of illustrations, this book emphasizes the individuality and varied design of early American pine furniture. It should be welcomed," ANTIQUES. 413 illustrations and 55 working drawings. 475. 8 x 10¾.                                            T145 Clothbound **$10.00**

**THE HUMAN FIGURE, J. H. Vanderpoel.** Every important artistic element of the human figure is pointed out in minutely detailed word descriptions in this classic text and illustrated as well in 430 pencil and charcoal drawings. Thus the text of this book directs your attention to all the characteristic features and subtle differences of the male and female (adults, children, and aged persons), as though a master artist were telling you what to look for at each stage. 2nd edition, revised and enlarged by George Bridgman. Foreword. 430 illustrations. 143pp. 6⅛ x 9¼.                                                            T432 Paperbound **$1.50**

**LETTERING AND ALPHABETS, J. A. Cavanagh.** This unabridged reissue of LETTERING offers a full discussion, analysis, illustration of 89 basic hand lettering styles — styles derived from Caslons, Bodonis, Garamonds, Gothic, Black Letter, Oriental, and many others. Upper and lower cases, numerals and common signs pictured. Hundreds of technical hints on make-up, construction, artistic validity, strokes, pens, brushes, white areas, etc. May be reproduced without permission! 89 complete alphabets; 72 lettered specimens. 121pp. 9¾ x 8. T53 Paperbound **$1.25**

**STICKS AND STONES, Lewis Mumford.** A survey of the forces that have conditioned American architecture and altered its forms. The author discusses the medieval tradition in early New England villages; the Renaissance influence which developed with the rise of the merchant class; the classical influence of Jefferson's time; the "Mechanicsvilles" of Poe's generation; the Brown Decades; the philosophy of the Imperial facade; and finally the modern machine age. "A truly remarkable book," SAT. REV. OF LITERATURE. 2nd revised edition. 21 illustrations. xvii + 228pp. 5⅜ x 8.                                              T202 Paperbound **$1.60**

**THE STANDARD BOOK OF QUILT MAKING AND COLLECTING, Marguerite Ickis.** A complete easy-to-follow guide with all the information you need to make beautiful, useful quilts. How to plan, design, cut, sew, appliqué, avoid sewing problems, use rag bag, make borders, tuft, every other aspect. Over 100 traditional quilts shown, including over 40 full-size patterns. At-home hobby for fun, profit. Index. 483 illus. 1 color plate. 287pp. 6¾ x 9½.
T582 Paperbound **$2.00**

**THE BOOK OF SIGNS, Rudolf Koch.** Formerly $20 to $25 on the out-of-print market, now only $1.00 in this unabridged new edition! 493 symbols from ancient manuscripts, medieval cathedrals, coins, catacombs, pottery, etc. Crosses, monograms of Roman emperors, astrological, chemical, botanical, runes, housemarks, and 7 other categories. Invaluable for handicraft workers, illustrators, scholars, etc., this material may be reproduced without permission. 493 illustrations by Fritz Kredel. 104pp. 6½ x 9¼.                      T162 Paperbound **$1.00**

**PRIMITIVE ART, Franz Boas.** This authoritative and exhaustive work by a great American anthropologist covers the entire gamut of primitive art. Pottery, leatherwork, metal work, stone work, wood, basketry, are treated in detail. Theories of primitive art, historical depth in art history, technical virtuosity, unconscious levels of patterning, symbolism, styles, literature, music, dance, etc. A must book for the interested layman, the anthropologist, artist, handicrafter (hundreds of unusual motifs), and the historian. Over 900 illustrations (50 ceramic vessels, 12 totem poles, etc.). 376pp. 5⅜ x 8.                          T25 Paperbound **$1.95**

# Fiction

**FLATLAND, E. A. Abbott.** A science-fiction classic of life in a 2-dimensional world that is also a first-rate introduction to such aspects of modern science as relativity and hyperspace. Political, moral, satirical, and humorous overtones have made FLATLAND fascinating reading for thousands. 7th edition. New introduction by Banesh Hoffmann. 16 illustrations. 128pp. 5⅜ x 8.
T1 Paperbound **$1.00**

**THE WONDERFUL WIZARD OF OZ, L. F. Baum.** Only edition in print with all the original W. W. Denslow illustrations in full color—as much a part of "The Wizard" as Tenniel's drawings are of "Alice in Wonderland." "The Wizard" is still America's best-loved fairy tale, in which, as the author expresses it, "The wonderment and joy are retained and the heartaches and nightmares left out." Now today's young readers can enjoy every word and wonderful picture of the original book. New introduction by Martin Gardner. A Baum bibliography. 23 full-page color plates. viii + 268pp. 5⅜ x 8.
T691 Paperbound **$1.45**

**THE MARVELOUS LAND OF OZ, L. F. Baum.** This is the equally enchanting sequel to the "Wizard," continuing the adventures of the Scarecrow and the Tin Woodman. The hero this time is a little boy named Tip, and all the delightful Oz magic is still present. This is the Oz book with the Animated Saw-Horse, the Woggle-Bug, and Jack Pumpkinhead. All the original John R. Neill illustrations, 10 in full color. 287 pp. 5⅜ x 8.
T692 Paperbound **$1.45**

**FIVE GREAT DOG NOVELS, edited by Blanche Cirker.** The complete original texts of five classic dog novels that have delighted and thrilled millions of children and adults throughout the world with their stories of loyalty, adventure, and courage. Full texts of Jack London's "The Call of the Wild"; John Brown's "Rab and His Friends"; Alfred Ollivant's "Bob, Son of Battle"; Marshall Saunders's "Beautiful Joe"; and Ouida's "A Dog of Flanders." 21 Illustrations from the original editions. 495pp. 5⅜ x 8.
T777 Paperbound **$1.50**

**TO THE SUN? and OFF ON A COMET!, Jules Verne.** Complete texts of two of the most imaginative flights into fancy in world literature display the high adventure that have kept Verne's novels read for nearly a century. Only unabridged edition of the best translation, by Edward Roth. Large, easily readable type. 50 illustrations selected from first editions. 462pp. 5⅜ x 8.
T634 Paperbound **$1.75**

**FROM THE EARTH TO THE MOON and ALL AROUND THE MOON, Jules Verne.** Complete editions of 2 of Verne's most successful novels, in finest Edward Roth translations, now available after many years out of print. Verne's visions of submarines, airplanes, television, rockets, interplanetary travel; of scientific and not-so-scientific beliefs; of peculiarities of Americans; all delight and engross us today as much as when they first appeared. Large, easily readable type. 42 illus. from first French edition. 476pp. 5⅜ x 8.
T633 Paperbound **$1.75**

**THE CRUISE OF THE CACHALOT, Frank T. Bullen.** Out of the experiences of many years on the high-seas, First Mate Bullen created this novel of adventure aboard an American whaler, shipping out of New Bedford, Mass., when American whaling was at the height of its splendor. Originally published in 1899, the story of the round-the-world cruise of the "Cachalot" in pursuit of the sperm whale has thrilled generations of readers. A maritime classic that will fascinate anyone interested in reading about the sea or looking for a solid old-fashioned yarn, while the vivid recreation of a brief but important chapter of Americana and the British author's often biting commentary on nineteenth-century Yankee mores offer insights into the colorful era of America's coming of age. 8 plates. xiii + 271pp. 5⅜ x 8½.
T774 Paperbound **$1.00**

**28 SCIENCE FICTION STORIES OF H. G. WELLS.** Two full unabridged novels, MEN LIKE GODS and STAR BEGOTTEN, plus 26 short stories by the master science-fiction writer of all time! Stories of space, time, invention, exploration, future adventure—an indispensable part of the library of everyone interested in science and adventure. PARTIAL CONTENTS: Men Like Gods, The Country of the Blind, In the Abyss, The Crystal Egg, The Man Who Could Work Miracles, A Story of the Days to Come, The Valley of Spiders, and 21 more! 928pp. 5⅜ x 8.
T265 Clothbound **$3.95**

**DAVID HARUM, E. N. Westcott.** This novel of one of the most lovable, humorous characters in American literature is a prime example of regional humor. It continues to delight people who like their humor dry, their characters quaint, and their plots ingenuous. First book edition to contain complete novel plus chapter found after author's death. Illustrations from first illustrated edition. 192pp. 5⅜ x 8.
T580 Paperbound **$1.15**

**GESTA ROMANORUM, trans. by Charles Swan, ed. by Wynnard Hooper.** 181 tales of Greeks, Romans, Britons, Biblical characters, comprise one of greatest medieval story collections, source of plots for writers including Shakespeare, Chaucer, Gower, etc. Imaginative tales of wars, incest, thwarted love, magic, fantasy, allegory, humor, tell about kings, prostitutes, philosophers, fair damsels, knights, Noah, pirates, all walks, stations of life. Introduction. Notes. 500pp. 5⅜ x 8.
T535 Paperbound **$1.85**

# Music

**A GENERAL HISTORY OF MUSIC, Charles Burney.** A detailed coverage of music from the Greeks up to 1789, with full information on all types of music: sacred and secular, vocal and instrumental, operatic and symphonic. Theory, notation, forms, instruments, innovators, composers, performers, typical and important works, and much more in an easy, entertaining style. Burney covered much of Europe and spoke with hundreds of authorities and composers so that this work is more than a compilation of records . . . it is a living work of careful and first-hand scholarship. Its account of thoroughbass (18th century) Italian music is probably still the best introduction on the subject. A recent NEW YORK TIMES review said, "Surprisingly few of Burney's statements have been invalidated by modern research . . . still of great value." Edited and corrected by Frank Mercer. 35 figures. Indices. 1915pp. 5⅜ x 8. 2 volumes.                                     T36 The Set, Clothbound **$12.50**

**A DICTIONARY OF HYMNOLOGY, John Julian.** This exhaustive and scholarly work has become known as an invaluable source of hundreds of thousands of important and often difficult to obtain facts on the history and use of hymns in the western world. Everyone interested in hymns will be fascinated by the accounts of famous hymns and hymn writers and amazed by the amount of practical information he will find. More than 30,000 entries on individual hymns, giving authorship, date and circumstances of composition, publication, textual variations, translations, denominational and ritual usage, etc. Biographies of more than 9,000 hymn writers, and essays on important topics such as Christmas carols and children's hymns, and much other unusual and valuable information. A 200 page double-columned index of first lines — the largest in print. Total of 1786 pages in two reinforced clothbound volumes. 6¼ x 9¼.
The set, T333 Clothbound **$15.00**

**MUSIC IN MEDIEVAL BRITAIN, F. Ll. Harrison.** The most thorough, up-to-date, and accurate treatment of the subject ever published, beautifully illustrated. Complete account of institutions and choirs; carols, masses, and motets; liturgy and plainsong; and polyphonic music from the Norman Conquest to the Reformation. Discusses the various schools of music and their reciprocal influences; the origin and development of new ritual forms; development and use of instruments; and new evidence on many problems of the period. Reproductions of scores, over 200 excerpts from medieval melodies. Rules of harmony and dissonance; influence of Continental styles; great composers (Dunstable, Cornysh, Fairfax, etc.); and much more. Register and index of more than 400 musicians. Index of titles. General Index. 225-item bibliography. 6 Appendices. xix + 491pp. 5⅝ x 8¾.                 T705 Clothbound **$10.00**

**THE MUSIC OF SPAIN, Gilbert Chase.** Only book in English to give concise, comprehensive account of Iberian music; new Chapter covers music since 1941. Victoria, Albéniz, Cabezón, Pedrell, Turina, hundreds of other composers; popular and folk music; the Gypsies; the guitar; dance, theatre, opera, with only extensive discussion in English of the Zarzuela; virtuosi such as Casals; much more. "Distinguished . . . readable," Saturday Review. 400-item bibliography. Index. 27 photos. 383pp. 5⅜ x 8.          T549 Paperbound **$2.00**

**ON STUDYING SINGING, Sergius Kagen.** An intelligent method of voice-training, which leads you around pitfalls that waste your time, money, and effort. Exposes rigid, mechanical systems, baseless theories, deleterious exercises. "Logical, clear, convincing . . . dead right," Virgil Thomson, N.Y. Herald Tribune. "I recommend this volume highly," Maggie Teyte, Saturday Review. 119pp. 5⅜ x 8.                          T622 Paperbound **$1.25**

*Dover publishes books on art, music, philosophy, literature, languages, history, social sciences, psychology, handcrafts, orientalia, puzzles and entertainments, chess, pets and gardens, books explaining science, intermediate and higher mathematics mathematical physics, engineering, biological sciences, earth sciences, classics of science, etc. Write to:*

Dept. catrr.
Dover Publications, Inc.
180 Varick Street, N. Y. 14, N. Y.